GARDENING TIPS OF A LIFETIME

Fred Loads' Gardening tips of a lifetime

Hamlyn
London · New York · Sydney · Toronto

To Moyra and Bill for their
long-suffering tolerance

Line drawings by The Hayward Art Group

The publishers would like to thank
Pitman Publishing Limited for permission to use
the quote on pages 26 and 27

First published in 1980 by
The Hamlyn Publishing Group Limited
London · New York · Sydney · Toronto
Astronaut House, Feltham, Middlesex

ISBN 0 600 38795 X

Phototypeset in 10 on 12pt Linotron Plantin by
Filmtype Services Limited, Scarborough, England
Printed and bound by New Interlitho, Milan, Italy

Contents

ONE

Making a Good Beginning 7

TWO

Soil Cultivation 15

THREE

Manures and Fertilisers 25

FOUR

Lawns 43

FIVE

Shrubs and Flowers 65

SIX

The Vegetable Garden 101

SEVEN

The Fruit Garden 139

Index 173

Making a Good Beginning

How does one begin to write a gardening book? I've got hundreds of them and glancing through a few dozen I have to smile when I read that the site should be carefully selected, not exposed and gently sloping to the south. The choice of soil, too, needs equally careful consideration. All I can say to this is that at no time have I ever had a choice. As an apprentice, journeyman or head gardener, the gardens were all there long before I was even thought of.

Eventually when I bought or lived in several other houses, new or partly worn, I had no say in where they should be placed – I just had to make the best of it; no matter if the builder had trampled the soil to death, ruined the top soil, dug up mountains of clay, made lime pits, spilled diesel oil from the cement mixer or chopped up hedges and roots of old trees to form breeding grounds for the bootlace fungus. A wise old gardener who was full of country lore came to my rescue; this little bit of advice has stood me in good stead throughout my gardening life, 'Any fool can make work'.

New gardeners, and often not-so-new gardeners, start off full of enthusiasm but create monsters which, in time, devour them. To them I would add the suggestion that you should never start anything in the garden in a hurry. At least wait until you have some idea in your own mind what you want from your patch of earth. Better still, try to get some of your ideas down on paper.

Nowadays, the modern home gardener has, I think, more to contend with than Capability Brown, that landscaping wizard of the 18th century who found capabilities in most situations. Some of the circumstances relate to the age of the owner; personally I would never make a garden for someone of retiring age in the same way as I would for someone who was just starting married life. In any case, whether it is brand new and full of builders' rubbish, totally neglected or, probably worst of all, a badly designed garden that has been well kept and was somebody's pride and joy, you have to decide whether to perpetuate this or make it your own. This is a decision only you can make.

So, you are a beginner, new to gardening perhaps and with ideas about the sort of thing that you would like to have, often with little chance of ever getting it. A garden can give practically everything that

7

the human heart can desire because it is probably the one place in the world that you can make your own; only please don't make a labour of it. As soon as it becomes a chore there is something wrong with either you or your garden. When I say this, people usually turn round and say 'Ah, but it's alright for you, you know what to do and when to do it'. That may be so but I'll guarantee to make a gardener out of anybody provided he is genuinely interested.

It makes no difference if your garden is only a window box or a bit of soil in the back yard. I know an old lady who has been struggling to grow two lettuce plants in a tin of dirt perched on the top of a backyard wall. They are going to be so bitter and dirty that nobody will ever eat them but for the first time in her life she has known the thrill and the joy of watching a plant emerge from a tiny seed, knowing she has coaxed it into life.

Looking at the soil

I have just mentioned a tin of dirt; well that's how many people think of soil – dirt, muck, mud, soil, earth, good earth. It depends on who you are; mothers and small boys for example look at the same substance from different angles. But the gardener has only one way of looking at it – and when I say gardener I am not thinking of the professional, but anybody who is a gardener at heart. The soil is our raw material; the factory from which, with the help of all sorts of forces, we can conjure up all the colours of the rainbow and every scent imaginable as well as good food. This is possible because the green plant is the only living thing that can manufacture food directly from the earth's natural resources. In fact, if all the green plants just stopped growing, all other life would quickly cease.

The different sorts of soils we find are the result of millions of years' work. They nearly all started off as solid rock. Then frost, the heat of the sun, rain, sea water and the acids from plants broke them down to varying degrees of fineness. So we get silts, which have very fine particles; clay, with particles a shade bigger; and coarse, gritty sand. On top of this, innumerable plants and trees have grown up, died, rotted down and got mixed in with all this finely ground rock. So, when you are faced with that awful looking stuff outside your new house, just console yourself with the thought that there are possibilities in the worst looking soil.

However, there is even more to soil than this; if it was just a collection of sand, clay, stones and rotted vegetation it would still be of some use for growing plants in, but it also contains countless numbers of living organisms. By these, I don't mean those creepy crawlies that run and wriggle about in and on top of the ground; I mean something much smaller – microscopic in fact. Although they are so small, they are extremely important for if they get killed accidentally or deliberately then the soil becomes dead or sterile.

Here's a way of proving it. Put a tin lid full of soil from the garden in the oven and bake it thoroughly, then smooth it out, water it and sow some seeds on it. They will germinate and grow for a few days and then die. But if you put just a teaspoonful of unbaked soil in the corner of the tin you will find that the little plants will grow quite well in this. If the soil is left for several weeks and kept moist, the living organisms will spread quite happily through the baked soil and it will become fertile again. Later on I will tell you how we make use of this knowledge in practical gardening.

Therefore, a gardener's first job is to make these living organisms happy and comfortable in the soil and provide them with fresh air, food and water. They must have this before you can think about growing plants and I will try to show you how we can give them the right conditions to multiply and work for us. I cannot stress too much how important it is to get the soil into good 'heart' and good heart means good health.

Whilst you are leaning over your gate ruminating, you might have a look round and see what sort of trees and weeds grow naturally because this will give you some indication of what the soil is like before ever you put spade or fork into it. For instance, the beech thrives where there's lime and this indicates that stone fruits such as plums and cherries will be perfectly happy. Naturally-occurring hawthorn means that apple trees and roses will do well because they are all related. Then, take a look downwards at the weeds as these, too, will tell a story. Dandelions and docks, for example, are happy in a moist sticky clay, whilst nettles and chickweed flourish in loose, open soil and fat hen loves sandy conditions.

Well, perhaps you can't tell one weed from t'other, so let's have a look at the soil itself. Get a trowel and a basin or container of some sort and take samples of the soil from about 2 in down from the surface at various parts of the plot. Or if it's a very big one divide it up into convenient sized squares, 20 ft by 20 ft, and take about five samples – one 2 or 3 ft inwards from each corner and one from the centre. Put them all in your container, mix them up thoroughly and then sift the soil that you've collected through a ¼-in sieve. You can then proceed with what is known as mechanical analysis.

You can also have a chemical analysis done later on, but for my part, I like to feel the soil and find out its physical characteristics. Into a large jam jar put about four dessertspoonfuls of the mixture, fill the jar three quarters full with water and stir up the soil without breaking down all the lumps. Then stand it somewhere undisturbed for twenty four hours. After this time you will see that it has settled out into layers of stones, sand, clay and humus. The little stones and the heavier particles will settle quickly and will be found at the bottom of

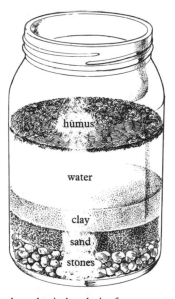

A mechanical analysis of a soil sample. The soil settles out into clearly-defined layers after 24 hours showing the proportions of the main constituents

9

the jar, and the organic matter or humus will float on the top. The finer particles of the humus will settle above the clay as a dark sediment. You may find that after twenty four hours the water is still cloudy and this will indicate that there is a fair amount of clay because the clay and silt particles are very fine indeed and take a long time to settle out. If there is no humus or organic matter either settled or floating you know that your soil is going to need as much organic matter as you can possibly give it.

If the water is nice and clear then you are lucky, but if it remains cloudy then mix a spoonful of hydrated lime in about a glassful of water, stir it well and add a spoonful or two of this to your jam jar. You will find that the fine particles will curdle, or more correctly, flocculate, and sink to form a layer on top of the sediment. This shows that your soil needs some lime, particularly if you want to grow vegetables. Unless you know the history of a particular garden then it is always worthwhile making this simple test.

At the same time as you are rubbing the soil samples through the sieve or, if you haven't got a sieve, through your hands, you will get a real feel of the soil texture. You should be able to tell whether it feels gritty and therefore contains a fair proportion of sand, or soapy if it is made up of clay or silt. If it feels greasy and is dark in colour then it could well be peaty. Furthermore, if you let your hands dry with the soil on them, you can actually read the soil's character so that next time you meet these conditions you will have a better understanding. This will stand you in good stead when it comes to seed sowing, pricking off seedlings and making up various mixtures. Don't be afraid of getting your hands dirty, garden wearing gloves later on if you like but greet the soil initially like a friend with your hands.

Later on as you gain more experience you can learn not only how to feel the soil but to feel plants as well. Just by a touch or caress they will tell you whether they want water or feed and if they are happy or healthy. Sounds daft I know, to talk about caressing plants but watch an old gardener going amongst his plants in the greenhouse or in the garden touching here, stroking there. He's not doing this just because he loves them or is expressing his affection, like stroking the cat, but more simply to say, 'Hello, how are you and how do you feel today?' And they will tell him. For instance, a tomato leaf when overcharged with nitrogen is dark and brittle and will crack if partially folded. A limp flabby leaf is as indicative as a limp handshake.

Tools of the trade

It doesn't take an expert to decide the sort of garden with which you have been saddled or blessed: brand new and untouched by human hand, a neglected derelict patch or a previously well-kept garden gone to seed. In the latter case you will have to decide whether to replant or carry on just as it is and clean it up, but the first two will need work, very often with a capital 'W'. Before you do anything else you are going to need something to work with, and that means tools. There is often a great temptation to call in mechanical aids and you may be advised to do this. However, I am strongly against it for the simple reason that even if the going is straightforward there are all sorts of things that should not be buried or chopped up. I am thinking of old roots, lurking lumps of iron or old bricks in the new garden – all potential killers – and in the derelict garden pernicious weeds such as couch grass which, if they get chopped up will only increase the problem because with such things as bindweed, couch grass or ground elder (bishop weed) any piece that has two ends will root and then you will have compounded your troubles.

So, let's see what sort of tools you are going to need. Garden tools are expensive and if you plan to buy only one or two at a time then the first buy should be a spade and a garden fork. There is no need to pick the biggest and heaviest in the belief that if you get a bigger one then you will be able to dig up more soil at one go. Instead, choose one to suit your weight and don't consider it a reproach to your virtility even if you select a lady's spade.

It always strikes me as odd that in every other occupation a newcomer to the job is taught how to use the tools of the trade. Yet every year thousands of people come to gardening who have never handled a gardening implement before and either expect or think they know how to use and care for the tools by instinct. True, most of the basic tools of our trade are simple but I can't help noticing that many folk develop bad habits and are what we say in Norfolk 'cack-handed'. This means handling the tools awkwardly and inefficiently.

When choosing tools, the best advice I can give to newcomers to the game is to take with them an experienced person, so that they at least start off with right tools of the correct weight. In spite of the efforts of the manufacturers of gardening tools, there are still some badly designed ones offered for sale. For instance, spades with thick, heavy blades with a ridge on the top. The idea being, of course, that this ridge will prevent damage to the boots and this encourages the belief that the waist of the foot should be used to exert pressure when digging instead of the heel. The trouble is that these thick-bladed, heavy spades are usually unbalanced and damp, clayey soil builds up under this narrow ridge and makes it more difficult to work. A significant factor too, is the choice of grip, and this will depend mainly on the size of your hand. Some wrists are not as supple as others, some people have short fingers whilst others have broad hands. Most people today prefer the 'D' split handle for maximum comfort, but if you have a broad hand, it may not be advisable to confine it in this type

The correct position for digging is with the heel exerting pressure on the shoulder of the spade

11

because of chafing the forefinger. This might suggest to you that a 'T' handle would be a better choice.

Check the point where the wood joins the metal; this is absolutely vital, not only with regard to the strength of the tool but also because, when working with a spade, the action of the handle is very much like that of a piston. If you regard the closed hand (left hand for a right-handed person) as the cylinder and the spade handle as the piston then it is easy to see why this must be smooth – even if you are only using a spade for a short time. Even if gloves are worn, it is essential for any tool to work freely without snagging or chafing and to do this there must be a smooth union between wood and metal. Incidentally, you may have noticed a reference to 'solid socket' in the description of various designs of tool. This is a technical term which indicates an extremely efficient and very strong method of attaching handle to blade and distinguishes it from the strapped design.

The spade The spade must be well balanced. To test this find the point of balance by resting the shaft of the spade just above the blade in the palm of the left hand, then lay the back of the blade flat on the floor – the handle should be some 12 to 13 in from the ground. If it is less than this the crank will make the spade too straight and uncomfortable to work. Choose a light spade. This is particularly important for those who are not using it every day and, more especially, if the soil to be worked is a stiff clay. A good spade is expensive but the outlay will be worthwhile as it will last a lifetime. Spades, like most other tools are well finished nowadays, but even so, I like to rub over all the woodwork and all the corners with a fine emery or glass paper, paying particular attention to the joints between wood and metal and to any rivets. After this give a rub over with linseed oil and you will have a tool that will not raise blisters on your hands. All you have to do then is to keep it clean.

A sharp spade makes the job of digging easier and a good spade should never be used for anything else, certainly not for chopping up and banging away at bricks or stones or used as a lever to heave out roots and rocks. My own spade, aptly named 'The King of Spades',

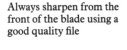
Always sharpen from the front of the blade using a good quality file

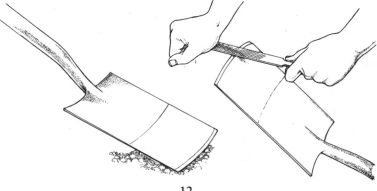

has been in use for over 30 years and is as sharp as a razor. And talking about sharpening: there is only one way to sharpen a spade and that is on the inside of the blade. To sharpen, get a good file, lay the spade on its back and either get someone to hold it on a bench or put it in a vice. Incidentally, if you do put it in a vice put it between two pieces of wood or the jaws of the vice will roughen up the smooth metal shaft and may even distort it. Sharpen to a chisel edge and do not touch the back of the blade with the file. The abrasion caused by wear will tend to make it self-sharpening and so sharpening with a file need only be done on rare occasions.

When you start work in the garden it's worth remembering that to get the greatest depth, the spade should be thrust vertically into the ground, preferably with the heel. The spadeful of soil has to be levered before it is turned over, so the greater the leverage the easier it is to loosen the spadeful of earth. When digging, moisture is a good lubricant and if your garden is of heavy clay or silt, then it pays to have a bucket of water handy to dip the spade into occasionally.

The spade, of course, is not a fine-weather tool and because so much care has gone into its making – and let's face it tools are not cheap these days – it pays to keep it in tip-top order. In the case of a spade this simply means keeping it free from rust. True, a spade will take a long time to rust away, even if left exposed to the elements, but with the corrosive chemicals in the soil, particularly artificial fertilisers, the surface becomes pitted – and this can even happen overnight. It is not so much the appearance that is important but the actual friction when in use. The easier the blade penetrates or is withdrawn from the soil the easier it will be to use. So, the brighter and shinier the spade the easier it will work. A wedge-shaped piece of hardwood such as box or beech makes a useful scraper. This may sometimes also be used during digging. Before hanging up, wash and dry the spade if very dirty and then rub it with an oily rag which you can keep near your tool rack. Alternatively, spray with an aerosol rust preventative.

The fork Next in order of usefulness comes the garden fork and this might be regarded as complementary to the spade, much in the same way as the dinner fork is complementary to the knife. The fork can double up for the spade and it is often easier and more effective to dig wet, heavy clay or silty soil with a fork. Using a fork in this way has another advantage in that no hard pan can be left as the points of the tines exert a scratching movement rather than a scraping action when the tool is thrust into the soil to its extremity. The fork, too, is extremely valuable in breaking down soil which has been either ploughed or roughly dug. Other obvious jobs are lifting root crops, such as potatoes, levering plants and weeds out of the ground and for loosening up the surface, as well as collecting rubbish. A garden fork is also invaluable for aerating lawns.

Hoes Coming on to the subject of hoes, I still prefer a wooden shaft to a tubular steel one. Here again, in selecting a tool, the tubular steel shaft with a rubber grip is quite satisfactory for occasional use, but where it has to be used for long periods then wooden shafts of either hickory or ash will be found to be much kinder to the hands. Every effort should be made to keep the shaft as straight as one would a fishing rod so do not put the hoe down where a barrow can be wheeled over it because if the handle becomes distorted it is almost as bad as having a twisted gun barrel and no great accuracy can be achieved.

I may be sticking my neck out here, but my observations lead me to believe that nine out of ten people have little idea how to use a hoe or, indeed, why they are using it. They have been exhorted to hoe, to chop down weeds and to produce a surface mulch to prevent loss of moisture. There are two main types of hoe; the Dutch hoe, which one pushes and the draw hoe, which one drags or draws. These both come in various widths. Through misuse, most hoes become unserviceable after only a few years' wear as the corners have been completely worn off and it is the corners which are so vital in the accurate picking off of weeds close up to crops. The hoe should be used in such a way that the whole blade does the job and not just the corners. The angle at which the hoe is held and the angle of the blade in relation to the ground, determine the type of cut made and the job it is intended to do. In practice this means the difference between penetrating the ground about $\frac{1}{4}$ to $\frac{1}{2}$ in and actually cultivating the soil to a depth of 2 in or more.

Where hoeing is to be used on a fairly large area, there is nothing to beat a well-maintained and correctly-angled draw hoe, preferably of the swan-necked type. The angle of the blade is, of course, set in the factory but it is not set or adjusted for individual needs. Where a large area has to be hoed for the suppression of weeds, then when the shaft is held at a convenient angle to the user the blade of the hoe should be flat with the ground. Where cultivation is to be deeper than this, then the blade is angled so that it cuts down rather than scrapes along the surface. Both Dutch and draw hoes are sharpened on the inside of the blade as, here again, the abrasion takes care of the outer surface.

The rake This is a craftsman's tool. It is sheer joy to watch a craftsman rake an onion bed and leave it as level and smooth as a billiard table as well as being fine and silky to the depth of the teeth. A good twelve-tine rake with square shoulders and a good handle is essential. Keep the handle true and straight by hanging. Never leave it lying about and never stand a rake up against a post, fence or wall with the teeth facing towards you. If you don't understand what this means and you ever chance to step on the teeth with your toe, you will get such a crack on the nose that you will ever after remember to turn the back of the rake towards you when resting it upright.

14

Soil Cultivation

As a boy I couldn't get out of school fast enough when the fields were being ploughed with a steam plough. This involved two wonderful traction engines, one at each side of the field with a six-furrow plough being pulled between them on a wire rope. This, of course, had very little to do with gardening but it brought home to me what was meant by complete inversion.

I am not against the use of mechanical tools, motorised or electrically driven, and have used practically every make on the market. I have even used some that never got there, including a motorised spade which would, once set in motion, operate on its own right across the garden turning over chunks of soil weighing more than half a hundredweight. However, for the ordinary gardener, man or woman, the fork and the spade are still the best implements. I mention the fork as a digging tool because under certain conditions, for instance, on heavy, wet or sticky land, the fork is the easiest to use. It can also be used for breaking up the secondary layer or spit after the top one has been turned over by the spade. The spade, is, in my opinion, still the best implement for turning or inverting the soil.

Digging and manuring

Digging is an art, as well as a job of work because not only is the soil inverted and weeds buried but the whole plot, under the skilful hands of the craftsman, can be completely levelled. It is far better to do this with a spade when the digging is first done rather than to move hundredweights of soil afterwards by raking just to get a level plot. Nobody can dig well unless they have taken out a good trench first because not only is the soil on the spade completely inverted, it is also moved forward 9 to 12 in.

An easy stance and a rhythmic action can make the job of digging easier and the 'bites' or the width of the spadeful should be regulated, not only to the state or condition of the soil, but also to the strength of the digger. To get the full benefit of digging, the spade should be inserted vertically and this is where attention to the 'crank' or angle of the blade to the shaft comes in. The spade should always be pushed into the soil to the full depth of the blade so that maximum root run can be obtained. Furthermore, if the spadeful of soil is thrown forward 9 in or so, every spadeful of soil then advances yearly so that perhaps in twenty years the soil has been taken from one end of the plot to the other. This has the advantage of mixing the soil to the benefit of the crops grown. To make digging easier cut a slice by jabbing the spade at right angles to the line of the trench to approximately the width of the spade. This enables the spadeful or spit to be turned forward in one lump without it falling apart. On very light soils this is not always possible, unless the soil has been consolidated, but special tools such as a digging shovel can be used. A digging shovel has curved edges to the blade thus enabling it to retain the volume of soil.

Unless the soil is being roughly dug and left as it is, it will be necessary to break down each spadeful. One reason for this being that if the soil is clayey and the weather is dry, the chunk can bake like a brick, and unless rain falls it is almost impossible to break it down later. So as each spadeful of earth is turned over and thrown forward it should be chopped with the side and edge of the spade to break it up. Of course, the amount of chopping required for each spadeful is dependant upon the season, time of year and the character of the soil. Light to medium soils require very little breaking up but a heavy moisture-retentive one must be chopped if it is eventually to break down and form a tilth. This is one of the reasons why it is advised that digging should be carried out in the autumn so that the action of the winter weather can reduce the newly broken earth to a friable condition by the spring. It is the heavy clay soils which benefit most from autumn digging and being left to the repeated action of freeze and thaw throughout the winter. This makes them more workable by the time spring comes. If digging is left until the spring a heavy tenacious clay soil will turn over in large solid lumps and even with hard work there is very little chance of it forming a good tilth during that season. Light soil is of a different nature and very often spring digging will produce a good friable soil ready for seed sowing within a few weeks.

Double digging is seldom done nowadays, and was really more useful on worn-out soils, which had been cultivated for a hundred years or more. It consists of bringing the second spit to the surface and burying the worn-out top soil. Much was made of this double digging, very often by writers who thought that the idea was to bring up soil from the bottom, because·it was better than the top soil. This is very rarely so, and in much of the land used for building the second spit is best left where it is but, as I have indicated, breaking it up with a fork ensures better drainage.

There are also some useful tricks for placing different manures or composts in and on the slope of the trench. Different types of manure will be discussed in Chapter 3, but suffice to say now that the long strawy stuff is best put in the bottom of the trench and along the lower part of the slope whilst well-rotted manure, well-rotted compost, leafmould or peat can be spread over the whole face of the sloping side of the trench. It will be seen that the layer of organic material will extend diagonally through the soil so that the roots of any crop must come into contact with it. Long strawy manure is inevitably new and unless it has been in the soil some three to four months it could definitely be harmful to the crop above it, for that reason it is tucked down a spade depth out of harm's way and giving it a chance to decay before the plant roots penetrate to that depth. Similarly, if you are applying fertiliser to the soil whilst digging, it should be applied on the forward slope of the trench for the same reason that well-decayed manure is spread on the slope. This may seem only a little thing but it is very important, for not only does it provide nourishment for the

Digging the plot

Any plot of land to be dug can be converted at least approximately into a rectangle. Divide the area roughly down its length with a line, as indicated on the diagram, taking out a trench a full spade's depth at top A and piling it on the end of B. A single trench of these dimensions is suitable for ordinary straightforward digging, but if the area to be dug is very weedy or a lot of rubbish is to be buried, then widen the trench by a half a spade's width still keeping the same depth. Such a trench enables one to incorporate not only weeds but manure can also be forked into the bottom.

   To get the best out of the operation of digging, skim off the top 2 in of the platform on which the digger is standing and put this into the deepest part of the trench. This gets rid of weed seeds and debris as well as any larvae, pupae or eggs which may be laid by insects and pests in the top inch or so of soil. Dig down the length of A to C and if you have done the job properly you should finish up at C with a trench comparable in size to the one that you took out at A. Now starting at end D take out a similar trench to the first one and fill in the trench now left at C. Proceed back to B where you will find a heap of soil awaiting you to fill in the trench which you should still have.

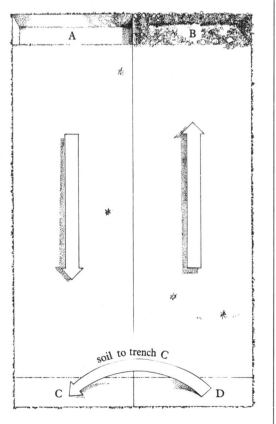

plants but for all the millions of bacteria, fungi and small creatures such as earthworms which inhabit the soil.

In the past too much emphasis has been placed on the importance of burying the manure completely in the bottom of the trench and too little attention has been paid to the value gained from its even distribution throughout the whole of the soil. It is often recommended that the manure be spread before digging commences, but when the soil and manure are wet and sticky you can finish with more on your boots than in the soil. If the job has to be done whatever the weather, try to get the manure carted out onto the land and tipped into heaps. It will then lose less of its volatile components than if it is spread out. Then it can easily be put into the trench with a fork and boots are kept clean. If you have a willing helper, then you can leave it in the barrow and he can spread it along the trench. This was one of my first jobs as a garden boy.

Ridging

This is a method adopted on wet, badly-drained soils and consists of heaping up or ridging the soil, which enables the moisture to drain out, air to pass through and frost to penetrate the ridge. It also exposes a greater area to weathering conditions, and in a new garden cuts out a work stage; if potatoes are to be the following crop they can be planted in the hollows between the ridges. It is not essential to put in manure at the time of ridging, the manure can be stacked, composted with leaves and garden refuse and then filled in to the hollows or trenches between the ridges in spring. This works very well, particularly if the area is to be used for potatoes as well-rotted compost can be put actually over the tubers. For exhibitors or those who wish to grow superlative crops of peas, beans and celery for which a good deep root run is essential, add the manure and then dig between the ridges normally. When the ridges are split and the soil is levelled, you will have an excellent site for these particular crops. Just in case it sounds a very formidable operation, ridging is a job which seldom needs to be done as the benefits are lasting and it is no harder or more dificult than ordinary straightforward digging.

After the initial spade work has been done most soils benefit from the surface being kept on the move and various appliances, both mechanical and hand operated, are available to help out. This is where the mechanical rotary hoes fitted with blades or tines come into their own; they really mechanise hoeing. Keeping the soil open allows it to breathe, rain to penetrate and helps to conserve moisture in the soil. This may sound contradictory but on heavy soils which have dried out, cracks can go down to a considerable depth and the moisture evaporates from the sides of these causing a great deal of moisture to be lost. A fine surface tilth prevents this cracking. It also benefits the various bacteria and fungi in the soil as virtually all the beneficial elements thrive on oxygen. The more you help them the more they will help you.

You can easily find proof that these various bacteria and fungi thrive in the top 5 to 7 in of the soil by looking at old posts. Posts which are otherwise very durable often rot off at, or just below, soil level. The top may be perfectly sound and, on being dug up, the part in the soil 2 ft or more down may also be as sound as the day it was put in, whilst the section at soil level can be completely rotted through. This is due to the active bacteria and fungi which cannot live out of the soil or in the airless conditions of the deeper subsoil beneath.

Not only does organic matter provide food for the various organisms in the soil, it also helps to retain moisture, particularly when it reaches the state gardeners describe as humus. This is organic matter which has decayed and broken down to a point when it is little more than a jelly-like film. Soil, no matter what the texture, is essentially mineral and made up of solid particles; if we can get humus between these particles it will help to keep the very fine ones (which occur in clay and silt) apart and allow better drainage. Between the larger particles of sand and grit it acts as a blotting paper and holds the moisture. So although it sounds contradictory to say humus assists

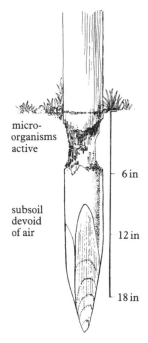

micro-organisms active

subsoil devoid of air

6 in

12 in

18 in

Ridging

This is the procedure to follow: put down a garden line, take out a trench at the end of the plot (A), three spade blades wide, dig the middle width (D) in the usual way, throwing the soil from the first trench forward to A. Then dig widths B and C turning them over on to the middle width (D). Complete the area to be ridged by digging successive strips in this way. As ridging is hard and time-consuming work, my advice is to do a little of this each year. It is better to utilise trench crops such as celery, leeks, peas and beans as a means of eventually trenching all the ground, and this will be found under vegetables.

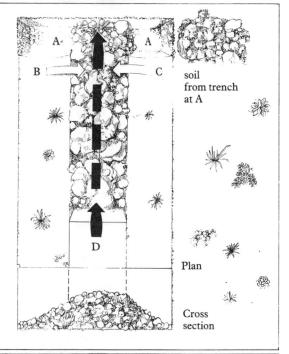

soil from trench at A

Plan

Cross section

drainage and at the same time holds moisture, this is a fact and anything that can be done to produce humus-rich conditions should be done.

Mulching

The title of this chapter, Soil Cultivation, may appear a bit far fetched because the cultivation of crops would seem to be the main aim of gardening. However, it is just as essential to cultivate the soil as the crops that grow in it. Soil cultivation touches on both the mechanical condition and the chemical constituents and to this end mulching can help enormously. A mulch was, at one time, always composed of loose organic material spread over the soil, mainly over the root area of the plant or crops grown, to conserve soil moisture. It was composed of partially-rotted or rotted organic material, manure or compost and any plant food elements washed out by rain into the soil were a bonus. Incidentally there is very little soluble material in peat but provided it is coarse and open, this is an excellent mulching material. Organic material will, ultimately, decay and be assimilated into the soil. Before this happens it can be chewed by small animals, such as woodlice, and portions can be carried down by larger animals, such as earthworms, so much so that in the course of a season a 2- to 3-in layer can be dragged down. I don't know whether we copy the earthworm by incorporating organic matter into the soil or whether they copy us, but the net result is that the soil benefits both chemically and mechanically.

Great claims are made about the value of the various types of earthworm with their burrowing, their swallowing and voiding waste products and much of this cannot be denied. They can also be a confounded nuisance to the gardener by spoiling the surfaces of lawns or upsetting the soil in pots. Nevertheless, for at least 75 per cent of the time, earthworms perform an extremely valuable and free service and should be encouraged. Fortunately, their needs are more or less the same as those of plants. Personally, when exploring the possibilities of a soil I like to find a wholesome crop of worms when digging up a few spadefuls, as I know they wouldn't be in the soil unless adequate supplies of organic matter were present.

Earlier I stated that mulches were formerly organic. However, nowadays many man-made substances can be used including granulated plastic foam materials or sheet plastic. But these, in my opinion, are merely substitutes for the genuine article if only on the score that they have no residual value and can be a nuisance if blown about by the wind. There are certain rules for mulching and because the primary object of the mulch is to conserve the moisture in the soil it is no good applying one to dry ground. Similarly a mulch can also act as insulating material so it is a mistake to mulch the soil surface whilst the ground is cold. It prevents the sun from warming up the soil, or at least delays it, so wait until the plants indicate the time is right. The calendar is of no help here. It is no good saying that mulches should be applied during the first week in April because so much depends on the season, climatic conditions and latitude. As soon as the tree, shrub or plant is growing a mulch should be applied. This is indicated by elongation of stem or by the production of new growth and bursting buds.

Surface cultivation

Opinions are divided on the value of surface cultivation by scarifiers, hoes and mechanical tools and, in my experience, this depends a great deal on the texture of the soil and how it has been used or abused. For example, provided the soil is naturally friable or has been made so by many years of repeated manipulation, manoeuvring and cultivation I have observed no difference in the yield whether the surface soil is stirred or not. To make this point, three separate methods were used on the same crop: surface hoeing to remove weeds and loosen the surface; covering the area with black polythene; controlling the weeds by spraying. The result was that the actual yield was almost identical in all three cases.

A bed of antirrhinums gave a similar result. Part of the bed was occasionally hand weeded whilst the rest was hoed regularly; the results came out in favour of hand weeding. On the other hand, hoeing gave the best results on heavier soils during dry hot weather. Therefore in order to use the most suitable methods of cultivation one is thrown back upon the experience and knowledge of one's own soil and climatic conditions. Unprotected light or sandy soils are, in my opinion, best left alone as the breaking of the surface seal releases moisture from the soil. Heavy clay or silty soils which crack when dry, will benefit from having the surface cultivated shallowly to provide a fine tilth. Again, after heavy rain this tilth may be formed into a sort of crust on the surface which must be broken up as it acts as a seal preventing air from entering the soil.

Consolidation of the soil

It is often said that you can recognise policemen and gardeners by the size of their feet. Whether the job produces the size of feet or whether people with large feet became gardeners and policemen I have never found out, but whether feet are large or small they are certainly most useful to the gardener. Not only the feet but the footwear helps too.

The broader the footwear the better, and in some cases it is desirable to increase this by strapping boards under the soles to avoid over consolidation. Nowadays these are seldom used.

To me, consolidation is neglected in so many instances today and I invite those new to vegetable growing to consider this aspect. It is the introduction and use of motorised cultivators and rotavators which makes consolidation more essential, particularly in the vegetable garden. I have seen 'gardeners' walk over newly rotavated soil and sink up to their ankles and then wonder why on earth they cannot grow good-hearted cabbages and firm sprouts. Possibly not one gardener in ten thousand these days would ever dream of dragging a roller over the vegetable plot, but it would certainly do much more good there than on the lawn. I have watched my father and scores of his age group preparing soil for the onion bed, for lawns and for brassica crops, side stepping literally for hours backwards and forwards across the garden. I have filled in many hours like this myself preparing ground for crops which require a firm soil. When preparing stations for individual rows of sprouts on recently cultivated or dug soil, the technique of using 9-in planks and running the roller up and down the planks seems to be a thing of the past. But after this treatment we certainly got good sprouts.

In my experience, consolidating the soil, particularly for certain crops which enjoy firm soil conditions, is just as important as digging, aerating and breaking up soil clods. What is also not generally appreciated is that large quantities of partially-decayed compost or manure which have been dug in will further decay after being attacked by bacteria and fungi and will leave the soil spongy. This means that even where soil has been trampled down hard it will still be honeycombed with air spaces after the material has rotted. Without consolidation, roots will wander into cavities and dry up as they grow faster than the soil settles naturally by the action of rain and so they never get a good grip on the soil. Similarly when roses, trees and bushes are planted, it is always recommended and should be the accepted practice that they should be trodden in firmly. If a fair amount of organic matter such as peat is used it is even more important to firm the soil thoroughly without paddling down the top surface.

There are several reasons why garden soil, particularly in the vegetable garden, is not consolidated as was the practice a generation or more ago. One is that often unsuitable garden footwear is used, light shoes with thin soles or the best wellington boots, instead of thick heavy boots. The time factor also enters into it – everybody is in a hurry to get the job done – and the wide use of mechanical cultivators doesn't help. There is nothing wrong with these but the rapid rotary movement of tines and blades pulverises the soil whilst it mixes in the manure. But either the soil must be allowed to settle by itself naturally, which takes several weeks or even months, or this process must be accelerated by rolling or treading. Two crops especially spring to mind as examples where consolidation pays off; sprouts, which if planted in loose puffy soil tend to topple over or produce blown sprouts instead of tight buttons, and tomatoes. With the latter the fruit becomes large and distorted with heavy crops of leaves on gross coarse plants. By consolidating the soil the fruits are of even shape and size with smaller leaves and fewer side shoots.

After any firming always lightly loosen up the soil surface, for over consolidation can be equally as harmful as loose soil. This can often occur when the soil is very wet. Again this depends on the composition of the soil. Roughly, soil types fall into three main groups. Silt, where the soil particles are extremely fine, clays where the particles are still very fine but not so fine as silt and sandy soils where the individual grains are much larger. As a rule the sandy soils cannot be over compacted either when wet or dry, but silts and clays are very susceptible to compaction when wet, especially if they are short of organic matter. This was brought home to me when visiting a nursery where a lot of treading had taken place between the rows of plants. When the crops were lifted water was standing in every footmark and wheel track and yet the soil beneath was extremely dry. This was a classic case of surface soil puddling.

This is one of the worst features of house building in the winter time or following heavy rain. The soil around the house, even if of reasonable texture before the builders start, can be damaged for several years. It is made worse when the excavated soil from the bottoms of trenches is left on the surface and compacted by many feet or by the wheels of vehicles. Where this has happened it is not advisable to dig the area. For by turning the floating or puddled material to the bottom it could lay for many years forming a barrier to root penetration and water seepage. Far better to fork up the top 3 in and leave this exposed to the ameliorating effects of frost and winds or, in the springtime, to showers and sunshine. Of course, this may delay the preparation of the garden but it is well worthwhile, especially if there is a lawn to be laid.

Even if the climate is ideal for working, the soil conditions may be completely unsuitable and it is better to leave it until they improve. This can even happen when there are pruning jobs to be done, for after paddling around a tree, both feet and soil can be in a shocking condition. Under such circumstances it is better to spread a few thick sacks on which to walk to spread the weight and to prevent this puddling of the surface soil. I use 2-in plastic mesh fencing. You can also get too much consolidation when treading in trees and shrubs at planting time when the soil is 'plastic'.

The observant may have noticed that deep footmarks made on wet soil will fill up with water which may remain there for days or even

23

weeks. As a result, in extreme cases green algae may form in these deep indented footmarks. This can happen, too, amongst rose trees when shortening them back in late autumn or early winter. When working in such conditions it pays either to wear boards on one's feet or to make short portable duck boards about 4 ft long and 18 in wide. I find that two of these made of 3 in lathes with 2 in spacing are easier to manoeuvre and better to use than planks.

Certainly no wheeling of a narrow-wheeled barrow should be done over grass when it is extremely sodden. Barrows with an inflatable tyre are far better, but of course not everyone has this more expensive type. If any wheeling must be done on the lawn, then either planks or plastic mesh should be laid down first. I keep a roll of 2-in plastic mesh for this purpose – the type that is usually sold for training clematis. Incidentally, if you employ this technique, unroll the netting and then turn it over against its curl. The ends can be secured by two bamboo canes pushed into the ground so that the mesh is kept taut.

Manures and Fertilisers

I made my entry into the garden scene via the manure heap and this is perhaps why I am more conscious than most of its value. It seemed to me, at the early age of eight, and this opinion has remained with me throughout my life, that manure, compost and fertiliser were the mainspring on which the soil quality and crops depended. My earliest recollection of a garden was not the beauty of the flowers but the little blue and red barrow my father made specially for me and a little short-handled fire shovel with which I went out onto the country roads collecting horse droppings.

Today it seems unbelievable, but back in 1910 in country districts where the motive power on the farm was either horses or the occasional steam traction engine, the clip clop of horse hooves on the flint roads could be heard from before dawn to after dusk. Manure was carted out from the bullock sheds and cow byres, turnips and mangolds were brought in and corn and hay were carted, all by teams of horses. My job, immediately school was over, was to dash home, at least a mile, collect my little barrow and get as much manure as possible wheeled on to the garden before it got dark, and for this I received one half penny per barrow load. There was keen competition and kids of my own age used to vie with one another to obtain information on which roads the greatest number of horses would be travelling so that barrows could be filled up in the shortest time. Horse manure, or muck as we knew it, was the stuff that made the garden tick. Fertilisers were virtually unknown, and, of course, far too expensive to buy and even the name meant nothing to most of the rural community. So the needs of the garden revolved round the horse droppings, muck heap and the muck hole.

Because of this early imprinting I can never understand why animal manures, whatever their origin, should be separated from organic material designated as compost. Compost is only as good as the material which is put into it and the more material which has had some animal contact the better, even if it is only the cleanings from the pet rabbit hutch or a few bantams or pigeons. Very often it is this which can act as a starter to a heap of garden debris, like yeast leavening bread. A shovelful of poultry or pigeon droppings introduced daily or weekly into the heap will make it infinitely better.

The long dissertations in the old gardening books about the qualities of the various types of organic manure such as horse manure, cow manure or pig manure and how they should be used and on what soils, I am afraid no longer apply. This is for the simple reason that as towns get bigger, so the source of the supply gets further away from the garden and it is no longer feasible or economic to bring this stuff from the country to the urban areas. It was almost a gardener's charter or bible at one time that a long strawy manure from the stable was the best for heavy land and cow and pig manure was best for light soils. Today, local bye-laws would prohibit having a load of pig manure tipped on the pavement to then be wheeled on to the garden at leisure. And, of course, the neighbours would likely and rightly complain. This all means that the would-be gardener is now thrown back on to his own resources. What then can be put into the compost heap? How essential is organic matter in the soil? As far as the plants themselves are concerned and as a short-term measure, I don't think it matters at all. Plants appear to grow happily without it and anyone who has seen buddleias growing strongly in walls high above the ground and 20- or 30-year-old shrubs and small trees growing in the tops of chimneys or towers and in crevices in rocks, cannot help but marvel at the persistence of life.

I am certain that the soil itself suffers and when deprived of organic matter gradually loses its ability to hold moisture, eventually becoming a desert. There cannot be anything very wrong with the routine practice which has stood the test of hundreds of years and is based on the return of organic matter in some form to the soil if only to keep it healthy. Continuous manoeuvring of the soil and the addition of organic matter can be relied upon to keep the soil healthy, and any additional compounds in the form of nitrogen, phosphates, potash and trace elements are an added bonus.

The soils in this country and in most other European countries can bear witness to this but one has only to go further afield to see how vast areas can be ruined by crude slash-and-burn techniques. This involves taking crop after crop from the land until it is exhausted and then moving on somewhere else. Here in England we can no longer afford these short-sighted practices. Plant analysis reveals there can be nearly a hundred different chemicals in minute proportions in plant tissue. Of these, there seem but a few which are essential.

To illustrate these points I cannot do better than quote from The Foundation Principles of Good Gardening by an old friend R. P. Faulkner, who used to be head gardener at the University College of Nottingham:

'*The primary task of the husbandman is to make his soil fertile and keep it fertile. Anyone can obtain large crops from a piece of good virgin soil, but to obtain good crops year after year, through good seasons and bad, is a very different proposition. Moreover, the gardener is often expected to bring into production soils which are of very indifferent quality – heavy tenacious clays or thin hot sands.*

Fertility of the soil for our common crops has two aspects, distinct and separate, yet complementary, and of equal importance. There is the aspect of the soil as the source of a great many very important nutrients, and there is the aspect of it as the home of plant life. We must pay equal attention to both aspects. In manuring our soils we must keep ever before our eyes next year's crops, and the years to come after, as well as this year's. In selecting the materials we propose to apply we must consider not only their value as sources of plant foods, but their effects on the life of the soil, and what such effects are likely to be on its fundamental character. If we ignore such factors as aeration, moisture-retention, temperature, and a soil condition which makes for free root expansion – in a word, the physical condition of the soil – and apply substances whose sole value is their plant food content, then we run a grave risk of ruining the physical condition of the soil, and when we have done this we shall find that our crops will be poor, although we load the soil with concentrated plant foods. Conversely, if we consider only the physical condition and ignore the nutrient-content aspects, then our crops will be smaller than they ought to be. In both we have to bear in mind that the conditions prevailing in our garden soil are to a certain extent artificial.

Nature does not dig in preparation for each year's re-clothing of the earth, neither does she waste the wealth of the soil, so that the tenets of modern hygiene may be obeyed. The losses from cultivated soils are greater than obtains in uncultivated soils, for the movement of water is usually more rapid, thus leading to leaching out of plant foods to a greater extent and a good deal of the vegetation removed is entirely lost; it does not return to the soil under the conditions of the western civilization in any shape or form.'

Making compost

Having been initiated into gardening via the manure heap and with a name like mine, which my school mates associated with loads of . . ., it seemed perhaps fate that when I went to a training college in Southern India I should follow in the footsteps of the king of the compost makers, Sir Albert Howard. Perhaps I should explain. I joined the army and became an instructor in education and was sent to a training college for teachers in Wellington, Southern India, adjacent to Coonoor where Sir Albert Howard was installing his compost bins using what is known as the Indore method of compost making. I should also explain that in the army during those early days of 1920, a second class Certificate of Education was essential to receive an extra 6d per day, and for county regiments particularly, gardening could be taken as an alternative to mathematics which was not usually the high spot of the farm-labourer-type soldier. As a result we had large model school gardens where we were instructed on teaching gardening. As dung in the East was mainly used as fuel and still is, every scrap of organic matter was valuable, hence the great interest in composting.

Despite being knee deep in manure and compost for most of my gardening life I have never been blind to the fact that supplements in the form of concentrated fertilisers are beneficial if used wisely. I am not a compost fanatic, but appreciate its value.

With all this talk of compost, how then does one make it? Nowadays there are all sorts of devices and claims made for various structures and additives which have some validity but at least 75 per cent of the claims made can be discounted. In fact, all that is needed is a supply of organic material, which is anything that has once lived be it animal or vegetable, a piece of solid earth and the ability to make a stack.

It is amusing to see how things come full circle and now the 'muck hole' has again come into its own, although the system is advertised under much more refined names. It simply means digging a hole and putting in the refuse. It is, in fact, a solid-sided container. In the case of the 'muck hole' and the 'muck heap' the hole was simply a method of containing the daily refuse, the fluff from the carpets (swept by hand of course), the feathers from the chicken or duck for Sunday lunch, egg shells, rhubarb leaves, potato peelings; in fact everything went into the hole.

I grew up in an area where there were no flush toilets or indeed any indoor toilets at all, neither in the village houses nor the great houses. All washing water was laboriously carried upstairs in the great houses and carried down again, together with human waste. This volume of liquid and solid matter had to be conveyed by hand from the big house and you can imagine the extra burden when there were balls and shooting parties. This work, for some strange reason, fell on the gardeners. Therefore, the first job at 6 o'clock every morning, long before anyone was stirring, was to cart anything from ten to twenty heavy buckets of human waste to be disposed of in the garden. From this there was no escape! Carriers and the hole diggers used to alternate. Holes were dug deeply by the light of a candle lantern which meant, in the case of the great houses, the vegetable garden would be trenched 3 ft deep or more continuously over the centuries. From this essential operation grew the technique of trenching and putting in manure.

Anyone who has listened to lectures by General Horrocks will know that in many cases towns and fortresses fell, not because they were taken by the enemy but because of the breakdown of the sewage system. One can therefore readily grasp the need for organised waste

disposal and actually see how gardens have suffered since the introduction of piping waste to the central sewage works. The 'muck-hole'
was the day-to-day collecting point and when it was full it was forked
out and the contents stacked in a square-sided heap adjacent to the
hole. The hole was then ready to receive its daily quota of organic
matter again. One quickly learned that it was advisable to chop up
long material such as old chrysanthemum sticks, pea haulms and
hedge clippings. This was for the simple and practical reason that it
was much easier to fork it out rather than tug half-rotted lengths of
material several feet long with the risk that they would snap back and
plaster you with partially decayed goo. It was also found that the
chopped-up material, whether cut with a sharp spade or with a
chopping hook and a block of wood, decayed more evenly and heated
up better than the long pieces.

There was no need for artificial containers as people were used to
making high stacks of hay and straw. The picture is different now.
Houses and gardens are cheek by jowl, noisome matter is not
acceptable, indeed not talked about, and the operator not so skilled.
So some form of containment is almost essential.

Soil is still the best base on which to make a compost heap and if
you don't want to go to the lengths of digging a hole, just use one
portion of the area designated for compost to tip any of the material
available, old leaves, lawn mowings, grass, weeds or any other organic
matter, into a pile. Then maybe once a week or once a fortnight,
depending on the amount of material, shake the pile out with a fork,
mix it up thoroughly and make it into a stack or put it into a simple
container made from four broom shanks and a 13-ft length of plastic
mesh. I prefer this method to tipping everything into the container

Four broom shanks and a
length of durable plastic
netting make a simple but
effective compost container

straight away because in a small garden there is never enough material added at one time to create any sort of fermentation or heating up and the mix is not good enough. For example, you can get a thick layer of grass cuttings during the mowing season or a thick layer of leaves in the autumn and although it is one more extra job, it is well worth the mixing and turning periodically if you want really good compost.

The ideal compost is made from aerobic fermentation where the material comes out dry and sweet and not foul smelling. It should be brown and when rubbed through the hands be almost like tobacco. My colleagues swear that I smoke mine. The other sort of stuff is graced by the name of anaerobic (without air) and is very often a wet, rotten, sloppy mess, no good for anything.

Owners of small gardens often complain that for the amount of waste they get it just isn't worth the bother and others say they haven't room for a compost heap. Frankly I can't accept either excuse. Making compost involves a certain amount of trouble, this is undeniable, but well-made compost, on analysis, is as near an alternative to manure as most of us are likely to get.

To suggestions that certain things such as rhubarb leaves and privet should not go into the heap, my answer is that anything that has once lived, except perhaps rubber, can be composted. Some materials may take longer than others to break down and if they are not sufficiently decayed, they can be shaken out when they appear and put at the bottom of the next heap.

The use of peat

During the last 50 years the production and use of peat in the garden, which started as a trickle, has become a flood and is possibly now at its peak. If the supply was inexhaustible then I would feel some concern about its continued application to soils and by its indiscriminate and uneducated use. However, I am not worried for the simple reason that it is a very finite material and possibly in 50 years time, the new gardener will be asking, 'What is peat?'

It is very big business at the moment and peat-based composts have now taken the place of soil-based composts (pity the one word compost has to be given to two separate and distinct formulations). In fact my only complaint about the peat supplied today is that it is not available in different grades with regard to size. For the ordinary garden much of it is far too finely ground and has been developed in this way to meet the gigantic appetite of commercial growers who use only fine peat. In the soil 2 lb per sq yd is ample for a yearly application.

Peat is of vegetable origin and, like compost, the quality is only as good as the materials from which it has been made plus the circumstances and conditions under which it has been laid down. Geologically, peat is not a very old material but curiously very little peat as we know it is found in the New World. Although there are literally hundreds of different types of peat, as far as the gardener is concerned there are three main types; these are sedge peat, moss peat and blended peat. Sedge peat is easily identified as it is darker, softer and more easily broken down than the moss peats which are light in colour, often drier and coarser in texture. From a practical point of view the main differences are that sedge peat is more readily broken down in the soil and, as a consequence, more quickly available to the plants but it has not the lasting quality of the moss peats. The third type is the blended peat which either occurs naturally in the bog or is deliberately mixed. Personally I prefer the natural blended mixture as giving the best of both worlds.

Peats vary enormously in their layer formation and are usually extremely acid and have to be weathered, which entails exposing them to rain, frost and sun to reduce the acidity. The stacking also drains out the surplus acidic water.

Peat or other organic materials generally break up heavy soils, making them warmer and less moisture retentive but on the other hand they bind loose soils and make them moister and cooler. They assist water retention, encourage bacterial action and allow oxygen to be admitted, which is just as vital to the roots as it is to the leaves. On the debit side, too much peat tends to make soils acid and encourages the growth and formation of mosses and liverworts on some soils and lawns. Too much peat can also make the soil too fluffy and loose and can alter the balance of the soil, both mechanically and chemically.

Peat should not be regarded as a plant food and must be supplemented by chemical fertilisers or animal manures. Mixed with manure, dried blood, fish meal, bonemeal or mixed in with the compost heap it forms a valuable addition to all soils. In fact an excellent alternative to manure can be made by adding about 15 lb of fertiliser to every 100 lb peat. This should be well mixed and turned continually and allowed to stand for a week or two and then applied at the rate of 2 lb per sq yd where it is required.

A frequent question is asked about the validity of the claims that peat or lignite products break down heavy soils and eliminate digging. This idea is by no means new and has been advocated for over 100 years. Any organic matter encourages the worm population and bacterial and fungal activity. The worms will carry down enormous quantities of it and in doing so they make tunnels and in time they carry the organic matter down to the same position as obtained by digging over with a spade or fork. In this way the soil is enriched and improved. Bacteria are encouraged, drainage is improved and the soil aerated. This can be regarded as a long term excercise but is, nevertheless, effective. However, all plants need their regular supplies of nitrogen, phosphates and potash, whichever way you apply them either as organic or inorganic material. The organic gardeners can use fish meal, bonemeal and dried blood and those who have no particular prejudice can make use of the chemical fertilisers.

Of recent years peat-based composts have been used as an alternative to natural soils as a basis for potting composts and growing mediums and an extension of this has been the growing bag. Basically, these are plastic bags of varying sizes filled with a mixture of peat, sand and slow-release fertilisers. They are recommended for the growing of a particular crop for one season. However, for various reasons it is not advisable to use these for a second year as it is virtually impossible for the ordinary gardener to replace the fertilisers which have been lost during the growing season. Therefore, in my opinion, after use the best place for these is the compost heap. Mixed into the other ingredients the contents will supply finely divided organic matter plus the residual chemicals that have not been used or leached out.

Green manuring

The first and obvious green crop for digging in is weeds. When digging in these or other forms of green manure you need a wider trench than normal so that the green stuff can be skimmed off with about 2 in of soil, turned into the bottom, given a few quick chops with a spade and clean soil turned over on top. The whole area is then left absolutely clean with no weeds or bits and pieces sticking out of the soil to go to seed and create more weeding in the future. The criterion of a good digger is this clean finish.

An ideal time to sow for green manuring is directly after harvesting a previous crop, the soil is still moist and warm and all that is necessary is to scatter on the seed and rake it in. The clovers and vetches will, in addition to providing humus, supply nitrogen to the soil. The new super rape called Akela is available now and if you cannot buy this direct then your normal supplier can obtain it for you from a specialist seedsman.

To obtain the best value from green manuring the crop should be dug in when in full leaf and before the stems become woody and the leaf area deteriorates. For this reason I like the clovers which continue green well into the winter months and can be dug in at leisure. Another good subject for green manuring is the annual lupin which, being a legume too, also produces nitrogenous nodules on its roots.

Perhaps one of the reasons why this ancient method of providing humus is not as widely used as it should be is the difficulty in obtaining small quantities of the seeds. Many allotment societies and gardening clubs buy in bulk to distribute to their members. Mustard and rape, however, are readily available and the value of the green stuff is out of all proportion to the small amount you have to pay for the seeds. Chickweed may not be your favourite weed, but very often, particularly if the autumn is damp, masses of this may accumulate in rows of peas and so here the method is obvious. Don't try to chop it up and rake it off as this only spreads the seeds. Instead dig out a trench, skim off both the pea haulms and the chickweed, and bury them at the bottom. There is nothing in the rule book which says that all the crops have to be cleared before you can dig and the safest place for weeds is a good 10 in below the surface. On sandy soils which do not benefit from early digging in the same way that heavy soils do, it would be better to use a clover mixture which will keep green over winter and can then be dug in during the early months of the year. Exposing light soils to heavy winter rains tends to leach out soluble nutrients such as nitrogen.

If you have a large garden with some dirty corners, plant comfrey. This is a perennial which can be mown regularly and is used either to

Strip digging

Somehow the modern home gardener seems very reluctant to take out a trench even for strip digging but if you think about it carefully, there is no need to cart soil from one end of the garden to the other to fill in the trench. Strip digging, particularly after peas or similar crops, involves taking out a trench about 6 ft wide. This soil is put to one side in a pile. Then dig across the garden, come back up another strip and the heap of soil is waiting there for you to fill in the trench. Strip digging reduces the weed population the following year and pests such as cabbage root maggot and carrot fly are relegated to the depths.

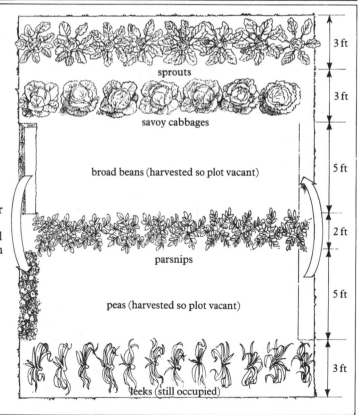

sprouts — 3 ft

savoy cabbages — 3 ft

broad beans (harvested so plot vacant) — 5 ft

parsnips — 2 ft

peas (harvested so plot vacant) — 5 ft

leeks (still occupied) — 3 ft

dig in green or to provide a constant source of materials for your compost heap. As comfrey grows vigorously it will eventually smother out weeds. The flower is quite attractive in its own right. It will also stand a certain amount of shade and can be a good barrier crop against invasive weeds. Altogether it is a most useful plant even apart from its medicinal qualities.

There is no need to scatter fertiliser or even lime on your green manuring. Save this for dusting on the soil surface and raking in a fortnight before you sow or plant the following season.

Fertilisers

The dividing line between manures and fertilisers is very finely drawn but as far as the practical gardener is concerned manures are widely regarded as being of organic origin, fertilisers of chemical origin. The fact that one could be the extract of the other is neither here nor there. There are fashions in fertilisers and in their distribution and availability. Since gardening, or horticulture, became big business, return on capital is often more persuasive than availability. Sadly, perhaps, this means that two-thirds of all the wisdom written about the use and application of chemical or artificial fertilisers is no longer relevant, for the simple reason that many of the compounds are no longer readily available. For example, the so-called straight fertilisers such as sulphate of ammonia are not easy to find. The main straights are nitrogenous fertilisers such as sulphate of ammonia and nitrate of soda, phosphates in the form of superphosphate and potash in the form of sulphate of potash. Their place has now been taken by granular compounds in various ratios either in equal parts as in the case of Growmore (formerly National Growmore) with its seven parts of each of the main fertilisers, or biased to suit a particular crop, say an extra dollop of potash in the case of a potash-loving crop such as potatoes.

More and more slow-release fertilisers are on the market and these give up their constituents over a long period and instead of being almost instantly available, as in the case of sulphate of ammonia, the nitrogen may be in several forms. In fact, some firms claim quick release, mid-term release and late release in one compound alone. Unfortunately experience has shown that there is a certain variability in this depending on temperature and the amount of moisture in the soil, and a slow-release fertiliser applied in the early part of the season with the intention of the nutrients being released throughout the growing period of the crop, may run out of steam during the first two or three weeks. This results in the crop getting an excess of nitrogen and then nothing.

Every fertiliser manufacturer has his own specific formulae for various crops and the gardener with limited experience is advised to use them specifically in the way that they are recommended on the pack and, as experience is gained, to supplement them with various straight fertilisers to suit the demands of a particular crop in a particular season under particular circumstances. There is very little danger of over-application, for the simple reason that unless you have a very deep purse you could not afford to do it.

Books of yesteryear with diagrams of which fertilisers to mix together and which fertilisers should not be mixed have gone by the board as few of them are available. The main thing to remember is that none of the fertilisers should come into contact with lime. The reason for this is simply a chemical one. When most fertilisers come into contact with lime a chemical change takes place and some of the elements are released either into the air or into the soil before the plants can make use of them. So if you apply fertiliser to the surface don't immediately apply lime. This goes for organic manures as well and a good rule is to separate applications of manure and fertiliser from lime either by space or lapse of time.

Reading the packet It is important to read and understand the analysis of modern compound fertilisers which by law is required to be printed on the packet. These fertilisers have been made up by chemists and experts in plant nutrition to suit the needs of a particular plant or group of plants. Bearing in mind what has been said about the need for nitrogen for leafy plants, read off the percentages of nitrogen, phosphates (sometimes expressed as phosphoric acid) and soluble potash. The way in which the analysis is printed varies slightly from company to company and indeed from country to country, but basically the message is the same. As an illustration a well-known grass fertiliser will be described as 36% nitrogen, 6% potash and 8% phosphoric acid. A fertiliser suitable for pot plants would be: 16% nitrogen (8% nitric-, 8% ammonic compound), 21% available phosphoric acid and 27% water soluble potash. A general fertiliser can be expressed in a slightly different way:

| Nitrogen N | Phosphoric Acid as P_2O_5 | | | Potash as K_2O |
	Water soluble	Insoluble in water	Total	
7.0%	6.0%	1.0%	7.0%	7.0%

And finally an organic fertiliser:
Nitrogen (N) 7.3%
Phosphorus Pentoxide (P_2O_5) 5.0% (P2.2%)
P_2O_5 (insoluble) 5.0% (P2.2%)
Potassium oxide (K_2O) 5.2% (K4.3%)

The recommended rate of dilution must also be studied, especially if they have to be mixed with water before application. The higher the nitrogen in the analysis, for example, the greater dilution. This need not lead to worry or confusion just so long as the recommendations are carried out. Powders and granules will take longer to act if left to be washed in by normal rainfall which may fall infrequently. Their action can be speeded up if they are washed in artificially using a hose pipe or watering can.

Foliar feeding Refined fertiliser elements plus minute traces of essential chemicals are available in highly concentrated solutions and often only a few drops per gallon are required. These are particularly useful during periods of drought when, due to lack of moisture in the soil, it is not possible for the plant to take in plant foods in solution by the roots. Foliar feeds are absorbed by the green parts of the plant only at the rate that the plant requires them. I must admit that in many instances this is an act of faith because without complete chemical analysis of the leaf it is mainly guess work. However, if this method of feeding is used then it is better done in the evening and, in particular, when the foliage is damp with dew.

Ash and soot

The use of oil for central heating and for the heating of greenhouses will soon deprive the gardener of two useful waste products of burning coal. The use of ashes for improving and ameliorating sticky soils is often argued furiously among gardeners, but personally, I have always found many uses for the right sort of ash. My early gardening career was spent in some of the great country houses, and from the various stoke holes which heated the greenhouses, conservatories and from the big house itself, ash disposal was a major problem. All garden paths, particularly in the kitchen garden, were ashed but the main walks were afterwards covered with gravel. The benches in the greenhouses were covered with ashes and they were laid under the benches and on all the back drives.

The right sort of ash for the garden is gritty and for general purposes containing lumps no greater than ½ in and no smaller than ⅛ in. In fact, all ashes were put through two riddles, and the larger lumps of clinkers were crushed up and the sharpest saved to put around the succulent growths of delphiniums and lupins to keep off slugs. Some of the finer stuff, when dry, was used for the storing of beetroot, carrots and even dahlia tubers. A fine gritty mixture when well weathered provides an ideal medium for the rooting of all types of cuttings. Nowadays, and indeed in those far-off days, ashes were used for the ring culture of not only tomatoes, but other plants as well.

Many corporations possess a screening plant for recovering cinders which are sold back to people. The fine screenings from these corporation plants is excellent material for topdressing grass, and is widely used by farmers. If the dust is sifted out again through ⅛ in sieve it is excellent for mixing with heavy clay, and can be used as generously as one sixth by volume. For example, to an area 3 ft by 3 ft

Collecting ashes

Nowadays, and indeed in those far-off days, ashes were used for the ring culture of not only tomatoes, but other plants as well. In spite of the conversion to oil burning, there are still large quantities of ash and even burnt shale for virtually the cost of carting, and many domestic boilers can still produce worthwhile supplies. In a less affluent period I can remember the time when virtually every household had a wooden box with a sifter top into which the domestic ashes were tipped and all the burnable cinders retained. Now they go into the dustbin where they are collected by various corporations and sold back to the allotment holders for greenhouse boiler fuel.

If you want to collect your own ashes, then get a box about the size of a tea chest, affix two strong runners inside some 4½ in from the top. Make a frame about 4 in deep half the width of the box. Fasten across the bottom of the frame some ¼-in mesh and tip the cinders into this. They are riddled by moving the sieve along the runners and this will, of course, reduce dust. You will be agreeably surprised that your fuel bill is considerably reduced as a result. The mesh will allow the passage of pieces suitable for garden use, as very fine dust by itself is of little value as it tends to go pasty and clog the soil. All the same, there is considerable value in fine ashes. They will be found of considerable use on thin or heavy soils, especially in the wetter parts of the country.

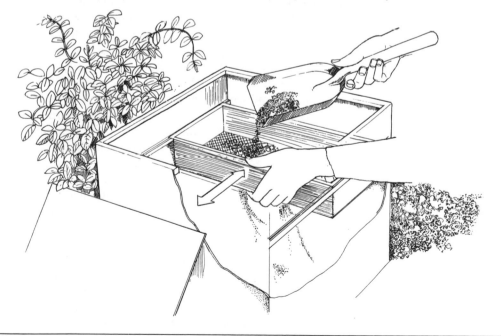

by 1½ ft deep may be added around two barrow loads of gritty ash.

The whole thing about the addition of coal ashes to soil is that it must not be overdone, as apart from the chemical action on the soil the crumb structure will be ruined. Continue with the long-term practice of adding as much humus as possible in the form of compost, manure and peat. Work the soil as much as possible before planting up with permanent subjects and regard the addition of coal ash as a short-term measure to open up the clay to provide drainage and to enable air to get in.

Soot Like many of the gardeners of the old school I still have a sneaking regard for the qualities of soot, knowing well that the claims are in the main over-rated. However, although soot, as with many other things, can be reduced to a chemical formula it does not always explain why plants benefit from such simple things. Possibly one of the reasons is that the elements are contained in such minute proportions and can be assimilated by the plant both through the roots and through the leaves.

Soot, I suppose, can be regarded as one of the very first so-called bag fertilisers and was used as a source of nitrogen long before the existence of the more concentrated fertilisers such as sulphate of ammonia. The value of soot in terms of nitrogen is practically negligible as it only contains two or three per cent. But because it was so cheap it became a source of nitrogen for the garden. Its value, though, does not end with nitrogen as it contains many mineral constituents whilst its solid matter is appreciable. Gardeners in industrial areas where there is a continual build up which acidifies the soil, have little good to say about soot except that it does confer on plants an almost complete immunity from fungal diseases. One point in its favour is that it is easily obtainable and anyone with a coal-burning fire is sure of a regular if small supply.

Soot newly swept from a chimney can be definitely harmful both to the roots and leaves of plants although up to 1½ lb per sq yd can be applied to vacant land during winter digging. Soot should be kept dry preferably stored in an open box in an open shed. In the soil it acts as a mild fumigant and fungicide, dusted around young seedlings it gives a certain protection from slugs and acts as a mild stimulant to growth. It can be mixed with lime so a small amount of ammonia vapour is released which benefits the plants and discourages soil pests. Weathered soot dusted on the dew-dampened foliage of celery and parsnips discourages attacks of the leaf miners, and dusted along rows of carrots, onions and cabbages it gives some protection against the female root flies.

It is as a source of liquid manure or soot water that it is perhaps most prized. It can be used both as a spray and for occasional watering to give plant foliage a good colour and in the case of chrysanthemums and celery it makes the foliage bitter and so discourages the attention of the leaf mining fly. To make soot water put about two shovelsful of soot in a coarse-meshed sack. Suspend this in a barrel of water to obtain the clear straw- or beer-coloured water. If the solution is very strong it should be diluted but the barrel which contains the liquid should not be kept topped up or it will become almost worthless. A black syrup is not soot water and will clog the surface of the soil and do more harm than good. As a spray for foliage plants soot water is excellent, both in the greenhouse and outdoors and so, perhaps in spite of newer fertilisers and insecticides, there is still room for a certain amount of soot in the garden.

Leaves – their storage and use

I am very much a leafmould man, due perhaps to the fact that all my early gardening life was spent on estates where raking leaves off shrubbery paths and burrowing into drifts of lovely leafmould several feet deep was a way of life. Few people experience that today but in most gardens there are always some leaves available. There is food for plants in all decaying leaves which vary more in texture than in nutriment, although there is probably more calcium in those of horsechestnut than any others.

The value perhaps lies more in the texture. It is often stated in articles and encyclopedias that oak and beech leaves are to be preferred, but they seldom state why. The actual reason is the texture, they last longer than most and break down into discs rather than mush. For example, take the texture of the beech leaf compared with that of the apple or hawthorn.

The beech leaf dries crisply and the first stage is the break up into discs, which when added to potting composts keep it open and break down comparatively slowly. On the other hand, the apple and the thorn leaves are soft with no stiffness and the whole leaf curls up and eventually decays. This means that most of the home-gathered leaves are soft unless you have access to a road lined with beech trees or a bit of adjacent parkland or open space where beech and oak leaves can be collected and stacked separately to form leafmould. Given the choice I prefer leafmould and dried leaves any time to peat or any other alternative organic matter.

Three types of leaves which I always avoid are ash, horsechestnut and willow. Not so much because of the leaf blades but because the thick stalks take at least twelve months to break down and decay and ash contains a certain amount of acidity which could be detrimental. However, a few of any of these mixed in with a sort of mixed grill of leaves generally found in the ordinary garden is acceptable. If there is money to spare, a mincer to chop up all the organic debris is ideal.

I have never been very keen on putting lawn mowings into the compost heap which is kept for potting or for mulching because of the many seeds of *Poa annua* (annual meadow grass) it includes. In late autumn when there are fewer seeds I do welcome a few lawn mowings and I achieve this by letting the leaves fall on to the lawn and then with a rotary mower slash the leaves to shreds whilst mowing the grass. They become thoroughly mixed together and form the basis of really fine leafmould.

This mixture is either raked up or, in my case, collected into a large box and put into the compost bin. On top of every 4-in layer I sprinkle on a couple of handfuls of superphosphate. Superphosphate has two actions, it kills slugs and their eggs and helps to break down the compost, partly chemically and partly because of the minute traces of sulphuric acid it contains. It also supplies very valuable phosphates which are retained and not leached out and most garden soils are deficient in phosphates. A small amount of phosphate helps germinating seedlings and promotes sturdy growth. It has no ill effect on any other seedlings or plants which are potted up into it.

I am often asked if pine needles or those of other garden conifers, such as cupressus or metasequoia, can be added to the leaves. The answer is there is nothing detrimental in them, the only trouble being that they take about four times as long to decay as deciduous leaves because of the resin and turpentine they contain. Compost them separately and they form an ideal and durable mulch for most flowering shrubs. My favourite use for the true pine needles, however, is for the making of a topdressing for paths as they form a dry durable weed-free surface.

Salt as manure

Common salt (sodium chloride) is probably the oldest chemical fertiliser and yet little or nothing seems to be known about how and why it acts. In fact, sometimes it doesn't and certainly an excess will kill plants as effectively as any weedkiller. In this connection it is rather interesting to note that if a heavy application of salt is used as a weedkiller, after a period of time the weeds come back with double their original vigour.

The recognition of the manurial uses of salt dates back to the very earliest recorded times. There are many allusions to its use in the Old Testament, and again in the New, whilst according to writers such as Pliny, it was well known as a manure in Roman Italy. The Persians and the Chinese are recorded as having used it from time immemorial as a fertiliser, particularly for dates. It seems, too, on looking through ancient books that it was used for a number of purposes some beneficial and some as punishment. For example, it was customary for the ancient Jews and the Romans after a total conquest of a city or a nation, to spread salt thickly on the fields, after razing the buildings. Having access to considerable quantities in the 'salt' sea, one could follow their logical reasoning.

It has been described as an insecticide, a germicide and as an antiseptic. The Romans also used salt to spread on a spot where some great crime had been committed. I have traced its use in England back for hundreds of years and Lord Bacon had a lot to say about it whilst Coke of Norfolk used it in considerable quantities.

In my own lifetime, before 1914, large quantities of salt brought from Great Yarmouth, together with herring heads and innards, were carted on to the fields, especially where 'mangels' (mangolds) and sugar beet were grown. Apropos of this, two old village rustic characters, 'Old' Bob Burton and 'Old' Betty Greavner, used to stock up on salted herrings when they were scattered on the land. Old Bob, a hedger and ditcher, used to toast many a herring over his breakfast fire and most appetizing they smelt too on a cold frosty morning.

I have been intrigued with the use of salt in the garden and on various crops ever since that time. Broadly, my experience has been that it makes poor land poorer but heavily-manured land better. It assists in the flocculation of fine particles, much in the same way as lime, but it seems to act perhaps more as a digestive by making solutes (solution of chemicals) more readily available and more easily assimilated.

It appears to me that the action of salt as a manure is indirect and not direct. This is in a line with sugar and yeast residues which are often used to put girth on exhibition leeks. Salt, of course, went out of favour as a fertiliser with the introduction of more precise chemical fertilisers but for some crops I still use it, particularly on asparagus and beetroot. I also use it on over-wintering brassicas such as sprouts, savoys and cabbage, as well as spring-maturing broccoli.

The old gardener's measure was a cubic inch of salt to the square yard. The cubic inch was measured by making a square hole in a potato or turnip; I used a heaped teaspoonful. The main advantage as far as I'm concerned seems to be that it acts a bit like anti-freeze and makes the foliage less liable to damage by the alternate freezing and thawing which plays havoc with overwintering brassicas.

I found the following quote in an old book: 'common salt – chloride of sodium – applied in the spring at the rate of 20 bushels per acre has been found very beneficial to asparagus, broad beans, lettuce, onions, carrots, parsnips, potatoes and beets. Indeed, its properties are so generally useful, not only as promoting fertility but as to destroying slugs, that it is a good plan to sow the garden every March with this manure'. The flower garden is included in this recommendation: 'for some of the best practical gardeners recommend it for the stock, hyacinth, amaryllis, ixia, anemone, colchicum, narcissus and ranunculus. And in the fruit garden it has been found beneficial to almost every one of its tenants, especially the cherry and the apple. My own experiences are in a line with those of Professor C. M. Aikman, a Professor of Chemistry at Glasgow University, that 'there must be fertilising matter present in the soil if it is to act favourably'.

Studying the experience of Norfolk farmers of 100 years ago, it would seem that by greed they ultimately did more damage than good. They found, as many other people have found, that a small quantity of salt applied with heavy dressings of manure produced beneficial results on virtually all crops. They then reduced the quantity of manure and sold this and increased the quantity of salt, which was cheap, the result being that the crops and the soil became poor, hence the old jingle 'salt and lime without manure makes both land and farmer poor'.

In the early days of artificial fertilisers, salt was often used as an adulterant, especially in the fertiliser known as muriate of potash, sometimes described as agricultural salt. Salt can be found naturally in virtually everything, animal and vegetable alike. More and more we are finding out that it is the tiny microscopic amounts of a substance that can make or mar man, animal or vegetation and so it would appear to be the case with salt.

Lawns

In this year of grace few people can afford the luxury of selecting and buying a plot of land of their own on which to build a house and lay out a garden complete with surrounding lawns. Instead, the house and garden come as packages, estates, either designed and laid out by private contractors or as municipal enterprises.

Invariably the fronts of the houses bordering on roads are levelled and turfed and even planted up by the contractor leaving only a small area at the back of the house, and even this is often roughly levelled. This is at best covered with a layer of top soil and at worst merely smeared over with a token depth of soil which can be suspect. In the days when a lorry was loaded by hand and the top soil taken from the top, it was usually reasonable, but now the lorry is loaded with a mechanical shovel which scoops anything in its path and tips it into the lorry to be spread as a top layer on a dozen gardens. Turf, where it is laid, is often of the poorest quality, full of rough grass and weeds and literally rammed down to make it reasonably level. Therefore, one often has to remake a lawn rather than to make it from scratch. Fortunately, grass, as the old proverb has it, will grow anywhere except on a busy street. The soil need not be rich but for preference it should be uniform in texture, and not given to waterlogging.

Drainage

Nowadays, housing sites are invariably drained and roads laid out before building starts. This means that if there are any pockets of excessive wetness, particularly where a low area has been filled in, there is just nowhere that the individual who owns the plot can drain it away. However, a few day's observation will soon settle if the area to be converted into a lawn is in need of extra draining simply by digging a few holes 12 to 18 in deep and observing if these fill up with water. If they do, then water is draining from somewhere else. Observation of the surface after heavy rain will also give a clue to the drainage capacity. If water remains on the surface after heavy rain longer than twenty four hours then something must be done about it.

If, after testing, surplus water presents a problem then, in an enclosed garden alongside others, there is often nowhere outside the garden where the excess water can be drained. This means that the only answer is a sump. This can take two forms, it can either be a hole or a trench. However tempting it may be never break into existing drains via manholes as this could lead to a lot of trouble and even more expense. If you decide to make a hole it should be at the lowest part of the garden and as far away from the house as possible.

For all normal gardens attached to a house built since 1945, a hole 3 ft deep and 3 ft square will suffice. The bottom should be broken up for the simple reason that if the area is waterlogged then the sub-soil will be clay or silt. In a new garden there is invariably enough rubbish, brick ends, lumps of concrete or similar debris on the building site to

Types of sumps

Draining by way of a sump is very suitable if you are making a path and most people like to have a hard path. It involves excavating the full length of the path, not necessarily the full width, but about 1½ ft wide and 2 ft deep. The trench is filled with rubble and the path laid on top. Any number of shallower drains can be let into this sump from other points in the garden. The drains can be commercially available perforated plastic drainpipes which are far

more convenient than the foot-long field tiles. Homemade drains can easily be made by placing two bricks on edge with one on top.

Faggot drains similar to those made by the Romans are another possibility. These are made of cuttings from hedges or coppices and will last a long, long time in clay. Where the drainage is not too bad clippings from a privet hedge or old chrysanthemum stalks laid lengthways will serve very well.

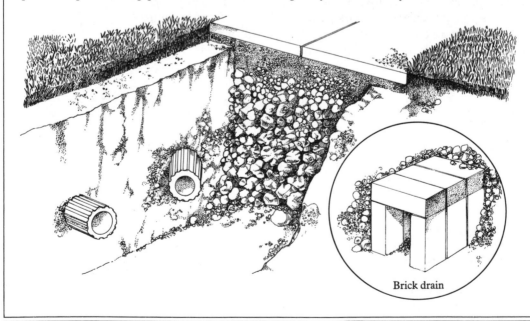

Brick drain

fill the hole to within 12 in of the surface. Place the big stuff at the bottom, small stuff at the top and if it can be topped with chippings or gravel so much the better. Fill in the top with a little of the clay mixed with soil and taper off to the best soil for the last 6 in.

Improving a badly-laid lawn

Let us divide the area already grassed and the area to be grassed into two separate parts. If the front of the house has been turfed and you have paid for it on the cost of the house, it would be unreasonable to suggest you take it up to see what it is laid on, or to re-lay it with special or better turf. Under normal circumstances it would be better to leave it because no matter how bad the turf is it can always be improved by cultivation. Obviously this means that any dressing, feeding or aerating must be done from the top.

Turfing by a builder is usually done by a sub-contractor or, in the case of a large firm, by a specialist department. So no matter what time of the year you take possession, the best thing that you can do is to dress the grass with coarse sand. This will level out irregularities and help to nullify or alleviate the pressure that is often used in the course of construction. Follow this up during the growing season, which extends from the end of February to the end of September, with a dressing of a summer compound lawn fertiliser at the rate of about 2 oz per sq yd. Only in extreme cases will it be necessary to dig it all up and start again. Obviously this could be a very expensive and time-consuming job. When starting from scratch, it pays to do a bit of exploratory work, even if the surface is covered with what looks like good soil.

Improving the soil

It must be remembered that to bury pipes, drains and cables, trenches are necessary and most likely have been dug by a mechanical digger and infilled the same way. So it is too much to hope that the sub-soil has been returned to the bottom of the trench leaving the top soil at the top. Although at first sight it appears that the contractor or builder has done you a great service by spreading out top soil all over the surface it may conceal horrors which will only manifest themselves when shrubs fail to grow and the grass grows well in some areas and badly or not at all in others. So although it takes time, it is worthwhile making exploratory holes to a depth of about 1½ ft to see just what does lie underneath the surface.

This surface layer of reasonable-looking soil so kindly spread by the builder can be a snare and a delusion because immediately under it may be an impermeable layer of clay, an area used as a lime pit or where a cement mixer has been standing and diesel oil has leaked all over the place. The result is that the unsuspecting new owner will carefully rake this top layer, sprinkle it with peat and fertiliser and eventually with grass seed and watch it shade to green as the seeds germinate. It is when the roots meet the impermeable or poisonous layer that the trouble starts. So it is essential that there should be no such layers and any top soil should be forked into the soil or rubbish underneath. Better still the top soil should be scraped into heaps and the underlying soil should be dug or forked over and exposed to the weather for as long as possible. Incidentally, exposure to sun and wind is almost as good as exposure to frost and winter weather for ameliorating the soil. Having tested the underlayer for excess water, re-spread the top soil and fork this into the top 6 in at least. This may well prove discouraging because if a thin layer, say 3 in thick, is laid over an area of mixed rubbish and clay the resultant surface will look terrible and not nearly as pleasing as the layer of top soil spread by the builder. However, the results in later years I can assure you will be far, far better than trying to establish a lawn in a thin layer of reasonable soil over what is literally a load of old rubbish.

Seed

For ordinary mortals the house has a front and a back, a front garden and a back garden, a front lawn and a back lawn. Front lawns, like shop windows, are intended to be eye catching. The back lawn is often more for use than ornament and invariably where there are children and pets it is subjected to a great deal of wear. This means that finer, though not such hard-wearing, varieties of grass can be used for the purely ornamental front lawn. Newer and better strains of grass seed are being evolved every year and varieties are now available for specific purposes; for example, under trees, in shade, on dry sandy soils and there are even grasses which are greener and better in the winter than they are in the summer. It therefore behoves anyone who has a pride in a grass lawn to enquire more closely into the characteristics of the grass seed they propose to sow. It is worth this extra trouble because the lawn is there for as long as the house lasts. You may change your flower beds and their contents but seldom does one change the lawn.

It used to be said, with truth, that rye grasses should never be included in a good seed mixture but this no longer holds good because dwarf leafy rye grass strains are now available. But don't be fobbed off with any old packet of cheap lawn seed. As with most commodities the higher the price you pay the better the quality.

The time of sowing of grass seed in the British Isles is roughly from the end of March to the end of April and from late August to the end of September. However, during a cool showery season sowings can be made during any of the summer months as long as you avoid hot dry periods. Any time when there has been a shower of rain during midsummer germination is quick and with modern sprinkler systems growth can be maintained.

Turfing

Out of the active growing season from early October until early March, depending on prevailing weather conditions and when the soil is workable, turf may be laid. There is no doubt that turfing establishes a new lawn much more quickly because it is simply the transference of the top layer of grass and roots from one place to another. Turves root quickly into the ground and into one another provided, or course, they have been properly prepared. In a matter of months one can walk or run about on a turfed lawn.

There is, however, a question of cost and quality of turf. Good turf is cultivated but there is also a lot of rubbish about and unless it is of good quality, free from weeds and 'boxed' (cut to squares or strips of equal size and of equal thickness) then you are in for a lot of trouble and extra work. Small quantities, say under 10 yd, of turf may be quite expensive for the simple reason that 10 yd takes as much carrying on a lorry as 100 sq yd and the cost of transport is high. Turf, when supplied by a turf specialist is usually cut by machinery and the turves may be in strips 3 ft long or measuring 12 in square. The main difficulty is that the soil on which the turf is growing seldom matches that on which it is laid. However, this has now been overcome by using a neutral growing medium and the turf can be supplied in rolls of up to 3 m long and 1 m wide under the trade name Bravura Turf.

This is possible because the turf is grown on a strong mesh in which the roots interlock with a backing sheet. There is, therefore, no severence from the ground and the roots have been grown horizontally instead of vertically. This means that immediately the plastic backing is peeled off and the turf laid on the new growing surface, the roots penetrate within a matter of minutes and in twenty four hours are an inch down. As a lawn it may be walked or played on within five weeks of laying instead of the usual 12 to 18 months. Perhaps the biggest asset of this technique is that at the time of ordering you can specify the particular type or mixture of grasses so your lawn is literally made to order.

Turf grown on mesh can be laid straight down onto previously prepared soil once the backing has been peeled off

Unorthodox lawn making

There is another method of making a lawn which I have used many times myself and this is 'cannibalising'. This is particularly useful when it is required to enlarge a lawn using the same type of turf so that the division between the new and the old is not apparent. If a strip is added to a lawn and seed is used, then the extension would probably show for ten or more years and even if turf is used it may take a good many years before the lawn looks a complete unit. Cannibalising means using portions of the existing lawn chopped up into small pieces, planting them about 8 in apart. Although this sounds a difficult job, in practice it is the easiest method of making a lawn that I know.

This method can also be used when making a lawn from scratch and requires only about one sixth of the amount of turf which would be required if whole turves were laid edge to edge. It is perfectly possible to make a lawn of cultivated turf by this method using a fraction of the quantity of turf and, of course, costs proportionally less. In fact 1 sq ft will produce about nine mini-turves.

The soil should be prepared in the normal manner; that is well dug and if the soil is badly drained, then the sub-soil should be broken up. Even if the sub-soil is hard and tenacious all that may be required is to take out narrow trenches about 6 ft apart. Break up the bottom of these with a fork and add ashes, clinker or rubble, so that in effect these breaks are lower than the hard pan. Water will then percolate through the top layer onto the hard pan and eventually find its way to the deeper broken up and porous levels. This method has the advantage that such a lawn does not dry up nearly so readily in dry weather as a completely drained lawn. Normally, however, it is sufficient just to dig and if the soil has been cultivated previously there is no need to add manure, fertiliser or anything else. On very light and hungry soils composed of a mixture of sub-soil brought up by the builder, it pays to fork over thoroughly and add peat at the rate of 2 lb per sq yd and allow the soil to lay rough for a few weeks.

A pre-seeding fertiliser should be raked in at the rate of 1 oz per sq yd a fortnight before planting. After levelling, raking and a light rolling, the surface should be raked to a depth of about 2 in, which is the normal length of the teeth of a good rake. This ensures the actual surface is loose whilst the body of the soil is firm. A normal-sized turf can then be roughly chopped up with a sharp edging iron to produce pieces of any shape roughly 2 in by 2 in. These can be placed on the surface of the soil, grass side up, from 6 to 9 in apart. All that remains to be done is to step firmly and squarely on each piece, pressing it into the soft, loose surface. When the area has been completed it can be rolled to consolidate the lawn and firm in the pieces.

I find it best to do this job during the early part of the year so that growth can start straight away. I have had a lawn, many lawns, in fact, and grass paths made in this way, completely covered by grass at the end of the summer.

Groundsmen and bowling-green keepers make use of this method to provide a reserve turf patch, and in a very short time they have at their disposal an excellent supply of good quality turf which is indistinguishable from their greens. This method too has the advantage that large quantities can be transported in sacks and used either

Edges and weed gullies

Where a hard path bounds a lawn and the lawn has been repeatedly trimmed with an edging iron, sooner or later a gully or space between the edge of the lawn and the edge of the path develops. Ideally the edge of the lawn should be protected by a 2-in wide concrete curb to just below the level of the grass so that it does not damage the lawn mower. The leaves of the grass can then be allowed to grow over the hard edging and be trimmed regularly with edging shears. Metal edging is not recommended as this bends and quickly becomes sharp and a danger particularly to small children.

If a gully has developed this can lead to endless weeding which will have to be done by hand as chemicals could damage the turf. It is best to fill it in. Start by making a cut with an edging iron some 9 in from the edge of the lawn. The gully should then be filled in with soil and the turf lifted, either in a continuous length or cut up into sections, whichever is more convenient, and pulled forward on to the path. This will leave a well-defined gully

behind the strip of turf.

This space between the permanent lawn and the strip which has been moved forward should be filled with soil with a little coarse sand mixed into the surface. Then, either sow with grass seed if it can be matched up with the old lawn, or, better still, cut off a further 2-in strip from the lawn side. Cut this up

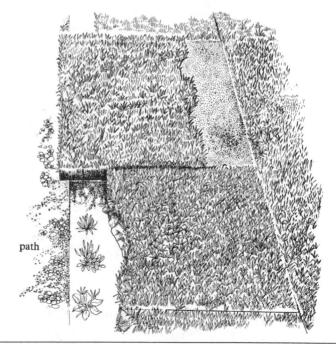

path

into squares and press them into the soil with the foot, grass side up of course. It will quickly fill in the space and in a few months there will be no noticeable difference in the type and texture of the grass. On the other hand, newly-sown grass may show up as an annoyingly different strip for several years.

for patching or making new lawns of special turf with much less of the burden and expense incurred from using full turves.

Mowers and mowing

Excellent lawns can be quickly ruined by bad mowing; even the best mower in the world can ruin a lawn if misused. One of the worst features of power-driven mowers is the effect of glazing. If the grass or the soil is wet the power drive should be released and the mower carefully turned round manually. If this is not done the spinning of the roller causes glazing, a sealing of the soil, and soon grasses die out and moss becomes established.

The more frequently the lawn is cut the better. Three times a week or a minimum of twice a week during the growing season is ideal. However, if under circumstances such as continuous wet weather, holidays or sickness the lawn is not cut regularly then the machine should be adjusted and no attempt should be made to make one cut at a low setting suffice. Grasses are living plants and can be damaged by badly adjusted or blunt mowers but the damage does not end with the chewing effect of badly adjusted blades. Every ragged end of the grass blade becomes very vulnerable to attacks by a multiplicity of diseases.

Types of mowers There are two main types of mowing machines. The first is the cylinder mower where a multi-bladed cylinder revolves against a stationary bottom or sole plate. The other is a spinning rotary mower with two or more cutting edges which depend for their ability to cut on the speed at which it revolves. This flail-like action does not produce the best appearance or the finest textured lawn but a well-maintained mower will keep the grass under control and in reasonable condition for a work and play lawn. For the purely ornamental lawn and for the purist, the cylinder mower with its scissor-like action produces the finest finish and the quality of the cut is determined by the number of blades. For example a ten-bladed cylinder mower will give a far superior cut to a machine with only five blades.

Stripes on the lawn have become an advertising gimmick in recent years and great play is made of this effect on television. It is purely visual and is simply caused by the roller of a cylinder mower pressing the blades of grass, first in one direction and then in the reverse, so that the light is reflected from different angles of the grass blades.

At least every two years a cylinder mower should be sent to a suitable firm for overhaul and maintenance, preferably as soon as the cutting season has ended in early October. No attempt should be made to sharpen either blades, cylinder or sole plate, no matter how tempting the adverts which suggest this can be done. Neither can a cylinder be sharpened on a lathe, as this produces the wrong cutting angle. The correct angle can only be obtained by having the cylinder stationary and the abrasive grinder revolve round the cylinder. Furthermore, the blades are extremely hard and if either of the blades, rotary or straight, can be touched by a file then they have got past the stage of usefulness.

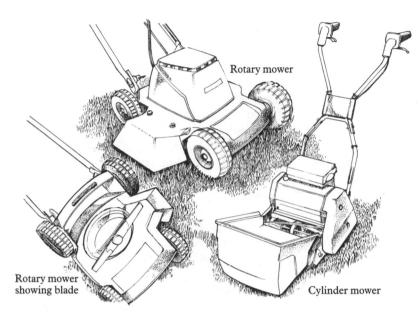

Rotary mower

Rotary mower showing blade

Cylinder mower

The cylinder mower gives the finest finish to a lawn but rotary mowers are becoming increasingly popular and cope well with rough grass. The rotary cutting blade is enclosed for safety but is easy to clean

Grass cuttings To leave these on the lawn or to collect them is not only a cause of controversy but often of real anxiety. The fact is that if the grass is cut not less than twice a week they may be safely left on. Not only is this an advantage during periods of drought but after fourteen to sixteen days the nitrogen in the cut grass is returned to the soil. I have proved this to my own satisfaction and had it confirmed by the agronomist, Professor James Beard of Michigan University.

I divided up my lawn into two. One half was cut three times a week without a collecting box whilst on the other half all the grass clippings were collected. This experiment was continued for twelve years and at the end of the period the half where the grass was not collected was in better condition and almost completely free from moss and thatch. Both halves received the same treatment with fertiliser and top-dressing. The safest guide with regard to leaving grass clippings on is that if they are visible two days after cutting then the lawn should be brushed or raked to remove any surplus.

Moss

All the scores of different algae, liverworts and mosses are collectively known as moss to the ordinary home gardener. They form on lawns, paths, walls, crazy paving, tops of pots, seed boxes, garden frames and even on woodwork. Judging from my letters and meeting people at lectures and shows, many people are worried to death about it. In fact quite a number have said they are sure there is more moss about now than ever before. This could be perfectly true, because these low growths are amongst the most primitive of all growing plants. They have a great capacity for survival and in remote ages played a big part in the formation of soil. They are flowerless plants and do not make seed, but they can be propagated by vegetative means, that is by division and spores. The latter are so tiny they are everywhere, up in the sky, thousands of feet down in mines and caves, in water, in everything we eat or breathe. Many of them have an affinity for anything that has been burned and my experience is that if mosses of various kinds are more widely disseminated than they used to be this may well come from the wider use of peat.

As the one-time owner of a peat bog I have had a good opportunity to study moss formation. Through the ages peat deposits have been burned, either by natural visitations such as lightning, or more recently by man. Immediately following the burning, huge areas are covered with various types of mosses and liverworts (the moisture-loving sphagnum is not included in this category as this requires special conditions). Many upland areas drain into reservoirs and though harming no one, thousands of millions of spores are disseminated in tap water. There are also millions of spores blowing about in the atmosphere to take into account and these are responsible for the greening of soil in seed pans, boxes, pots and where the hose pipe is used on the lawn or flower beds. At some time most gardens have received peat of some sort or another and this too carries its quota of spores.

How harmful then is moss on the surface of the soil? Quite frankly, I think an awful lot of people worry unnecessarily about it. True, it is dangerous on paths and crazy paving because it makes them slippery. When raising slow-germinating seeds such as those of roses, the moss may inhibit the growth of the seedlings by smothering the soil and excluding the air and forming a mat which cannot be pierced by the seedlings. But under shrubs, roses and strong-growing herbaceous plants, I have not been able to find that it does any harm whatsoever.

The formation of moss will become more widespread following the use of chemical weedkiller, because after more than five years of experimental work, I find that mosses will re-establish themselves more quickly than the higher plants such as grasses and weeds. This, I know, already worries a lot of people, but my own close observations have satisfied me that provided the soil is stirred at least once a year moss will not seal the soil to exclude air or rainwater. Topdressings of acid fertilisers also encourage the growth of mosses. In fact their very formation is an indication that the surface of the soil, at least, is rich in nitrogen.

Mosses on crazy paving can be eliminated by sprinkling with mercurised lawn sand and on concrete paths, drives, hard tennis courts by watering or spraying with an ordinary tar oil winter wash. Various proprietary bleaches, such as chloride of lime, will also remove dangerous and disfiguring mosses. However, care must be taken when using caustic materials as if they drain into vegetation, such as lawn edges or borders, they can cause harm. Damage can also be done to carpets by walking on treated paths and then going indoors.

Mosses on lawns are a separate problem and although one is repeatedly advised to examine the drainage, this is only one small part of the problem. Mosses can and do appear on the best drained lawns, depending on situation and environment. Bad drainage is often blamed for the appearance and growth of mosses. This, however, cannot be true of such situations as the sides of pots, the tops of stone walls, crazy paving and tree trunks where it often hangs in festoons. What is necessary for the formation of the majority of species of moss is ample moisture in the atmosphere. This means that certain districts are more prone to moss formation than others. On the shores of Lough Erne in Ireland for example I have seen moss 4 in deep on concrete gun emplacements with the moss breaking up the surface of the concrete. It also breaks up roofing tiles and fills up gutters.

As a pioneer plant it is extremely valuable as it adheres to rocks and, as just mentioned, unsightly lumps of concrete. It traps wind-blown soil and in the situation examined, formed the first home of such diverse plants as wild strawberries and primroses. Here is an extreme example of the growth of mosses on a well-drained surface. A gardener in this district lined his driveway with moss-covered stones. Birds took the moss from these for their nests and the buds and spores settled on the asbestos tiles on his bungalow and in two years the resulting growth had dissolved and destroyed the whole roof.

Moss disseminates by division of minute detachable buds and by spores. Thus, the vigorous raking of lawns so often advised may spread more new plants than destroy old ones. Assuming that the lawn is reasonably well drained, that is, water does not stand on the surface for more than twenty four hours after a heavy downpour, it is more important to encourage the growth of grasses than to tear the lawn apart by raking. Forking or hollow tining at least once every three years and annual top-dressings of sandy soil will do more good than severe raking. Certain acid peats as previously mentioned can encourage moss. Heavy liming is no cure either. In fact, as the best lawn grasses grow in slightly acid soil, liming will only encourage the production of the more leafy and stalky grasses.

Early feeding, say at the middle or end of February, is one way of killing moss as this encourages the early growth of the finer grasses. The coarser grasses, such as those grown by the farmer for cattle feed, start into growth some weeks later.

Various chemicals may be used for controlling moss, and perhaps the best of these is mercurised lawn sand which has the advantage of killing not only the moss and the small viable buds but destroys the

Aerating the lawn

No doubt you have read from time to time, that lawns require spiking or aerating, both to let air into the soil where it gets a lot of traffic and to improve drainage. Today there are a number of special hollow-tined forks and similar devices for this job. Even so this can be a very arduous task where the lawn is of any size.

In this case a special spiked roller is an easier tool to use, but as these are used only once a year few people will want to go to the expense of buying one. It is, however, perfectly possible to make a very effective spiked roller at little cost which will last a lifetime. The cylinder of the roller is made from an ordinary five-gallon oil drum, and spikes from ordinary pipe holdfasts. These are tapered spikes approximately 3 in long, with a semi-circular loop at the other end which when knocked into a wall holds the pipe. The thickness of the oil drum is immaterial as in time it will rust away, but it is important that the drum should be free from dents. It is essential that there should be an opening at one end big enough for the hand to be inserted, but failing this, the end of the drum can either be removed by melting the solder or cutting a hole. A large hole may be made by drilling a number of small holes in a large circle then knocking through the small separating pieces with a cold chisel.

To accommodate the axle of the roller a hole should be made exactly in the centre of each end of the drum, the size of the hole depending on the diameter of the pipe available. I found that a 1-in pipe is sufficient and an iron bar can

Hollow-tined fork

be pushed through the pipe as the axle proper. This leaves scope for plenty of ingenuity in attaching a handle. I adapted the handle of an old mowing machine but that of a pram or push chair will work quite well. If no fixed handles are available it is perfectly possible to pull the spiked roller with a rope, but in this case a spacing bar must be used to stop the rope spores as well. This is best applied in April at the rate of about 3 oz per sq yd. Where the moss is extremely dense it may be necessary to loosen and carefully rake some out, because when it is dead and in districts of high rainfall it tends to settle as a solid mass or film which excludes air. Air is absolutely essential to the roots of grass plants and the density of the moss growth will determine the severity of the treatment needed to overcome it.

It may take two or three years to eliminate dense moss by forking, sanding and adding small amounts of fine grass seed with the solid topdressing. I recommend adding ¼ oz of seed to 2 lb of a sand and

chafing on the edges of the roller as the ends of the rope will be attached to the axis.

The holdfasts can be purchased from any ironmonger's shop and the spikes of these should be about 3 to 3½ in long and the number required will depend on the circumference of the cylinder. The spikes should be arranged in rows and spaced alternately about 4 in apart in the rows and about 5 in between the rows which will simulate forking. The position of the holes is best marked out first with chalk on the outside of the drum. When the positions of the holes have been determined make the holes themselves by using one of the holdfasts as a punch and driving the spike right through to its widest point. Do this, of course, from the outside. It will be found that the spike of the holdfast is broader than it is thick. Therefore make the holes, which will be rectangular in shape, so that the longest side is parallel with the end of the drum. This may sound fairly complicated but in practice is perfectly simple.

When all the holes have been made, stand the cylinder on its end on two bricks or a soft surface to allow the end of the pipe which carries the axle to protrude about 2 in. Then insert the holdfasts from the inside of the drum. Tap them gently through until the curved part which normally holds the pipe is up against the inside of the drum. Then mix a sufficient amount of sand and cement to fill the drum, using one part cement to one part sand to three parts fine granite chippings or clean gravel. Make this rather on the moist side and fill in and tamp down gently with a cane or stick to make sure that the cement mixture is pressed in between the loop of the holdfast and the inside

of the drum. Complete the filling and leave standing on end until the cement is set hard. In a few years the metal cylinder or drum is bound to rust away but by this time the cement will be stone hard and it is more of an advantage than otherwise. For a smaller lawn, of course, a smaller cylinder can be made and very often the handles can be taken off the lawn mower and temporarily attached to the roller.

When not in use stand the roller on end for if it is left on the grass the buried spikes will rust more quickly. Try not to drag the spiked roller over a stone or tarmac path as this will not only chip up the surface but blunt the spikes.

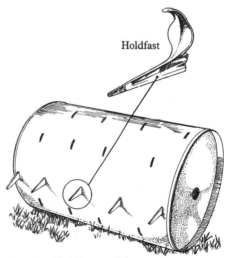

Holdfast

thin edge of holdfast parallel to direction of travel

soil mixture. A method used and recommended by the Turf Research Association is to make up a compost of a 6-in layer of good loam, interspersed with 2 in of farmyard manure and more soil. This is allowed to mature for twelve months and is then sliced down and sieved before applying. Spent mushroom compost may be used, but this should be free from chalk lumps. In gardens where soil is difficult to come by the old soil knocked out of the pots of chrysanthemums and tomatoes may be used to advantage. Stack this for twelve months and then sieve it through a ¼ in sieve before using.

Generally a complete fertiliser, preferably organic based, is better for the promotion of good grass than large quantities of sulphate of ammonia which in time tends to kill out the finer grasses and encourage weeds. My own experience with fine lawns is that no violent action should be taken at any time. By this I mean making any application of large quantities of fertilisers, dressings or lime, with which to try and achieve a rapid change in soil and herbage conditions. The soil and herbage of a lawn should be in a state of equilibrium and it can easily be disturbed, thus the maintenance of a lawn is one of the trickiest jobs in gardening.

Playing surfaces and lawns used for the family to romp about on, can easily be compacted if used extensively when the surface is wet and sticky. This compaction of the surface forms an ideal place for the development of algae, which is the beginning of moss formation. Raised bumps in the lawn or ridges which are scalped by the mower are also nursery beds for mosses which are then carried all over the lawn. Often these can be reduced by filling up the hollows on each side of the hump or, in extreme cases, removing the hump. All these are contributory causes to moss formation, and are points to be watched, but I feel there is no single cause for moss-grown lawns.

Insect pests of turf

One of the contributing factors to the reputation of the good turf grasses which we can grow in the British Isles is the fact that we seldom suffer from extremes of weather, such as excessive heat or continued drought. However, one of the first lines of defence against pests, as with all other plants, is to produce strong healthy growth.

Although turf is a continual attraction for insects, it can support a large population without serious harm particularly if it is in good condition, poor, hungry and unthrifty turf is vulnerable and likely to get worse. Damage can take several forms, some indirect such as root disturbance by ants and moles. Cutworms and similar pests may bite the stems through at soil level, wireworms and chafer grubs damage the roots causing large bare patches to appear whilst others may merely suck the sap from the leaves.

Ants can be a nuisance on the lawn where the soil is light and dry. They may be controlled, without using insecticides, merely by seeing that the lawn has plenty of water applied, preferably using a sprinkler; they just do not like the moisture and move out. In practice this can present difficulties because the ground is too wet for children to play or people to sit on whilst the sprinkler is operating. The alternative is to use one of the various proprietary insecticides of which chlordane or carbaryl is the active ingredient. Where the grass is used as a play area as distinct from a purely ornamental lawn, carbaryl is probably the most desirable to use.

Ants may be all over the lawn but they have nests and these can be located by sprinking a little granulated sugar around. The ants will seize the sugar and can be visibly traced as they carry it to their nest. This is then treated in a more concentrated fashion rather than dusting or spraying all over the lawn. Malathion or derris are suitable for this task, the latter can be used either as a liquid or powder. What usually happens in the case of ants on the lawn is that their tunnels allow the soil to dry out around the roots of the plants, often causing the grass to die. They can also prevent it from germinating by feeding on the seeds or by storing them in their nests. Personally I mix sugar with any of the powders I use for this purpose so that the ants can carry the insecticide down into the nest.

During a dry spell wasps may often damage lawns by their nest-building habits. They are very energetic and they dig holes about ¾ in in diameter and mound up the excavated soil around the entrance. The holes are usually about 6 in deep and then branch out terminating in round cells. If a powder insecticide is used, push the powder down into the hole with a little bit of stick through a small funnel and smooth out the soil. Apply a liquid with a small hand sprayer that can be pumped with the finger.

In most cases it is the grubs or larvae of the insect, be it moth or beetle, which damage the grass. Wireworms, the larvae of click beetles, can cause a great deal of damage to newly-sown lawns. They are sometimes found on established lawns too, usually near the edge of a flower bed from which they migrate to eat the tender grass roots. Here again, carbaryl will give good control. To make the treatment more effective it pays to prick the soil with a fork to a depth of about 2 in as they seldom go deeper than this.

Wireworms

In some areas leatherjackets, the larvae of the daddy longlegs, cause quite a lot of damage and there may be as many as 200 to the square yard. Where use of an insecticide is not desirable then they can often be controlled by the use of a garden roller which literally squashes the soft grubs. On a fine evening on a badly infected patch one can see these larvae pop up through the soil; you can actually see the mature insects emerging and after a few minutes rest and drying out, pump up their wings and fly away.

Leatherjackets

57

Nematodes cause more damage to turf than is generally realised. They are tiny insignificant worm-like creatures which live at different depths in the soil and are thus virtually impossible to control. They seem fonder of foreign grasses than our native varieties and hybrids. In America, where grass farms may be anything up to two thousand acres in extent, nematodes cause millions of pounds worth of damage every year to cultivated turf. There is no effective control yet.

Worms can cause both damage and annoyance and in particular the types of worm which voids its casts on the surface. The control of these earthworms has been a controversial subject ever since I can remember, some people arguing that they drain the soil and should be encouraged and preserved. The facts are these: the burrowing worm passes soil through its body and voids it in the form of the familiar worm casts. In the process of being digested, toxic substances are added and for just over a week this substance is capable of killing grasses. After exposure to sun, wind and rain it becomes fertile. In the meantime, however, due to the plastic nature of the cast, air is excluded and the grasses beneath can die out over an area sometimes 3 in in diameter. Nature being what she is attempts to fill this in, often very quickly with weed seeds. I remember an old groundsman from a research station telling me some thirty years ago that 'a wormy lawn is a weedy lawn' and I can certainly vouch for this. Worm casts also clog up the rollers of mowers and if you don't want to destroy the worms then at least destroy the worm casts by brushing.

Worms also encourage moles. Worms themselves can be encouraged by heavy dressings of organic materials such as bonemeal or dried blood which they use as part of their diet. So if you want worms, then feed them and if you want moles then encourage the worms. Most of us, however, want a smooth weed-free lawn composed of fine grasses and anything that we can do to eliminate the worms is desirable. Worms are most vulnerable in the spring and autumn, when they come up from the depths to the surface in April and before they descend in October anything up to 2 ft to avoid the severe winter weather conditions. There are several proprietary substances available for destroying worms and sometimes one can be found incorporated in fertiliser compounds. Ornamental turf grass lawns can grow quite happily, and indeed better, without the assistance of worms. Personally, I have as much use for them in a good lawn as I have for a big fat worm in a plant pot.

Common turf diseases

There are quite a number of turf grass diseases, and ironically the better the turf and the more closely it is cut the more likely you are to attract one or more of them; so much so they have been described as man-made. Of the many diseases the three most common are fusarium patch, corticium, sometimes called red thread, and dollar spot. Of these three, two are late-summer and autumn diseases but can, like every other fungus disease, show themselves any time conditions are suitable. Fusarium or snow mould is one which is likely to appear after the winter or where snow has been lying on the grass, but the other two may be expected at any time, especially after the moist, muggy weather generally experienced in July.

Dollar spot This occurs on turf grasses virtually all over the world and the name was derived from the occurrence of dead bleached spots about the size of a silver dollar. The spots rarely get beyond that size but if not controlled they can become so numerous that they tend to join up and overlap resulting in large irregular areas of dead turf. They are particularly visible in the early morning when the grass is damp with dew and at this time wisps of the white threads of mycelium can be seen on the tips of the grass blades. The sun and the wind will dry the grass and the mycelium but it can persist in the cool beneath the grass blades. The disease gains entry through the cut leaf tips and if treated early can be prevented from travelling down, eventually to kill the whole plant. Blunt, badly set mower blades, especially of rotary mowers, can chew the tops off the leaf blades causing them to become whitened and so make it easier for the fungus to settle and attack.

Disease development is usually most rapid when the temperatures are fairly high, around 21°C (70°F) but, unfortunately, there are various strains of the fungus which can operate at lower temperatures. It is worse on lawns which have been starved but the resistance of grasses to fungus disease is significantly increased where the plants have received adequate nitrogen. Fortunately, dollar spot is not a disease that destroys grass quickly, especially if adequate nitrogen is provided. Personally, I find the best way of applying a nitrogenous fertiliser is in liquid form, such as a good soluble foliar feed. If the soil is dry it should first be wetted before the fertiliser is applied. Unfortunately, however, mowing without a grass box or using a rotary mower may cause the rapid spread of the disease. If it does develop try to avoid walking on the affected spots. There are a number of fungicidal compounds available suitable for controlling dollar spot and one of these should be applied without delay, according to the directions on the pack.

Corticium Also known as red thread, this is a disease of spring and summer and is especially prevalent during cool wet weather. It is readily identified by the coral pink gelatinous and sticky masses formed by the fungus on leaves and the sheaths of the grass plant. This jelly-like coating is often joined with a pink web of mycelium which, like dollar spot, is very conspicuous when the grass is wet. This disease will affect the leaves and the sheath, which is the point at which the leaves join the stem. The grass rapidly dies and takes on a light tan colour when dry. Corticium is easily spread by walking on the grass, by birds, animals, on the mower, by wind and various other agencies. Here again the application of nitrogenous fertiliser and prompt treatment with a suitable fungicide will clear up the trouble within a matter of weeks. The most important thing about all these diseases is to recognise them quickly and act promptly. If you have nothing else available, use the same sort of fungicides that you would spray on roses. This is better than nothing, especially if otherwise you have to wait until you can go into town to buy a turf fungicide specially for that purpose.

Pythium blight An annoying disease which you may often find on new grass, or newly-sown lawns, is one of the pythium blights. This is the same sort of trouble which gardeners call 'damping off'. This disease is favoured by cool wet days followed by a burst of sunshine and it is more active where there is an abundance of moisture and the plants are wet. Heavy dews, high humidity, muggy weather all favour its spread. Pythium blight does not seem to respond readily to the ordinary turf fungicides, but I have found that Cheshunt compound, also used against damping off, and permanganate of potash give good control.

A lawn that is well fed and where the grass plants are kept in reasonable condition is much more resistant to diseases and, if it does become attacked, it grows away much more quickly than one containing starved grasses. The recent introduction of a long-lasting lawn feed will be found to be a boon to those gardeners who always mean to feed the lawn but never get around to it. This fertiliser contains quick-acting ingredients and a proportion of slow-release nitrogen and other plant foods which are given up over the whole of the season, so that one quick application provides sufficient plant food for the rest of the season.

Fairy rings The legend attached to 'fairy rings' is much more attractive than the real cause. The legend says that the circle of dead grass is caused by the feet of gnomes and fairies dancing round the fairy queen throughout the night, killing the grass with their feet. To compensate mortals for this damage, the fairies make the grass grow thicker and greener. The fact is that fairy rings can be caused by not just one fungus disease, but by several. Mushroom-like fruits appear and whilst most of them are harmless, one of them, *Lepiota morgani,* is deadly poisonous if eaten. So to be on the safe side do not let children, or indeed anyone else, eat any of the little fungi which appear. Sometimes animals, particularly puppies, will gobble these up usually without any ill effect. But my advice is remove or destroy them with a brush or long cane whenever they are seen.

Fairy rings usually appear as circles or other-shaped areas of dark green grass in lawns that are normally on the moist side. A ring of dead grass may develop on the inside or the outside of the greener circle. During dry weather, especially in late summer or early autumn, the dead area is usually outside the green ring. The following spring, whilst the soil is still moist, the fungus occupies the soil outside the dead ring and there the growth of the grass is stimulated and dark green in colour. In addition, a second ring of green is sometimes seen inside the dead ring. After rain or heavy watering the mushroom-like fruiting bodies of the fungus which causes the disease may appear in the circle of green grass.

The first thing you see are tufts of stimulated green grass or maybe a cluster of mushrooms, depending on season and the amount of organic matter in the soil. The spores and mycelium grow only outwards from the central cluster in the surface foot or so of soil. Actually the advancing margin of the fungus is actively growing, the receding margin dying. The stimulation that shows up as greener grass is due to the increased amount of nitrogen which is made available to the grass by the fungus as it breaks down the organic matter in the soil. It uses up moisture to do this and so the soil in the dead area is usually drier and this contributes to the death of the plants.

Some fungal diseases are peculiar to some varieties of grass, often first starting on one type and then spreading to others, while others are universal killers such as the fairy ring fungus. How to get rid of fairy rings is a recurring question and it must be said straight away that there is no complete answer. One of the biggest problems of course is the depth to which the fungus penetrates which may be as much as 15 to 18 in but is, more generally, about one foot. The only sure way of getting rid of it is to excavate to this depth and then fill in with new soil; this, in my opinion, is not worth the trouble. A professional way of masking the accentuated green of the fairy rings is to make all the other grass look the same. This can be done by applying either a foliar feed of nitrogen or use some quick-acting stimulant such as nitro-chalk. Alternatively, copy our American friends, and simply dye the rest of the grass!

Another device I have used is the sub-irrigator which is merely a metal tube inserted in the end of the hose pipe. With this you can bore holes to a considerable depth. This is, in fact, a technique I use for watering shrubs without wetting the surface of the soil. Provided you use a container with a non-return valve you can inject suitable fungicides into the soil by this method. Jeyes fluid, Bray's emulsion and permanganate of potash are all safe controls I would recommend. It is possible to strip the turf from the infected area, break up the soil and saturate it with fungicide. However, I do not recommend this as the time of recovery is even longer and the damage more marked than if you let it alone.

Although the fairy rings are more pronounced and may be more irritating on a perfect sward, they are really less damaging than some of the less spectacular fungus diseases such as fusarium and red thread. I am a bit of a grass fanatic, but personally I still like to think that it is the fairies and not a nasty fungus which is responsible for the rings. When making a new lawn avoid burying wood chips and tree and shrub roots, as this can encourage the disease.

Solid topdressing

There are few lawns that do not benefit from a topdressing of solid material which is best applied after mowing ceases, approximately the end of September. The solid topdressing achieves several things. It helps to level up small irregularities in the surface, feeds the grasses and as the grass sheath tends to elongate on ordinary lawns which do not receive the same meticulous attention as, say, bowling greens, it helps the grasses to re-root at a higher level. Topdressing after spiking also helps to improve drainage and if the soil is heavy, helps to ameliorate the clay soil.

Ideally apply a light dressing, say 2 lb per sq yd every year, or, failing this, a slightly heavier dressing every three to five years. Even in hollows the depth of the dressing should never exceed the height of the grass. If nothing else is added coarse clean sand is beneficial on most lawns. Fine plasterers' or builders' sand should not be used and can be definitely harmful as it is too fine and puddles almost like clay when wet and sets hard when dry. Coarse sand, however, soon miraculously disappears when applied to the surface. The rate of application depends on the texture of the soil underneath, the heavier the soil the heavier the dressing. Using a 2-gal bucket as a measure, a bucketful to 2 sq yd is a reasonable application.

For a solid topdressing a good formula is equal parts coarse sand, fine peat and ordinary garden soil sifted through a ¼-in sieve and well mixed. Old chrysanthemum or tomato potting soil is ideal for this job for although it contains a small proportion of lime this is counteracted by the acidity of the peat and the summer dressings of acid fertilisers such as sulphate of ammonia.

My own practice when applying a topdressing is first to scatter lightly ¼ oz per sq yd of the finest grass seed that I can buy and then apply the dressing over this. This overseeding, as it is called, is a certain way of improving the worst lawns even if no solid topdressing is applied. The two together will very quickly turn a poor lawn into a good one, if you consider that one single grass seed, depending on variety, can make a plant 4 to 18 in in diameter in a single season. It is easy to see how the character of the lawn and the texture of the grass can be immeasurably improved.

Weeds on lawns

The introduction of hormone weedkillers has probably been of greater benefit to gardeners than any other invention, as all weeds can now be controlled by the application of one of these. Admittedly some weeds are more resistant than others. Daisies are particularly so but, as with other weeds, once the worst of them has been cleared it is worthwhile resorting to spot weeding, which is the treatment of individual weeds or clumps.

A counsel of perfection is to drop some form of indicator when mowing so that when cutting is completed the individual weeds can be effectively treated. My own practice is to drop little squares of folded kitchen foil and as these are collected the weeds are treated. A simple method of spot weeding is to mix up a selective hormone weedkiller in a bucket and, with an ordinary soft hand brush, to paint over the surface of the weed or clump with sufficient pressure to damage the protective bloom or patina on the leaf surface. This is to ensure that the effective elements in the weedkiller can reach the more vulnerable part of the leaf. Some weeds are so well protected that the weedkiller runs off in globules just as water runs off a cabbage leaf. This method is cheaper and less time consuming than watering or spraying isolated weeds or clumps with hormone weedkiller. One reason is that a watering can and its rose has to be thoroughly cleaned out after a hormone weedkiller is used otherwise incalculable damage can be done if it is inadvertently used for watering broad-leaved plants in other parts of the garden.

The best prevention against weeds, especially wind-blown seeds, is a good healthy dense sward so that they cannot reach the soil to germinate. Bare patches will be quickly covered by moss or provide a seed bed for weeds, so every effort should be made to keep a carpet-like growth of grass.

As the years roll by the treatment, non-treatment, or neglect of a lawn will cause it to change, influencing the character of the grasses and also the weeds which grow in it. In an earlier chapter I mentioned weeds as indicators and nowhere is this seen more clearly than on the lawn. Some plants, particularly of the clover family, like an alkaline (limy) soil. This can come about through habitually allowing the dog to chew bones on the lawn or it may be the result of patches of lime left by the builder or even lime rubble from an old building scattered on the soil and dug in. Therefore, in the case of clover clumps appearing it is of little use killing off the clover unless an attempt is made to acidify the soil and make it less to the liking of the lime-loving plants concerned.

This can be done by treating the area with lawn sand. This will also kill lawn weeds such as daisies, plantains, dandelions and other broad-leaved plants and at the same time will improve the quality of the grass. It is made up as follows:

> 35 parts by weight sulphate of ammonia
> 15 parts by weight calcined sulphate of iron
> 50 parts by weight dry sand

Mix this up thoroughly and apply when the surface of the leaves are damp with dew. For spot weeding just mix the sulphate of ammonia and sulphate of iron and apply a pinch to the centre of the weed.

Fertilisers

The application of any fertiliser should be made with an eye kept open for the weather. For example, materials are wasted and the whole operation abortive if rain falls within an hour or two of the application of weedkilling hormones although this is ideal for washing in fertiliser. However, fertilisers should never be applied to wet grass as the powder or granules can lodge and may cause burning. Similarly it is a waste of time applying fertiliser during very dry periods when grasses are not actively growing as scorching can occur.

Changes in soil characteristics influence the type of grass which will flourish or become debilitated and weeds too will follow this pattern. This is why no abrupt changes should be made either up or down the scale. No sudden applications of high concentrations of nitrogen in the form of sulphate of ammonia or attempts to correct acidity by heavy dressings of lime should be made. With a lawn it is gently, gently all the time; you can't get away with things in the same way as you do in the vegetable patch.

Shrubs and Flowers

Trees and shrubs may be regarded as the equivalent of furniture in the house which has to be functional as well as ornamental, not only to provide shelter but to give privacy and screen from noise. To me, colour and interest in winter is every bit as important as in spring and summer; perhaps more so, as even without scheming and trying you can have colour during these months. The choice is wide and is entirely yours, but the methods of planting and maintaining are common to all.

Garden centres, with their containerised trees and shrubs, have radically altered the stocking of gardens in many ways. One being that trees and shrubs, and even roses, are readily available for planting at any time, provided due care is exercised, with the minimum of root disturbance. This, of course, reduces losses and a garden can be quickly stocked. On the other hand, the choice of plants is severely restricted, often to the most common and readily saleable varieties and the sight of large quantities of shrubs induces impulse buying which is not always in the best interests of a planned garden display. When buying from a garden centre it is far better to go with a list of requirements rather than make the decision without reference to one's own garden plan.

When planting a container-grown plant, care should be taken when removing the plastic container. This is best done with a sharp knife, making an incision at the base and drawing the blade of the knife upwards on opposite sides and then peeling back the two halves. Where shrubs and trees have become root-bound and have grown through into the standing-out medium, these roots should be cleanly severed; not allowed to die and wither. If it is found that the roots have grown into a tight ball in the pot, as many as possible should be carefully teased out with a pointed stick before planting. At the same time take care not to break down the ball of soil unduly.

All containerised shrubs and trees should be thoroughly watered before planting and allowed to stand for an hour or two and then at least two gallons of water should be poured into the planting hole as the filling proceeds. Always make a hole at least twice the size of the root ball, and plant to the old soil mark, putting top soil in nearest the roots and spreading the worst soil over the rest of the garden area.

65

Peat or peat-based planting additives are usually available from the same garden centre and these should be mixed in with the soil rather than used to fill in the hole. After a good watering, use some of this material as a mulch over the surface to prevent any drying out. Evergreens and conifers, which are usually planted in April or October, should be watered more frequently as the top of the evergreen acts as an umbrella keeping rain off the root area. For spring planting this watering may have to be continued for at least a month.

Screening

Screening aurally and visually is becoming increasingly important. Even old country houses and estates suddenly find a motorway or a link road running through them, sometimes on an embankment as high as the house. With others, skyscrapers, cooling towers and pylons sprout up like mushrooms and spoil views which have been enjoyed for many years. Obviously it is impossible to cover these up, but a certain amount of screening can be done from the garden. The larger the garden the easier it is to do this.

There is still much to be said for the rule of thumb method adopted

Surveying the height of a screen

Very briefly the method is to sit in the house, provide your assistant with a 20-ft rod and get him to stand in a line between you and the object to be screened. Obviously the farther away he can move the better. The nearer your assistant moves to you the lower will be the height of the screen.

It would help to make marks on your rod and this can be done by merely tying strips of white rag at 1- or 2-ft intervals so that you can then get an idea of the height of the screen required to completely blot out the offending structure.

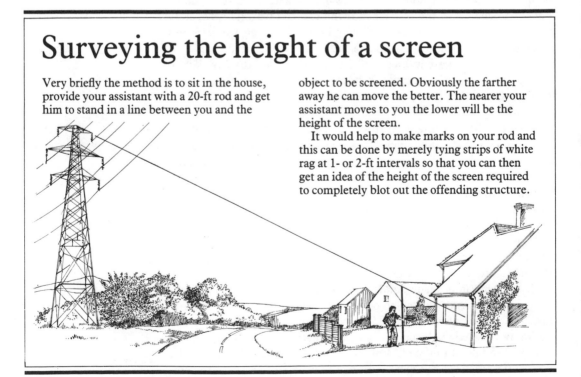

by some of our famous landscape gardeners and that is to employ the man with the pole. In your own case this may mean your wife or youngster holding a fishing rod or canes tied together. The screening materials available to the gardener are trees, shrubs or ornamental and rustic structures to blot out the offending building in the distance.

Suppose, for example, you have a garden 20 yd long and on looking out of the window you can see a block of flats being built half a mile away. Get your assistant to move into a position in a direct line between you and the building and then get him to walk back as far as is reasonable and practicable. You may find that at the end of the garden you need a screen 20 ft or more high; so get your assistant to advance slowly towards you and stop him when he has reached a point where you can interpose a suitable screen within your capacity.

Where houses are in a group it is often possible to co-operate with neighbours. In my own case I wished to screen off a newly erected pylon on one side and some not-very-attractive new houses on the other. I got together with two of my neighbours and for the cost of supplying two trees, one a metasequoia and the other a weeping willow planted some 75 yd away, I was able to screen off the offending objects. The trees were sited in the neighbour's gardens, having given due consideration to their planting scheme. I have reciprocated by planting a Corsican pine to stop the wind from funnelling between the end of their house and a neighbouring garage. Most of us live so closely together that co-operation is absolutely essential in case we trespass on one another's amenities. True, there is always the risk of the change of occupier and I have had the experience of a new, enthusiastic but inexperienced neighbour cutting down a tree and some shrubs, thus spoiling a screen which I had carefully built up.

When making or growing screens it is important that due consideration is given to the fact that trees will grow and, in addition to screening, they can easily cut out a desirable view. For most people who wish to screen against eyesores and noise, their first reaction and, in some cases, action is to plant evergreens and conifers as they reasonably argue that deciduous trees drop their leaves so in the winter there would be little screening either visually or against sound. This is not strictly true, as trees with fine twigs such as birch will, when well grown, break up sound just as effectively as something more solid. Such a screen is infinitely to be preferred in windy districts. Never forget that the wind does not blow constantly in one direction. So if you put up a solid barrier it may screen you when the wind is blowing in one direction but when it blows in another you may find that the backlash is more devastating than the direct wind, as eddies and vortices are created.

Even where the space is very limited narrow fastigiate trees (columnar or upright growing) occupy little space and grow tall very quickly. Obviously, if you can afford it, there are now available trees

20, 30 and even 40 ft high which will give you almost instant screening.

It should also be remembered that the change from peace and quiet to noise and movement is very acute during the first few weeks, but the senses do become dulled and what may seem intolerable at first, becomes bearable and, in time, almost unnoticed. There is also the feeling of being completely walled in which happens when a single row of dull dark green cupressus is planted completely round the house and garden. Larch, birch and Lombardy poplars are cheap and may be planted as close as 5 ft apart with the object of thinning later. Close planting makes them grow upwards very quickly and the various variegated acers and sycamores, as well as the very useful golden elm and golden willow soon provide effective and attractive screens. Added to this list can be the service tree, *Sorbus domestica*, and in most districts the mountain ash, *S. aucuparia*.

Covering pipes and posts

Unless you have a very modern house and even modern houses are not immune, you are bound to have a pipe problem. Architects and builders seem to take a delight in decorating the outside of houses with all sorts of pipes. An added difficulty is that they usually rise out of concrete and it is not always practicable to break it up in order to plant a climber or shrub to disguise at least part of the pipe. The biggest problem, however, is not the container for the plant but a method of training it up the pipe when it starts to climb. Not even self-clinging shrubs like to cling to metal or plastic and, indeed, pipes are not the only problems. Nowadays carports and extensions supported on pillars are common. This means that if a single stem of a climber is to be trained up one of these a nail has to be knocked into the brickwork or strings or wires tied round the circumference. This is obviously a nuisance and it is rather silly to use 8 ft of string to train a single rose or climber up; very soon there will be more string than climber. The problem also arises with pergola posts. Fortunately, with modern inventions it is now easy to clothe a pillar, pipe or clothes' post in a very short time with practically no trouble whatsoever. The best material for this purpose is 2-in mesh plastic netting. This material is flexible and kind to all plants and does not rust. It can be used to train bignonia, various types of clematis, loniceras and *Forsythia suspensa* with no trouble at all and to great effect.

Most climbers need no attention whatsoever as they seem to prefer to run up between the supporting cylinder of mesh and the post or pipe itself. For example, an 8-ft post can be completely covered in four months by the variegated *Lonicera japonica* Aureoreticulata. Where it is necessary to support the climbers this can be done simply

Hold plants against the mesh support with simple plastic-covered wire rings

by using plastic-covered wire rings made by wrapping the wire round a broom shank and cutting with a pair of strong garden scissors or tin snips (don't use good secateurs for this). Sweet peas and other annuals such as *Tropaeolum canariense* (canary creeper) can also be used to supplement and add colour to permanent climbers such as honeysuckles, various forms of non-clinging ampelopsis, vines and clematis. Incidentally, one of the loveliest and most useful roses for this purpose is Zéphirine Drouhin. In fact anything that climbs may be used, depending on the circumstances and the height of the column to be covered. Be careful with the choice of shrubs and plants as obviously it would be unwise to train a rampant-growing vine up something only 8 or 10 ft high and equally unwise to use a short-growing honeysuckle, like *Lonicera fragrantissima* up a pipe 25 ft tall.

Making a plastic mesh cylinder

Plastic netting is supplied in various colours and, for preference, tan or neutral shades should be used as, when it is exposed, the green accentuates the pipe or pillar. Measure round the post or pipe to be covered with a piece of string and add on at least an extra 4 in. Cylinders of the plastic mesh may be much larger than the actual circumference to be covered. Two-inch plastic netting is self supporting, but cut the cylinders from the width of the material rather than from the length as it is much easier to handle, also overlap the edges rather than join them edge to edge; the illustrations show clearly what is meant. Any number of cylinders can be placed one above the other without any risk of them slipping down, although, just for safety, the edges are best tied together. Lacing the edges together with nylon string, which again is virtually indestructible, gives the neatest join but plastic-covered wire can also be used, either as a lacing or individual ties.

The first cylinder is placed around the pipe and the bottom allowed to rest on the ground, the next cylinder is placed above, laced and affixed to the bottom one with one or two ties, and so on. In the case of a pipe which is affixed to a wall, the material may be cut to accommodate these braces and a smooth cylinder can easily be made.

Incidentally, if the pipe is in need of painting, do this before encircling it with plastic mesh. This is a common-sense precaution as no repainting should be necessary for a good many years after it is covered by a protective creeper, especially if particular attention is paid to the back of the pipe. Plastic pipes, of course, need no protection and have very long lives.

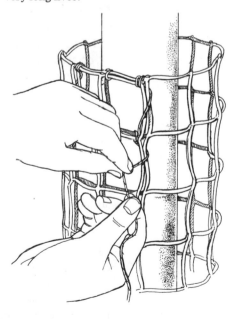

There are, I am sure, literally millions of pipes, posts and pillars which would be far better covered by an ornamental creeper or climber and are left exposed because of the initial work involved. Finally don't forget that it is virtually impossible for even a cat burglar to climb up a covered pipe.

Oil storage tanks

Whether oil storage tanks are placed up to the wall of the house or sited a few yards away in the garden, no-one can say that they are attractive, even if painted green. However, all utilitarian appliances or containers cannot be treated in any way that makes them not fully functional. I'm often asked if the fumes, which arise from tanks, are harmful to vegetation and so far I know of no case where this has proved to be so. The liquid itself, however, is definitely harmful and will kill foliage as effectively as any weedkiller. If the oil is allowed to run on the ground when the tank is being filled, drained or cleaned, then any roots touched by it may be damaged and if any quantity is spilled then plants may be killed.

There is an excusable and natural tendency to try to use quick growing subjects for screening, but it must be remembered that where vigorous subjects are used they will continue to grow long after they have covered the screen. I am thinking now of shrubs such as *Polygonum baldschuanicum* (Russian vine). This climber will grow 20 ft in a single season which means unless it is rigorously controlled the whole area will become a jungle and create a terrific amount of work besides making it awkward for access.

The trellis or screen itself needs to be substantial and durable and supporting posts, 3 in by 3 in or 4 in by 4 in are advisable. Longitudinal battens and wood trellis are then nailed on or, alternatively, 2-in mesh plastic netting attached. Personally, I have long since given up using green paint or green netting in the garden, preferring khaki or wood tan. Green draws attention and focuses the eye until it is completely covered, whilst browns or khaki melt into the background. This applies to stakes and posts too and, as these are uncovered for most of the time, they blend with the background of soil far better.

Tanks of course are more likely to be visible from upper windows than they are from the ground floor and there is no objection to taking trellis or rigid netting across the top provided, of course, sufficient headroom or space is left above the tank if the filler cap is on the top. Every site varies but in every case full use should be made of the natural conditions. In one instance I know, and with the co-operation of the firm concerned, the tank was actually built into the hillside with a rockery over the top and walling up the front, leaving only the valve

70

connections visible. This was so successful that nothing at all was visible and the front wall was ideal for training various shrubs such as *Cotoneaster horizontalis* and clematis. Incidentally, this container held 8000 gallons.

It is not necessary to use only clinging shrubs to screen walls or unsightly buildings. Many plants prefer to have their backs against a wall even though they are not actually climbers. Examples of these are *Garrya elliptica* and *Cytisus battandieri* both of which are evergreens and so give screening all the year round. Another trouble-free semi-climbing shrub which is a great favourite of mine is *Lonicera fragrantissima* which is evergreen most years and in favourable districts blooms practically all the year round. It never grows more than 8 ft high and all it requires is to be clipped over with the shears to within 4 or 5 in of the main branches every February. Although it is very tempting to use rambler and climbing roses to cover such a utility

Screening an island tank

I prefer to surround an island tank on the access side with either flag stones or some other sort of paving. This allows ease of operation with the hose pipe and connections which may be valves at the top or side, according to construction and type of installation.

Some heating installations are gravity fed which means that the tank is often elevated on piers. For this latter type the simplest screening is to put up trellis all round with an overlapping wall to screen the actual entry, as in the construction of a gents' lavatory. The flagged or concrete path allows entry and keeps anything growing on the trellis well away from contact with the tank. Oils of this type tend to creep over metal surfaces and it is useless trying to arrange climbers or creepers on the tank itself.

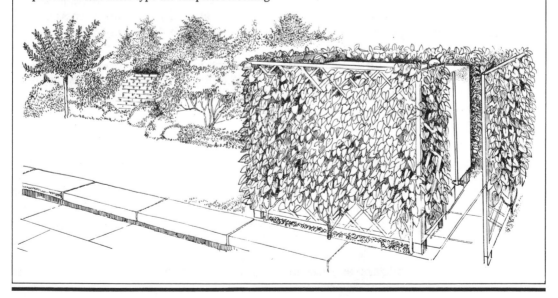

trellis, I advise against it, for no matter how well they are trained there are bound to be thorny growths which make the manoeuvring of a heavy oil supply pipe difficult and vexatious. One rose however which is perfect for such a position is Zéphirine Drouhin. This is completely thornless and makes very strong canes and growths which are easy to train and tie in and it needs little of the old wood cutting out.

There is nothing quite so effective as the ivies for providing evergreen cover and although this sounds Irish, the best of all evergreens requiring the least attention is the variety Buttercup (also known as Golden Cloud or Russell's Gold). This is the best golden ivy that I know, it has small leaves and requires the minimum of attention. This variety, incidentally, also makes an excellent carpeting plant and I know of one large bed in the centre of London which is absolutely covered with gold and looks effective all the year round. Other varieties are Marginata or Silver Queen and Tricolor (Marginata Rubra) which has grey-green leaves bordered with white and edged in winter with rosy red. As the ivies do not grow outwards, except in old age, they are better subjects for training up vertical supports than most other shrubs, including pyracantha which rapidly tends to reduce the space available between trellis and tank.

Screening walls

Walls are always a problem, whether they be the wall of a house, a shed, a dividing wall or that of an unsightly outbuilding. This is not because it is difficult to cover them adequately, but because of subsequent maintenance. For climbers and creepers the question of support is of paramount importance. To be really successful and efficient the structure on which they are to be trained must have at least as long a life as the climber itself. The condition of the wall, too, is important. On no account erect a screen or trellis on a crumbling wall for before very long it will either fall down or have to be pointed. So before considering climbers make sure that the wall fabric is sound and where high dividing walls are to be covered, see that the coping stones are secure.

One question which is always raised is 'Will the creeper or climber harm the wall?' One school of thought insists that clinging creepers such as Virginia creeper and ivy eat into the fabric of the wall. Personally, I have never found this to be the case. In fact, I know of several instances where a covering of ivy has protected the wall of a house for 60 years and when removed the whole wall had to be rendered waterproof. The ivy had protected it and kept the house warm all that time. Certainly invasive creepers should never be allowed to push under tiles or guttering, as the sheer pressure of growth will cause damage.

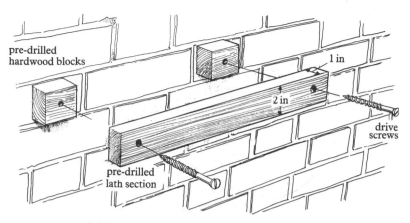

pre-drilled
hardwood blocks

1 in

2 in

drive
screws

pre-drilled
lath section

Fix hardwood blocks to the
wall to support laths against
which climbers or wall
shrubs can be trained.
Always drill holes into the
solid brick rather than the
softer mortar for really
secure fixing

Often climbers are planted against a wall without first making adequate provision for their support, with the result that one has to be constantly knocking in nails and tying up the new growths with bits of string as they appear. This does no good at all to the mortar and is a never-ending job. In the old days I have spent hundreds of hours nailing in peaches and nectarines with cast iron nails and strips of cloth so I know how damaging it can be, not only to the wall but also to one's fingers on a cold morning.

Any wood used should be treated with a non-toxic preservative, paying particular attention to sawn ends. On no account should crude creosote be used as this gives off harmful fumes and could kill plants. Where possible use red cedar or pitch pine for the main battens. Stone and brick walls absorb heat and provide snug dry shelters for many harmful insects and fungi, so always provide an air space behind the climbing shrub. This will also enable a certain amount of wall maintenance to be carried out. Before erecting the trellis prepare a number of hardwood blocks, such as oak or beech, soak these thoroughly in a bucket of wood preservative and allow them to dry out. They should then be drilled with a ¼-in bit and placed between the main batten and the wall. The wall must be drilled with a masonry bit and plugged with a plastic plug. This material can be bought in foot lengths and cut to suit the depth of the hole. The battens are then securely affixed to the wall with 4-in screws. Incidentally, when affixing anything to a wall, I prefer to drill into the solid brick, stone or cement rather than into the softer mortar or cement between the bricks. This ensures that no damage is done to the fabric of the wall.

Strong-growing coarse shrubs such as *Cytisus battandieri* can be trained and tied directly to a framework of battens. For twining shrubs such as clematis, honeysuckles or similar climbers, I prefer to cover the whole area with 2-in mesh plastic netting. This material has a long life but if used over a very hot wall or where the heat is intense, black mesh should be used. One advantage this material has over all others is that any shoots can be quickly and easily secured merely by using ordinary sweet-pea rings.

The method of fixing trellis or plastic netting, as well as the choice of plant and the method of securing, is all important. The object of planting climbers and creepers is that they will grow up and cover areas but if they are not kept under control they can become unmitigated nuisances. I receive any number of letters saying that honeysuckles or jasmines have got completely out of hand, weighted down by snow and dragged away from their supports, blown by the wind or are full of dead wood and what on earth can be done? I am afraid this sort of thing is bound to happen unless adequate and properly-constructed supports are provided. In fact, I would go so far as to say that if you are not prepared to spend time on the initial preparation of supports then forget all about putting up climbers. This does not mean that walls need not or should not be screened for there are plenty of shrubs which need little or no support which prefer to grow with their backs to a wall.

Backs-to-the-wall shrubs

It is with their backs to the wall that many otherwise tender shrubs meet on common ground and people who move from north to south will perhaps be surprised to find that they can grow comparatively tender shrubs. Quite obviously it is not possible to move the walls around to suit particular subjects, but it is possible to find a wide range of shrubs which can be accommodated in a particular situation. Many walls, for various reasons, cannot accommodate a trellis or dense framework so for practical reasons a skeleton framework is best. Treated wood, cedar, metal rods or tubes are preferable to wires which sag, rust fairly quickly unless of heavy gauge and require substantial supports well away from the wall with some device at one end, at least, to keep them strained tightly.

Of all the directions in which the wall may be facing, south to south-west is probably the kindest for several reasons. Although in many districts the prevailing wind blows from this direction, it is usually a mild wet wind. Furthermore, east- and south-facing walls usually receive the sun early. This, at first thought, would seem to be the best position, but during periods of cold freezing weather rapid thawing does more harm than good and a shrub on a sunless north-facing wall would fare better. Furthermore, a wall with a southern aspect, especially in mild districts, may become extremely hot. In these conditions the foliage, stems and roots dry up and pests such as red spider mites, which enjoy these hot dry situations, are encouraged.

One of the reasons why even tender shrubs can be grown near a wall

In order to see the full beauty of climbers that usually only bloom high up or on the other side of the wall, train them over a rail and let them hang down to form a flowering curtain

is that it retains a considerable amount of warmth. It does, in fact, act in the same way as a storage heater. Fortunate indeed are those lucky people with old walls which contain flues where heated air can be passed through the wall, maintaining warmth even during the coldest weather. These used to be a feature of old walled gardens and heat from the boiler fires could be deflected through these flues. This, of course, enabled early crops of peaches and nectarines to be produced.

Shrubs usually designated as wall shrubs are those which are fairly tall and erect in habit such as magnolias and *Cytisus battandieri*; *Kerria japonica* and *Forsythia suspensa* are also ideal subjects for wall covering. In a cold garden various varieties of ceanothus can thrive against a south-west facing wall when they easily succumb in other situations. There are non-clinging climbing shrubs which are of soft tender habit and persist in climbing up to the top of any wall, no matter how high, and absolutely refuse to bloom until they reach the top. This means they are bare at the base but, as with several types of ampelopsis, may be encouraged to grow up and then hang down. Where a wall or building needs to be screened and a vigorous shrub such as *Polygonum baldschuanicum* is used, it can soon get out of hand and just sit top-heavily on the top. The same technique is used for a tender climber. It is encouraged to go rapidly to the top where it is allowed to grow over a wire or rail supported on strong brackets some 9 in from the wall. The soft growths are grown over this and soon hang to the ground, remaining neat, unobtrusive and easily trained; the whole wall being screened from top to bottom with a curtain of living vegetation. Even during the winter months the stems are so dense that the wall will be completely screened.

Many wall shrubs fail to thrive or establish themselves because of lack of ground preparation. The soil at the base of a wall, especially with new or even very old buildings, is often full of builders' debris or lime rubble which may be completely unsuitable for such subjects as camellias or tree heaths which dislike lime. Soil preparation at the base of a wall is perhaps more important than the preparation of soil in an open garden. If it is thought necessary, the base of the wall itself may be protected from damp by using thick polythene fertiliser sacks, black polythene, sheets of glass fibre, roofing felt or any other waterproof material. Dig a planting hole of adequate size and break up the bottom. Fill in with good soil to suit the type of shrub being planted, checking to see whether such a subject will tolerate lime or not. Some shrubs such as *Garrya elliptica* or forsythia, will be satisfied with almost any ordinary soil. However, tree heaths, magnolias, and camellias need a high proportion of peat and compost and no lime whatsoever. One of the reasons for putting in the extra protection for the wall is that during dry periods it may be necessary to water thoroughly, especially where the bed adjoining the wall is bounded by a path or some obstruction which prevents the roots of the shrub from growing outwards.

Many people will have experienced the distressing fact that subjects such as rambler and climbing roses planted against a wall may suffer badly from mildew and other fungus diseases, the leaves look pale and unhealthy and are often attacked by aphids, red spider mites and various other pests which enjoy the shelter of the wall. Much of this is due to the baking which they receive and inadequate water supplies, so these points must be watched carefully. Shrubs or climbers against a dry wall often benefit from a regular mulch after the soil has been thoroughly wetted and the mulch applied in late April or early May. This goes a long way in preventing the drying out of the roots. The reverse may be true in other places where the wall may be exposed to driving rain or under a roof without a gutter where the water constantly drips. Under these circumstances the emphasis must be on good drainage.

Hedges

Unless one has a precise and well-ordered mind I think the constant trimming and cutting of a hedge is a job that one can well do without. Any sort of a hedge, if it is to be kept as a hedge, should be cut not less than three times a year and where it encircles a fairly large garden, what usually happens is that it doesn't get cut as often as it should. Every year it becomes a bigger burden and will soon get out of hand. True, there are mechanical aids but unfortunately these are not for everyone and although the various adaptors to electric drills do take care of a lot of chores, there is still the clearing up to be done. All the same, I would certainly prefer to have a varied and ornamental screen rather than a hedge to surround the back garden.

Where fields bound a garden then a tough hedge is needed, such as white thorn, blackthorn or myrobalan plum. The latter is a species of fruiting plum which can be used for a hedge and, armed as it is with spines 2 in long or more, will keep out cattle and virtually anything else. Incidentally, if you want to grow your own hedge then sow pear pips; pear seedings make a formidable hedge equipped with spiny branches and it can be clipped just like any other hedge. Gooseberries, too, make fine hedges and can be clipped and tended in just the same way as privet. For this purpose the small hairy varieties, such as the Lion or Golden Drop, are admirable. Practically every form of tree or shrub can be cut and used as a hedge as any countryman knows. Beech, hawthorn, hornbeam, holly and yew are excellent but all need cutting regularly. Even oaks and fir trees make hedges of a sort. *Lonicera nitida* makes a neat hedge but has no life, gaps often mysteriously appear after about five years and unless cut hard back and kept narrow it soon becomes ugly and is not a particularly good hedge in or near industrial areas.

Perhaps one of the loveliest of all hedges is made from pyracantha, the firethorn. This is often grown up the side of a house but it can be grown both as a separate bush and as hedging material and does not need to be clipped rigorously into shape, but huge sprays of berries can be cut off for house decoration. Another wonderful hedging shrub is *Chaenomeles japonica*, (flowering quince or cydonia) which is covered with beautiful apple blossom-like flowers in early spring, often followed by large fruits.

Then, of course, there are scores of shrub roses which can be used for this purpose and even less trouble are many of the polyantha and floribunda types. A variety which I have used very successfully is one called Flamingo which makes strong growths. An annual snip over with the secateurs will take care of pruning, but they should never be allowed to get so big that they get out of hand and encroach either on your side of the garden or on that of your neighbours unless it is by arrangement as some of these will make a barrier 6 to 8 ft wide. Even in a town a rose hedge can create the illusion that you are well into the country.

The cotoneasters and berberis provide an infinite variety of hedging material and require very little attention except for an annual cutting of large sprays of berries. *Berberis prattii* is a fine example. It starts in the spring with ornamental foliage of a bronzy colour, the flowers are bright primrose yellow followed by masses of coral berries and it is so full of thorns that not even a cat can worm its way through. My method is to buy fairly large specimens and then split them up. I train them in fans along two wires and then just leave them.

For windy positions and in the thickest of industrial pollution *Cotoneaster simonsii* will come up smiling every year, it grows to a natural height of 5 ft and can be trimmed if so desired or merely left alone. One of the most beautiful hedges I have ever seen was made from this and interplanted every 6 ft with *Jasminum nudiflorum*. This is the winter-flowering jasmine which blooms from late October until early May, and you can well imagine what it looks like in the winter time with sprays of bright yellow rambling amongst masses of brick-red berries. The primary object of a hedge I suppose is to define a boundary and to give privacy and if this can be achieved by giving beauty as well, so much the better.

You may say, 'What about the cost?' Well, this need not be heavy as practically everything I have mentioned roots readily from cuttings once you have got the stock plants and they can be taken in a number of ways and raised without any trouble. On the other hand small rooted cuttings can be bought. It is good advice to plant small. Most people ordering from a catalogue say they'll have something 3 to 4 ft high to start with, under the mistaken impression that this will make a better hedge more quickly. Nothing could be further from the truth because to do the hedge justice plants should always be cut down to about 12 or 15 in. Small plants 12 to 18 in high will be half to possibly a third of the price and will grow and establish themselves more quickly than big stuff.

Planting a hedge

It is not always appreciated that hedges and screens may last longer than a boundary fence and as they are to be there for such a long time it pays to prepare the ground properly. In many areas very little is needed beyond digging a trench deep enough to plant the shrubs and to break up the ground underneath to facilitate drainage. However, in some areas where the soil is shallow you may find almost solid clay only a few inches down. Even with this there is still no need to do anything very elaborate except to take out a wider trench so that you do not imprison the roots in a sort of grave and, whilst breaking up the clay underneath, work in some coarse peat or compost. Other materials such as old compost, grass, weeds, chrysanthemum stalks, privet clippings and such like are also suitable. They take some time to rot down and provide a good root run and a certain amount of long-lasting plant food.

When making a hedge you must decide whether you can afford a single or a double row of plants. A double row will make a thick hedge more quickly but is more expensive. It will require more cutting as it gets older and will probably have to be cut back more severely. To make an impenetrable hedge always plant your subjects at an angle of about 45 degrees rather than upright as you normally do. They may look rather queer for the first year and the main stem will remain at the angle of planting, but all axillary growths will be vertical and you will thus establish a framework of an impenetrable barrier.

Ideally a path should run alongside hedges that need regular clipping. This is necessary for two reasons; first to facilitate cutting, the use of steps and the sweeping up of clippings and secondly the construction of a good path close to the hedge will prevent the invasion of the roots into borders. The alternative is to grass close up to the hedge. It is unwise to put a border close up to a hedge which needs cutting at least three times a year as in time both will suffer.

To establish a really thick hedge plant at an angle of 45°. Mark out the line of the hedge with a length of string and take out the soil for the first planting hole and put it in a pile to one side. Proceed along the row, covering the roots of one plant with the soil taken from the next hole. The initial pile of soil is used to cover the roots of the final plant

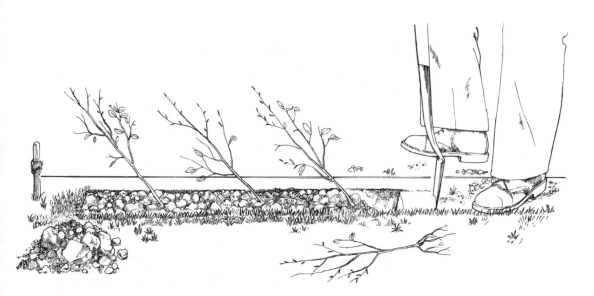

Fruit hedges

The question is will they last? Are they any good as a real hedge and do they produce any worthwhile fruit? I can best answer by quoting from my own experience. I remember my first gooseberry hedge some fifty-five years ago, prior to that my father had known it for over thirty years and even then it was old and well established. Although I left that garden fifty years ago, I still see it some four or five times a year and it has fruited continuously all this time. So it must be in the region of a hundred years old and is still approximately the same height, about 4½ ft. To the best of my knowledge it has been clipped regularly three times each year, in fact, treated like any other hedge.

A nice combination for a hedge is gooseberry, redcurrants and white currants. As these all fruit on both old and new wood, the cutting and trimming with shears is the same as spurring back with secateurs. The fact that the clipping is done when the bushes are in leaf does not seem to have any detrimental effect. Currant hedges by themselves are without solidity and tend to be springy and they also have a tendency to die back in the centre.

Gooseberry The best varieties of gooseberries for hedges are the vigorous erect growers, the quality of the fruit being a secondary consideration because, no matter how large the berries should be, they will always be on the small side when grown in this way. I find that the old variety Lion with the small juicy golden berries makes an excellent hedge as it is full of thorns, and stands any amount of hard cutting. These hedges also stand up to mildew which sometimes attacks them but the hedge can be drenched with spray and it is no worse than the powdery mildew which appears on thorn hedges.

To make up a gooseberry hedge from your own material strike cuttings without disbudding (this would normally be done to produce a bush on a leg) and plant these in a double row, 12 in apart at an angle of 45 degrees. When established, cut them back by about a third and, as the hedge takes shape, clip it two or three times a year as you would any other. The hedge will benefit particularly in its early stages by a dressing of sulphate of potash, 2 oz to the running yard, on each side. If you want something neat and narrow to take up the minimum amount of room then train gooseberries espalier fashion either in a single or a double row. Put in the rooted cuttings which have had the lower buds removed to produce a leg in the same way as you would for forming a bush. In case this technique is new, let me explain. Select a young growth about 9 to 12 in long for your cutting. Take about 3 in off the top, shortening back to a bud. If a heeled cutting has been taken, trim this or trim back to a bud. Remove all the lower buds leaving about four or five at the top. Insert the cuttings in open ground until they have rooted, then plant out 4 ft apart, securing each one to a cane about 4 ft high. Train horizontal branches along wires or canes; these will become the foundation of your espalier frame.

This cannot, of course, be done all in one season and it may take several years to get a four- or a five-tiered espalier. The horizontal branches can be from 4 to 8 in apart and you will be lucky indeed if they are all regular, but by training and perseverance a neat frame-work can be built up. These branches can then be treated much in the same way as a cordon. That is spurring back during dormancy and regulating new growth in the summer with finger and thumb. It sounds like a lengthy job but, in fact, is far less trouble than taking the side shoots out of tomatoes. The advantage of such a hedge when established is that it is virtually child and dog proof and only occupies about 6 in in width even when it is fully grown. I can assure you that such trained trees produce the heaviest crops and, if thinned out, the best-of-all exhibition berries.

Myrobalan plum This is one of the best of the fruit hedges. If left to produce a tree this will grow to 15 to 20 ft high and about 12 ft across, carrying crops of the most luscious round pinky-white fruits about 1½ in in diameter. Unfortunately these are seldom seen nowadays; I don't know why, because they are a wonderful dessert fruit, make beautiful preserves and cook equally well. However, when trimmed and cut hard back as a hedge, although they flower I have never seen them set any fruit. I have made several long hedges from this material round a fruit field. Every 10 yd or so I allowed one to grow up as a fruiting tree which in spring looked really beautiful and later produced good crops of fruit. If this is new to you, the name is *Prunus cerasifera* and it is often listed in the catalogue as myrobella.

Cane fruit Loganberry and blackberry hedges are common place and require little comment. In cold windy districts, however, I have found that the best way is not to trim out all the old wood each year, but use this as a foundation on which to tie the new growths. In time the older growths will die, but I have no objection to this as the outer part of the hedge is always covered with new growths. These must be tied in horizontally and thinned somewhat.

Care and Propagation

Timely attention to trees extends their life often by many years and reduces the danger of their falling down with all the risk to life and property which that might entail. Such surgery often applies only to trees of sentimental or historical value or because of their amenity value to a particular district. Where the problems are large it is often wiser to call in an expert.

Most people mourn the passing of a large tree or group of trees as they are like old friends, but there is a definite life to even the oldest living specimens. In many cases trees which pass from one owner to another are taken for granted. The cavities that develop at the base of a large limb or in a fork often go unnoticed becoming romantic hiding places for *billets doux* or the homes of birds and squirrels but they are also very often the beginning of the end of the tree. Water and snow enter these holes and in a few years the rot will spread down the centre of the tree. Or again, water standing in shallow holes during the winter freezes with sufficient expansion to burst the tissues still further and fungi and bacteria do the rest. In such cases, the most

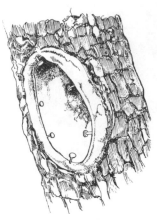

After an area of decay has been cleaned and treated, the hole is packed with cement to within 3 or 4 in of the entrance. A few nails are then partially banged in round the mouth and the filling is completed. The nails help key in the final layer of cement and ensure that it doesn't draw away from the wood

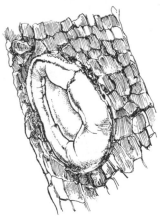

In time the wood will grow over the edges of the cement to form a callus

important job to do is to prevent the entry of water and to clean out the decay which may have already started, and for this purpose a wooden mallet and a fairly large gouge are required. For the uninitiated, a gouge is a curved sort of chisel and is much more suitable than an ordinary straight one because no unnecessary cuts are made when cleaning out a circular or a rounded hole.

Chip away all the decayed wood inside the hole until sound wood is reached. This should not be allowed to get wet again if the job cannot be completed in one day. Care should be taken not to damage unduly the outer edge of the hole where the bark is still actively growing. Next swab out the interior with neat Jeyes fluid or similar disinfectant using a short-handled woolly-headed mop, such as is used for cleaning out milk bottles. However, remember that the mop will not be fit for its original purpose again but will do nicely for applying oil and grease to tools and to blades of the lawn mower. After swabbing out the hole, paint the inside with bitumen paint. The neat disinfectant will sink into the wood and destroy any fungus spores and the bitumen will remain on the surface and so seal it, preventing the re-entry of any more spores or bacteria.

Complete the operation by filling the hole with cement, using a mixture of four parts coarse sand to one part of cement. The cement mixture should be used as dry as possible as a wet sloppy mixture may take months to dry out in a deep hole. Use a square-ended stick to ram it down as firmly as possible to exclude air. Fill the hole up to within 3 or 4 in of the entrance and then drive a few galvanised iron nails round the inside of the hole with the heads pointing to the centre, leaving 2 or 3 in of the head exposed. For a large hole, nails with wedge-shaped points are ideal and should be driven lengthwise of the grain. Continue tamping the cement gently amongst the nails leaving it slightly raised in the centre. If it is left flush with the edges of the hole and slightly higher in the centre it will shed the rain and also allow the cambium and bark to creep over the cement to form callus. This it will do in a year to two if the hole is only a small one. The same sort of technique may be applied to a branch which has rotted off but, here again, care must be taken to scrape out all the old rotten material as deeply as possible. The idea is to make it easier for the cambium and bark to grow over it and so completely heal the wound.

Lopping

The object of all pruning and lopping is to retain the character of the tree as well as the balance between root and head. If this is not done a very large root system deprived of its natural outlet through the branches may send up basal growths and suckers and it will be a continual fight to get rid of these, especially with such trees as willows, poplars and sycamores. Certain trees like oak and beech are better behaved and lower branches can be removed which are a danger or obstruct light without harming the symmetry of the tree too much.

When lopping large branches, it may be necessary to cut them down in sections and lower the cut portions to the ground by means of a rope slung over a higher branch. Even if the branch can be sawn off in one piece it is best to leave about 2 ft projecting from the trunk. This serves two purposes; the ladder may be leaned against this stump whilst the operation is in progress and the short spur will prevent the branch tearing off raggedly and injuring the trunk. Then, with the ladder leaning against the main trunk, the short stump can be sawn off as closely as possible to the trunk itself. When cutting off the limbs of valuable trees, I always rub down the cut surface with coarse sandpaper and trim the edges of the bark with a sharp knife as this allows it to be covered over much more quickly. Immediately after smoothing the surface, paint the cut portion with a good lead paint; Stockholm tar, which is prepared from wood and not coal, is ideal.

One word of warning, if the branches of a neighbour's tree annoy you, you are not at liberty to cut any further back than your boundary fence. However, it is far better to discuss the whole matter amicably with your neighbour and come to some understanding before you spoil a tree. Taking too many branches off your side of the fence may not only make the tree look lopsided but perhaps may cause it to fall.

Suckers and suckering

A sucker, by horticultural definition, is a shoot rising from underground which will develop into a new plant. Suckers are liable to appear on any subject which is grafted or budded so that one portion of the stock is below ground and the scion, or named part, is above ground. The roots of many trees and shrubs are capable of sending up suckers from underground roots and stems but these fall into a different category. It is the unwanted suckers of what is really a foreign plant that cause concern to many home gardeners. This includes roses, lilacs and cherries, to mention but three. A good nurseryman does everything in his power to see that his shrubs and trees are free, or have been freed, from suckers but naturally he has no control over what are produced once they get into the customer's garden.

Embedded beneath the bark or skin of the roots are dormant buds which can burst into growth if they are damaged or when the life and safety of the subject appears to be threatened by damage. These dormant buds can spring into activity out of sheer poverty of soil and very often cultivated grafted trees growing in poor ground will send up masses of suckers. Various strains of rootstocks carry within them varying degrees of susceptibility to suckering. A shaly or abrasive soil may also induce suckering, especially if the soil is loose and light and the top of the plant is allowed to waggle in the wind thus causing the roots to break.

Bad planting and deep cultivation, however, are the more likely causes of frequent suckering. The treatment of suckers can also influence their incidence. For instance, many is the time I have seen people hoeing their rose beds and on seeing a sucker they take a stabbing swipe at it with the Dutch hoe. This is the surest way of getting more, bigger and better suckers. To deal with the development of suckers on all grafted subjects would occupy a very large book as there are so many variables but, generally speaking, the behaviour and treatment of suckers appearing on roses will serve to indicate the best type of treatment in general. First, an idea of how and why they are produced may be helpful. As already stated, a vast number of plants are capable of producing growth buds from the roots and, of course, advantage is taken of this in propagating. Nature is wise in the provision of means to ensure continuity and buds, whether above or below ground, seldom appear singly. A casual examination will show that there is only one bud in the axil of the leaf or on a root, but if these are examined closely, and sometimes a hand lens is necessary, it will be found that there are generally two secondary buds, one on each side of the main bud. They are there to ensure that growth is continued. During severe weather quite a number of the first or primary buds of trees may be destroyed by frost or cold wind and then masses of buds appear in a short time and the whole head of the tree or shrub may be covered with shorter and smaller twiggy growth resulting from these secondary buds. The same sort of thing occurs with the underground buds.

As these growths or suckers may appear from inches or even feet below the surface they have, in effect, become stems with buds spaced all the way along them, just in the same way as they appear above ground. So if they are chopped off at or just below ground level these stem buds, in addition to basal buds, can and often do, sprout into active growth. This means that if you see a single sucker appearing above ground and you chop it off, the next group that appears may consist of two or even half a dozen growths and if these are chopped persistently then quite a thicket can develop. Unfortunately, once they have started they have a great advantage because they develop at a point below the place where the foster bud has been put in by the nurseryman, thus giving them first call on all the food supply. Because suckers are the natural and original growth there is an easy path for the food supplies and sap to move along and the artificially-placed bud is bypassed.

In budding or grafting there is bound to be not only variation in wood and growth substances, but some degree of callousing and rejection occurs even with compatible subjects. Where they are more incompatible and the rates of growth are different then a great deal of thickening occurs. In the case of a tree, if planks are sawn through the point of grafting then the whole complicated thickening of the grain can be easily seen. Incidentally, it is a very pleasant exercise to look around some of the trees grafted some 60 to 100 years ago when they knew less about compatibility. There are some excellent examples in the Embankment Gardens in London and at Kew. Sometimes the stem of the stock is thicker and the head smaller or it can be the reverse. When it was a common practice to graft pears onto thorns, very often the pear scion grew three times the size of the stock and the trees were blown over. However, this is another story and was only introduced to illustrate a point. The main thing is to try to remove the suckers so that they do not appear again; in the case of grafted trees and bushes, especially roses, avoid deep cultivation and deep, in this case, may be no more than 1 to 1½ in at the most. Avoid allowing the shrub to get top heavy so that it waves about in wind and rain, damaging and loosening the roots.

The only way to remove suckers satisfactorily is to dig down carefully with a trowel to find the point of attachment to the roots. Here again it is useless cutting off the sucker as, although you may remove the main growth, the guard or secondary buds still remain. They are, however, placed fairly closely to the main growth and if the sucker is grasped firmly and pulled away from the root it will come away with the heel bringing the embro buds with it. As most of the suckers will be firmly attached, steady and firm the plant with the feet at the time of pulling otherwise you may break more roots. Replace the soil and tread firmly. I have found from personal experience that since I discontinued hoeing and forking in between my roses and relied on chemical means for keeping weeds under control, I have certainly had no suckers whatsoever.

Honeyfungus

Honeyfungus, bootlace fungus or honey agaric (*Armillaria mellea*) call it what you will, is becoming a serious and widespread disease. As more and more houses are being built and gardens made, often on the site of old hedges, cleared shrubland or where trees have been removed, so the menace increases. Scarcely a day passes without a report of part of a hedge, sometimes even whole hedges or well-established shrubs collapsing and dying without apparent reason.

Like most other fungi it attacks the weaker plants or those which have been damaged or debilitated by being planted in badly-drained, waterlogged or otherwise unsuitable soil. The best safeguard is prevention, but unfortunately few amateur gardeners, particularly beginners, realise the potential danger in the remnants of old roots, old wood chips and debris from hedges and woods. Often, too, this is masked by the builder spreading a load of soil over the original half-cleared debris. It may take some years before the insidious bootlace-like growths wriggle through the soil in search of living victims.

What often happens is that this fungus becomes established on old tree stumps in bits of broken root and gradually spreads through the soil until it finds the damaged, dying or even dead roots of badly-planted trees or hedging materials. It then attacks and spreads to the living tissue. Offhand, I cannot think of any other disease which spreads so insidiously, is such a killer and is so difficult to treat. This is mainly due not only to its invasive nature, but also to the fact that the disease can spread from mushroom-like fruiting bodies which appear in late summer. These take the form of honey-coloured caps with brown scales and long yellowish stems. From these will be liberated spores which will infect other dead stumps and debris. From the source of infection long shiny black cord-like strands are sent out, like something out of science fiction. Any shrub or portion of hedge which mysteriously dies should be carefully dug up and promptly burned, even if it means lighting a fire especially for the purpose. It is of little use replanting, as the fungus can remain in the soil for many years and will attack all dead debris and be passed on to living tissue. It does not discriminate but seems to attack almost anything. However, it has a preference for privet, flowering currant and rhododendrons. It will attack herbaceous plants too, even going for rhubarb and daffodils, but as a rule these are only attacked on waterlogged soil.

The method of clearing the soil is laborious and difficult and the only way that I have been able to master it is in the case of a hedge or individual tree by taking out the soil to a depth of 2 ft and twice the width of the root area. To prevent re-infection polythene should be spread on either side of the trench or hole and the top soil is placed on one side and the sub-soil on the other. Take care not to walk about any more than can be helped during this operation. After the whole of the soil has been taken out, prepare formaldehyde or Bray's emulsion at the dilution of one part chemical to thirty parts water. Throw 3 in of soil back into the trench and soak this with the solution. Continue putting in the layers and soaking them until the job is completed. There may be other chemicals available which will do the job, but frankly I am not sure of them. I have used Jeyes fluid at the same dilution for this purpose and obtained partial control the first time of application as it changed the character of the growths. These became fanlike and were killed on the second application. Certainly no further planting should take place for at least another season even after treatment. The best preventative is to pick up every scrap of wood chip, root or old stump that it is possible to fork up and rake out.

Never plant in solid clay or waterlogged soil and always try to keep the shrubs growing actively. If you follow this advice you will go a long way to warding off attacks.

Layering

Layering is perhaps the most simple and useful form of increasing stock in the ordinary garden but, even with this method, techniques have been evolved for virtually all types of plants. There are some ten recognised techniques:

1. Simple bending	7. Notching
2. Tonguing and heeling	8. Arching
3. Ringing	9. Growing point layering
4. Strangulation	10. Marcotting
5. Twisting	11. Fracture
6. Piercing	12. Serpentine

The common advantage of these techniques is that the portion to be rooted is not at risk in that the portion, be it branch or tip, is not severed from the parent plant until it has made roots and is capable of supporting itself. This is particularly useful where cutting material is scarce or a subject takes a long time or is difficult to root for then the cuttings would be at risk. Furthermore, older material may be used which would not readily root if inserted as a cutting.

Personally, I know of no upper limit to the age and thickness at which certain subjects would fail to root by layering. I have seen trees getting on for 100 years old which have been successfully layered and cases can be frequently seen of apple trees and laburnums which have fallen down and have re-rooted along their stems. Certainly, this is the safest method of propagating for the not-so-skilled, or where facilities are not available, for it prevents many disappointments.

All the techniques are based on the principle of the partial arrest and disturbance of the sap passing along the stem at a point where roots are to be formed. Of course, in some plants roots will form at any point and all that is required is to cover them with a suitable rooting medium, but very often special techniques must be used to satisfy particular conditions. This takes the form of arresting the flow of sap and, incidentally, there are conflicting opinions as to why checking the sap should encourage rooting but the fact remains that in practice, if the bark and the layers beneath the bark are constricted either by wire, scraping, cutting, nicking or some other form of strangulation or fracture, sooner or later roots will form. The object, of course, is to induce these roots to form on the portion which is to be removed.

A simple method of layering is to take a branch or portion of the

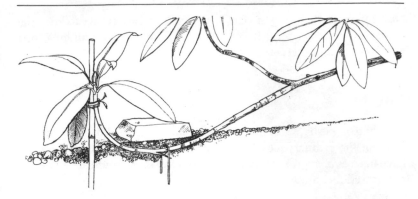

Layering a rhododendron using the tongue and heel method involves bending down a branch and slitting it partially through. This is bent back so the slit opens and is held down in the soil by means of a piece of bent wire. As rhododendrons take time to root the branch is held in position by a stone or brick. The end of the layered branch, supported by a stake, will eventually form a new plant that can be severed from its parent when a root system has been established

plant situated in a suitable position so that it can be bent down in order that a portion of the stem enters the ground. The piece actually buried must be roughened, nicked or slit and preferably bent up at as near a right angle as possible and secured to a stake. This bending further constricts the flow of sap. A hollow should be taken out of the soil and replaced with a mixture of peat and sand so that the bent or lacerated portion sits on this. Then it, in turn, is covered with more of the mixture and the soil replaced and firmed down. Subjects such as holly or rhododendrons may take a long time to root, so an easy way is to place a brick or flat stone on the portion to be rooted. This not only holds the branch in position but keeps the soil beneath the brick or stone cool and moist.

Layering, although actually simple in operation, is an immensely complicated process so far as root production is concerned, but for the operator it is enough to say that this is an almost 100 per cent sure way of ensuring vegetative reproduction of the plant in question. Advantage can often be taken of this natural stem rooting when it is desired to increase the size of a clump, even without actually severing the rooted portion after it has rooted. With the serpentine form of layering, this may be done with a long flexible branch so that a number of layers can be obtained at every point where the stem touches the ground. Tip layering is most useful for blackberries, loganberries and rambler roses. In this case, if the young actively-growing tip is pegged securely to the ground it will root quickly and readily. Aerial layering or marcotting is another story and outside the scope of this book.

Flowers in the Garden

If trees and shrubs are the furniture, then flowers are the soft furnishings and the lawn is the carpet. No one should worry unduly about arrangement and colour schemes as most colours in nature go together. The green of the foliage is always a saving grace and if you want a garden to look like a painter's brush rag, why not? Whatever you enjoy most is the important factor to consider.

Herbaceous and mixed borders

I look back rather nostalgically on the last really big herbaceous border that I designed and planted. It was some 98 yd long and 7 yd wide and was a real show piece backed by a mellow brick wall. The border was fronted with a red shale path, 6 ft wide, and edged with grey lavender and santolina on the other side. Such a border is virtually a full-time job for one man. What with the staking, tying, thinning and dead-heading, a true herbaceous border takes quite a lot of attention. To the purist the term herbaceous means herbaceous perennials, but strictly speaking herbaceous plants include annuals and also bulbs and dahlias.

For the ordinary garden, my own opinion is that a mixed border, which includes flowering shrubs as well as the whole range of spring and summer bedding plants and bulbs, is a far better proposition. Such a border provides colour for the whole of the year and there is no reason why such subjects as heaths cannot be included too. One advantage of herbaceous perennials is that with few exceptions they all enjoy the same type of soil and there is no need, as in a rockery, to provide pockets for lime haters or lime lovers. A few plants, such as the perennial scabious, require extra lime but such pockets may be localised and treated separately after planting.

Generally speaking, the same sort of treatment that would be given to a vegetable garden can be given when preparing the herbaceous border. Great play is often made of preparing the ground, but this is only of real importance when a new garden is being made or when a particularly bad site is being prepared. For convenience, herbaceous or mixed borders usually bound one or both sides of a lawn. But, where the garden is large enough, a central border which can be viewed on both sides makes a striking feature, and even an island site can be used to advantage. From the point of view of drainage and for setting off the plants it is desirable to raise the border slightly higher than the adjoining lawn or path and, better still, to slope it from back to front. A border which is planted regularly with tall subjects at the back sloping down to dwarf subjects at the front, looks too much like an exhibit at a flower show and is extremely artificial. A certain amount of thought and skill is necessary for the satisfactory arrangement of plants in borders. Most catalogues carry plans of suggested arrangements which will be found invaluable to the beginner.

The life of a border depends entirely on how it is cared for. A border which is planted and left may need lifting and dividing in about four years, but a well-maintained one can go on for twelve or fifteen years. I prefer to treat and replant the border piecemeal rather than to dig everything up and start all over again. The actual planting and preparing of a border is a straightforward commonsense job, and no great quantity of manure or fertiliser need be added; I prefer annual topdressing to a heavy initial application. My own suggestion is to use a barrowload of well-rotted manure or compost per 4 sq yd and to supplement this with 2 oz or a good handful of raw bonemeal and 4 oz basic slag per sq yd. This should be well mixed into the soil and the whole well trodden before and during planting.

The sort of thing I had in mind when I talked of piecemeal renovation was the regular division of strong rampant growers such as Michaelmas daisies and heleniums. Good varieties of lupins I prefer to propagate each year and replant when necessary. In a large border I prefer to plant in groups rather than clumps. I would like to illustrate this more fully. A clump of Michaelmas daisies requiring division is lifted and the soil shaken off. This invariably leaves a depression which should be topped up with a barrowload of soil from the vegetable garden, a little bonemeal and rotted manure added and well trodden in. Good individual rosettes with two or three growths are selected from the outside of the clump and planted 9 in apart. In a large border there may be ten to twelve such clumps, in a small border three to five or seven. Each of these clumps grows outwards eventually to form a large ornamental and striking group. In the case of lupins and delphiniums, which begin to deteriorate after about four years, cuttings are regularly taken in the spring. The young ones are planted close to, but not actually on, the site of the old plant. For example, there may be three delphiniums in a group adjacent to a clump of phlox. Some of the phlox may be removed and the young delphiniums placed nearby. Cuttings or divisions of phlox go into the reserve border and when the old delphiniums are taken up the new phlox plants are put in their place. This means a certain amount of juggling with space and materials, but although it sounds rather complicated, in practice it is not too much trouble. This treatment keeps the border perennially young and any replanting of a particular type or variety is given a different site. This is for two reasons; exhaustion of the soil by particular plants and the possible incidence of pests or diseases.

In a mixed border I like to reserve spaces for such things as dahlias and chrysanthemums and certain well-defined bays in the front of the border for annuals, spring and summer bedding and plots of bulbs, so that there is colour all through the year. I am not averse to using shrubs in such a mixed border and like to employ certain of the less-sprawling shrub roses. The so-called pillar roses, which are a compromise between the rambler and an ordinary bush-type rose, make wonderful columns. So do sweet peas which, if strategically placed, make a splendid splash of colour. In my opinion such a border is more colourful, far less trouble and requires less annual material than a series of beds devoted entirely to bedding plants. Clumps of annuals may be sown direct and at different times of the year, even as late as the end of June, to produce masses of beautiful fresh colour when the rest of the border is beginning to look a bit tatty. Generally not enough late sowing is done; it is usually one good do which uses up all the packets and results in half the plants being wasted. Far better to make three sowings, and this can easily be done from the same quantity and number of packets.

Nowhere in the garden is there such a concentration of roots and such intensive cultivation as in the herbaceous or mixed border. Yet far too often the plants themselves receive very little in the way of food. It is just as easy to apply manure and fertilisers to the surface of a herbaceous border as it is between the rows in the kitchen garden. The amount needed is comparatively small and the applications are spaced over a season. For example, three light dressings of Growmore fertiliser or fishmeal hoed in during the summer, followed by a regular autumn dressing of some organic matter, whether it be – best of all – well-rotted manure, well-rotted compost or a favourite mix made up of peat and fertiliser. A good standby topdressing for shrubs and herbaceous plants is to mix 30 lb of Growmore with a bale of peat. Break down the peat, damp it and then incorporate the fertiliser thoroughly and apply this at the rate of about 1 to 1½ lb per sq yd to the whole of the border.

Herbaceous borders, mixed borders and shrub borders should never be dug. After shortening back the tops and taking out the weeds, the topdressing should be applied and the whole surface lightly pricked over to a depth of about 2 in with a fork. For this sort of job I like to use either a flat-tined border fork or a five-tined curved Cheshire fork, so that despite the shallow depth the whole surface can be completely inverted, burying the weeds and weed seeds. Where bulbs are used in the border tulips can be lifted in the normal way as

When designing a mixed border make provision for annuals and bulbs at the front. Allocate bays for dahlias and chrysanthemums which will provide plenty of colour at the end of the season. Larger shrubs and pillar roses are most effective at the back where not only are they beautiful in their own right but they also provide a pleasant background

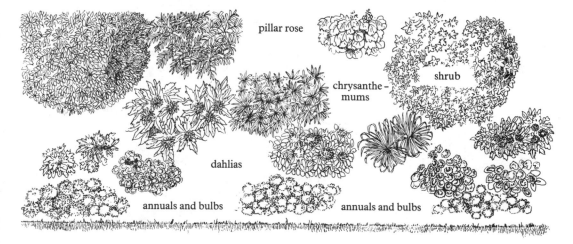

pillar rose

chrysanthe-
mums

shrub

dahlias

annuals and bulbs

annuals and bulbs

91

Sowing annuals

Probably the best way to sow is in drills, tracing these with a stick in oval or circular patterns about 1 ft in diameter for small borders and twice that for larger ones. Make the drills about ¾ in deep, that is the depth of a new penny on its edge, and sow the seeds very shallowly. Then make a little hole in the centre of the ring and put a few seeds in this. It may be that the soil at this shallow depth will be dry, even so do not water the area. This is a golden rule when sowing outdoors. Instead get a watering can without a rose, a kettle or even a teapot and fill in the drill with water. Let this subside and sow the seed, covering with dry soil. Seeds of any sort sown this way seldom need any more watering until they are quite large plants, even during a dry period.

When the young plants are about 2 in tall they should be thinned out drastically. Annual chrysanths need 9 to 12 in between plants, whilst Shirley poppies will do at 4 in. Quite a number may be transplanted to other parts of the garden, but poppies and eschscholzia are not satisfactory when moved. After thinning give them a feed of a heaped dessertspoonful of superphosphate in a gallon of water; this will encourage them to make a good root system.

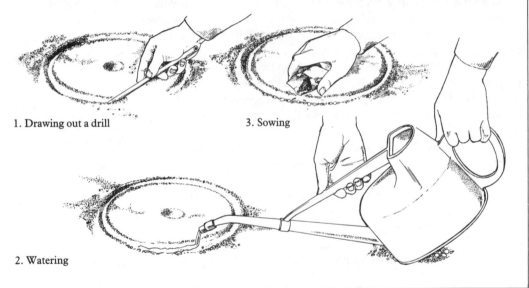

1. Drawing out a drill

3. Sowing

2. Watering

with ordinary spring bedding, but daffodils can be allowed to remain provided they are marked to avoid danger of skewering them during the autumn prick-over of the border.

Beds and bedding

Slightly-raised beds give a more effective display of the plants and, if cut out of grass, provide a decent clean sharp edge. So, assuming there is no need to lift the turf, this can be dug in and chopped up as the job proceeds. Add rotted manure, old potting soil or compost and, as the job proceeds, turn the soil to the centre to create a trench so that after the first spadeful or two you are digging round and round. Turn the soil slightly forward each time, gradually increasing the width and depth of the trench. Don't be at all worried if you finish up at the edge with a trench nearly the depth of your spade, this is as it should be.

Depending on the time of year, the bed can be left rough to break down of its own accord or, if required for immediate use, the soil can be broken up and trodden thoroughly. If it is to be used for summer and spring bedding, lightly dust with hydrated lime before raking.

Shaping beds

One of the most indispensible tools in the garden is a 6-ft lath marked off in feet and sub-divided into six inches, with six separate inches marked at one end. A useful lath would measure 1½ in wide and ¾ in thick which is substantial enough to stand an occasional wheeling over by the barrow.

Rectangular beds When initially making a new square or rectangular bed then the sides and the corners must be exact right angles and here a little mathematical formula comes in handy. Starting off from the base A and putting in a peg, measure along 3 ft and put in another peg. From point A again measure as near as you can judge to point C a distance of 4 ft. Then, putting down your lath from point B across to point C, measure 5 ft. If A–C does not just coincide adjust it and your line so that it meets at a point D. The formula is 3,4,5: from A to B is 3 ft, from A to D 4 ft and from B to D 5 ft.

With this little formula you can true up or make any rectangular bed by using your 6 ft lath and a piece of string or a garden line.

Oval beds Guessing how to draw out an oval bed is not easy, but here again with three pegs and a piece of string one can easily make a bed to the desired shape and size. Having decided on the size and shape of the ellipse, put in pegs at A and B and loop a piece of string or garden line over the two pegs tying the ends together. The tightness or slackness of this loop will decide on the type of elliptical bed that you make. The pegs A and B are fixed. Withdraw C from the ground and walk with this keeping the string taut. By doing this you will describe an elliptical bed. The distance from the straight line A–B to C will be half the width of the bed and this is where you make the adjustment to suit the shape of the bed. The greater the distance the more tubby will be the bed and the smaller the distance from the line A–B to C will give you a much narrower bed.

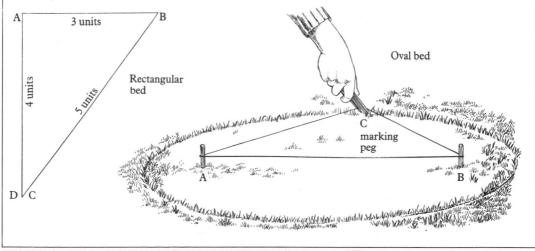

A   3 units   B

4 units

5 units

Rectangular bed

D C

Oval bed

C
marking peg

A   B

The extra deep trench at the edge of the bed will allow you to rake down any debris, stones, clods of soil or roots which can then be easily collected. Leave an edging about 3 to 4 in deep. To 'true' up the edge use a half-moon edging iron and then, to neaten off the job, turn the rake with the head downwards and go around with the back of the rake to the turf edge gently tamping down. Thereafter, when digging a circular bed, always start at the centre.

When it comes to planting out the procedure is somewhat changed. For circular and oval beds you start planting at the edge; in other words you put your border in first. For example, supposing you are planting up a circular bed with lobelia and antirrhinums. Get your bedding plants on to the bed. (Never mind about trampling it down, this will do more good than harm provided soil conditions are right. Most flower beds are left far too puffy with the result that the plants suffer as the soil settles.) Then decide on the distance to allow between plants and rows and mark out the positions of the first two rows using your trowel or measuring rod following the curve of the bed. After these have been planted it will be found that it is no longer possible to stagger the plants; that is putting one plant opposite each gap formed between the plants in the row in front. After the two outer circles have been planted all the other plants are just put in equidistant from one another with no attempt at making a circle or any other figure. Depending on the occupants of the bed, a 'dot' (taller-growing plant) is selected for the centre. Plant circular, oval and triangular beds this way and after planting, run over the whole surface with a small Dutch hoe.

Ground cover

Much has been written and spoken about the use of low-growing plants as ground cover; the implication being that the ground can be covered by quick-growing plants which will exclude weeds. Various prostrate subjects have been recommended such as heathers, *Cotoneaster dammeri* and vinca, all of which seem to offer the hard-pressed gardener a respite from controlling weeds between shrubs and trees. In theory this sounds excellent advice but there are many snags. Perhaps the greatest is that these plants need to be planted very closely together so that they establish themselves quickly before the weeds get there first. This does not matter a great deal when the area is small but if it is large then any weeding must be done by hand as neither tools nor weedkillers can be used amongst this dense planting, so initially it means more work.

Closely planted subjects naturally grow quickly together. This means that after two or three years they are choking one another and have to be drastically cut back or thinned out. At the same time they prevent any mulching or cultivation of the main body of trees and shrubs and actually rob them of food and moisture, so that the main planting suffers. Once perennial weeds become established amongst the ground cover, then the battle is completely lost as no corrective treatment can be given.

Having experimented and followed up various plantings for over twenty years I have come to the conclusion that the most useful and effective ground cover which excludes weeds without harming the main plantings are as follows, in order of effectiveness. Grass, which can be mown and have wild flowers, such as primroses, forget-me-nots and anemones, introduced into it. Trees and shrubs can be planted and as they increase the grass will gradually die out. All that is needed is to maintain a small area free from grass round the base of the tree or shrub. This can be done chemically and will allow space for feeding, mulching and watering. Wild strawberries are next in my order of usefulness and have proved very effective for sixteen years. The third subject is ivy which is also very suitable and can prove an excellent trap for fallen leaves. However, it has to be watched in case it starts to climb.

A technique which I have evolved in tackling a new garden, no matter what the soil conditions provided water is not standing, is to loosen the soil surface and sow with grass seed. This gives a breathing space so that the whole area can be tackled at leisure. I am not thinking of formal strips in front of the house but much of the very large area behind it. Mark out the lawn area proper, then lightly rotavate the rest or chip with a spade to create a tilth. Rake in the grass seed which, when it germinates, will form a sort of canvas on which any kind of picture can be painted. Then stand at each window of the house in turn, looking out and visualising what you would like to see. After this sit down with a catalogue and select trees and shrubs for colour, shape and form which will give pleasure as well as doing the job of screening. Mark these in with stakes and try to imagine what they will look like in ten or fifteen years' time. This doesn't come easily to some folk but trying to see them in the mind's eye is much better than having to shift them ten years later. In the meantime the grass is growing, there are no weed problems and an occasional run over with a rotary mower will keep your 'canvas' clean until you are ready to plant.

Having decided on the subjects and their location you can complete the scheme at leisure. Now that shrubs and trees are available in containers they can be bought singly and planted at any time of the year. Using this technique it does not matter if the job takes years to complete as there is nothing untoward or unsightly. There are no weeds to bother about and bulbs can be established if desired. Grassy paths can be pegged out and the whole job is a joy which can be taken up and dropped like a piece of knitting instead of carried out in a

95

frantic rush in a few weeks with the subsequent problem of having to keep down weeds and cultivate the soil between shrubs for years.

The winter garden

After the first frost all too often one tends to have a clean up and figuratively pull the shutters down to hide the garden; sort of 'that's-it-'til-next-summer' attitude. But gardens can be attractive in the winter and the best way, I think, to make them so is to create a corner for a winter garden. A sheltered position facing south or southwest where early morning sun can be avoided would be ideal if possible. The reason for this is that if any subjects do become frozen and are rapidly thawed they are almost certain to be damaged, but if they can thaw out gradually then less damage will be done. On the whole winter-flowering subjects are not the gaudy, flamboyant types of midsummer but are mainly made up of clusters of small, often sweetly-scented blooms. I mention this so that no one will feel cheated if winter-flowering shrubs do not provide such a mass of colour as we expect from spring and summer varieties. Their appeal in winter is more intimate and cheering. For instance, a warm corner in January with a clump of golden witch hazel (*Hamamelis mollis* or *H. japonica*) with a ground-work of pink or red erica is both colourful and cheerful. If the bed is edged with early-flowering bulbs of blue, such as chionodoxa, and clumps of muscari (grape hyacinths) are interplanted amongst the heaths, the interest and beauty of the bed is extended to the stage when early-spring flowering shrubs take over.

Erythronium dens-canis

Another charming combination is one or two *Viburnum tinus* (laurustinus), with chimonanthus (winter sweet) and pale pink flowering *Viburnum x bodnantense* underplanted with varieties of the dwarf *Iris reticulata*. Under such shrubs the Christmas rose and erythronium (dog's tooth violet) will be quite happy too and will give a display well into the spring. The beautiful hardy climber *Jasminum nudiflorum* must not be forgotten and, although mostly grown and trained up a wall or fence, it is very happy growing up an old tree stump either amongst or behind other flowering shrubs. It should not be trained up a straight larch pole as winter jasmine loses much of its charm if rigidly tied; far more effective is to let it scramble naturally over a twisted bough of oak or chestnut.

When planning a garden I like to arrange gardens within gardens so that there is always some interesting feature at every season of the year and not just a feast or a famine. Try to link these different gardens so that they fall naturally into successional flower. Let spring-flowering shrubs take over from the autumn- and winter-fruiting shrubs with their colourful leaves and bright berries. There are shrubs with coloured bark, like dogwoods and golden willow, which if cut down to the ground every year will provide masses of young growths which glow almost as brightly as a bonfire in the winter sunshine.

All these plants I have mentioned are especially valuable as they will grow and thrive even in cold northern districts or on the fringe of smoky industrial areas. In the purer air of the country the gold and silver foliage of conifers and the cupressus make excellent partners for winter-flowering shrubs. It needs only a little planning and no more expense to have a garden which is interesting and colourful in winter as well as during spring and summer.

Here is a longer list of plants which will add interest and colour to the garden from November until March: *Chimonanthus praecox, Clematis calycina, Cornus mas, Corylopsis spicata, Daphne mezereum,* some species of erica, *Garrya elliptica, Hamamelis mollis, Jasminum nudiflorum, Lonicera standishi, Mahonia bealei, Prunus x amygdalo-persica* Pollardi, *Prunus subhirtella* Autumnalis, some species of rhododendron including *Rhododendron praecox, Viburnum x bodnantense, Viburnum fragrans* and *Viburnum tinus.* Don't forget, too, that polythanthus will naturalise in grass just as well as the primrose and will seed and spread. Also that species crocus bloom weeks ahead of the larger vernal varieties. There is no need at all for the garden to be dull in winter.

Hamamelis mollis

Naturalising bulbs

Few sounds are more sickening than the clunk of a spade slicing through a clump of bulbs or few things more annoying than skewering them on the end of a fork. Having run through this gamut of emotions, I now plant my bulbs completely out of harm's way. My own choice is to arrange them around the base of shrubs, often in company with such things as heaths, primroses, violets or other similar low-growing perennials. Here they are perfectly safe and, provided they get an annual topdressing of a mixture of peat and a complete fertiliser such as Growmore, or a good garden compost supplemented by bonemeal, they will be quite happy for many years. The perennials indicate the presence of the bulbs beneath, so the danger of them being damaged is minimal. It is preferable not to overplant daffodils so that, if necessary, the ground can be sprayed with a total weedkiller after the foliage has died down.

For naturalising proper, and by proper I mean in woodland or in grass, the bulbs should be arranged as clumps within clumps. When in leaf this arrangement is not noticeable and the whole area looks to be a mass of flowers but still enables the grass to be mown. Planting is done by lifting flaps of grass on a hinge by cutting on three sides and turning back about a foot square of turf. The soil is loosened and some taken out. The bulbs are laid on their sides in the hole and topped

To naturalise bulbs in grass lift flaps of turf and loosen the exposed soil. Make a hole and lay a few bulbs on their sides. Cover them with soil and replace the turf, firming it with the feet

with a mixture of peat and sand or leafmould to which a little HCH powder has been added. The reason for laying the bulbs on their sides is so that there is no danger of damaging the nose of the bulb when the turf flap is trodden down. Have no fear, the bulbs will pull themselves upright and come up perfectly normally. After flowering, the seed pods are removed and the foliage inserted in plastic net sleeves. The whole area is then sprayed with a growth inhibitor containing maleic hydrazide which also prevents the grass from getting out of hand.

At some time or another most people like to dibble crocuses into grass, but scattered indiscriminately they look like sore fingers and large areas can remain untidy for a long time. Generally, however, where they are planted in this way people get so fed up with the untidiness that they run the mower over the not-yet-ripened corms with the result that the corms are unable to multiply or even produce flowers the following year. Personally, I like to plant drifts of crocuses so that they can not only multiply and draw down the newly-formed corms with their special prehensile roots but seed as well. Very often a percentage of seed-sown crocuses bloom after the second year. These too should be sited carefully and if there is a sloping bank so much the better. Never plant in straight lines.

Dry and hollow walls

These make ideal features in new gardens and can improve older ones at little cost. It is a pleasant job to create one during the summer months. The secret of construction is in keying the stones and if one has any doubts about the durability of mortarless structures one has only to look at the dividing walls in the fields of our northern and western counties. Let me first of all make it quite clear that I am speaking of two separate types of construction; the hollow wall which is filled with soil and subsequently planted and the dry-stone wall which is solid in construction but can still be used for growing plants in the crevices between the stones. However because of the small amount of soil, the type and variety of plant is extremely limited. In the hollow wall, on the other hand, almost any type of plant may be grown depending on the width and depth of soil. Many of the so-called hollow walls constructed by builders are far too shallow and more ornamental than practical. There is a limit to the height of mortarless walls and I suggest no more than 2½ ft to be reasonable and for a solid wall about 5½ ft.

Construction Like all other structures, such walls need a firm foundation and I always like to sink the first row of stones below soil level. Take out a trench to the required width, level off the bottom or in the case of a slope this can either be stepped down or sloped to follow the lie of the land provided it is not too steep. Loosen up the surface as one would prepare soil for sowing, removing any bumps, roots or large stones. The garden wall differs from that erected by the farmer in that soil is used between the joints to accommodate plants, whereas dry-stone walls do not present a solid face and strong winds can blow through them.

Stones of any thickness may be used but it saves a lot of trouble if these are sorted out into what are known as courses, which is another name for the thickness of the stone, for example 3- or 4-in courses. Any irregularities are taken up with the soil which is used as mortar. I like to use a soil which is as rich as possible. This is passed through a ½-in riddle to remove stones and lumps and then as much rotted compost as possible is added; extra sand is unnecessary. The idea is to produce a rather sticky fine compost which is spread on the top of the stones about an inch thick if the stones are flat and, where they are irregular, it can be built up to about an inch and a half. Where more building up is required small pieces of flat stone may be used. The outer face of the wall can either be built up square, that is using faced stones, or it can be as rough as you like to have it.

A hollow wall consists of two separate outer walls filled in with soil. As one can well imagine the weight of the soil has a tendency to press out the comparatively thin unsecured walls. To defeat this we use what are known as 'throughers'. These are long tie stones which stretch right across the gap between the two walls and the weight of the stones on top, together with the solidity given by the soil which is filled in after, maintains a perfectly rigid structure. Neglecting to put in these ties will result in the walls collapsing after frost or heavy rain. I may add that walls which I erected nearly thirty years ago are still perfectly sound and no amount of weather has disturbed them. The soil joints allow for expansion and contraction and, of course, provide perfect drainage. In dry districts I sometimes seal a number of the joints on the inside with clay which has been moistened and worked to the consistency of putty. Where rainfall is high this is unnecessary.

Planting When building such walls, I either decide in my own mind how the wall will be planted or a plan can be prepared on paper. This I consider important as it is far easier to plant as the job proceeds than to try to push in plants afterwards. Suppose, for example, you intend to plant aubrieta, iberis or other trailing plants along your third course. First spread the layer of soil then knock the plant out of the pot and tease out the roots, arranging the plant over a vertical joint. This allows it to spread downwards, sideways and backwards into the mass of soil. Each succeeding layer of stones should be set back, roughly about an inch from the one below as this not only gives stability but soil will fall onto these ledges and any number of plants will establish themselves even in this very small amount. It also makes it easier for sowing both annuals and perennials.

Seeds of annual and perennial plants can be incorporated in any wall with cracks simply by making little mud pellets from decent compost, pushing the seeds into these and then pressing the pellets well into the cracks of the wall. If you can syringe these for a day or two to keep them moist, so much the better, but you will be surprised how well many of even the difficult seeds germinate in what may seem almost impossible conditions. My advice is to avoid large-leafed plants such as nasturtiums; for although in theory they should look fine under these conditions, they often look untidy and unsightly. Alternate the plants hanging from the face of the wall by using some trailing plants and some tufted types but do not use small shrubs in the sides. These, including roses, can be used in hollow walls. I have one hollow wall planted up with the small polyantha-type rose, variety Willie Den Ouden, which has looked beautiful for the last twenty years. All this receives is the normal feeding and an annual top-dressing of a good compost such as J.I. potting compost No. 3 or an equivalent mixture.

Before planting in a wall spread a layer of soil over a course. Then tease out the roots of the plant and position it over a vertical joint. Cover the roots with more soil and lay the next course of stones

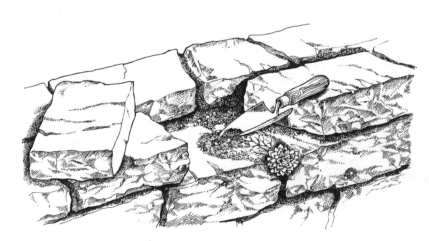

The Vegetable Garden

Vegetable plots, like gardens, come in all shapes and sizes and face every direction, mostly the wrong one, but once in position there is nothing one can do but accept the situation.

Planning the vegetable garden

Printed plans and articles in books are usually shown as rectangles or squares but this is mainly for convenience of putting them down on paper. However there are certain principles and practices to observe whatever the shape, whether it be a triangular corner site, or a long strip – which can often be a veritable wind tunnel – by the side of the house. The farther that the vegetable plot can be sited away from the house or overhanging trees the better. The shade caused by a building is preferable to that cast by trees because not only is there an overhead canopy with trees but also searching roots. A tall dividing hedge between gardens can cause similar problems. Permanent crops such as asparagus, rhubarb and horseradish should be located at one side of the garden so that they will not interfere with the regular digging, planting or cultivation of other vegetables.

In a situation where there is a prevailing wind or, worse still, draught, an artificial windbreak such as that provided by plastic mesh should be provided in preference to using fruit bushes. All the same, these can be used to supplement and re-inforce the main windbreak. Fortunately, the vegetable crop which lends itself for use as a windbreak, the broad bean, is the earliest crop sown and the toughest. It is good also to remember that every foot of height gives lateral wind protection of 8 ft. Thus a crop of broad beans, planted at the windy end of a plot, growing up to a height of 2½ ft will give some 20 ft of protection on their lee or sheltered side. It is usually recommended that broad beans be planted in a double row with the beans spaced 6 in apart. My plan for many years has been to plant a bed of broad beans, four plants wide, thus making a double row barrier. In an extremely windy area it is a good idea to stop the growth of the beans on the outer row by pinching out their tops when they are about a foot high. This creates a sloping side so that the broad leaves of the beans will

101

carry the wind upwards and over the top, thus improving the windbreak. It is essential to secure the beans by putting a string on each side and to take two more diagonally through the rows. This protection will make a significant difference to the earliness of the crops grown in its shelter. Another method of sheltering young plants is by drawing up soil with a hoe on each side or, if there is a prevailing wind, on the windward side of the crop.

It has been customary and even traditional to sow seeds of beetroot, carrots, spring onions and similar crops in single drills but a practice which I have developed and used for the last 40 years is to make wide drills. Using beetroot as an example; single plants in a thinned-out row have no protection and if they are spaced as recommended at up to a foot apart a great deal of the land is wasted. My drills for such subjects are a spade width and in fact can be made with a spade. On calculation this method produces roughly three and a half times more in terms of yield than from a single row.

To illustrate this point let's look at onions and beetroot. If onion seed is sown thinly over the broad drill spring onions can be pulled from the narrow bed for as long as they remain suitable for salads or even for flavouring and then the remainder allowed to develop. This produces bulbs ranging from little pickling onions to bulbs the size of an old-fashioned pocket watch on the outside of the broad drill. In the case of beetroot one wide row will produce young beets which can be pulled when about the size of golf balls on a regular basis. This gradually thins out the roots to about 4 or 5 in apart allowing sufficient room to grow on to maturity for storing. A number of firms now sell mixed packets; that is packets containing mixed varieties. This means you can have round, intermediate and long beet in one row which may be selectively thinned without waste as the thinnings can be used.

In addition to trebling the crop from virtually the same area of ground, they provide one another with mutual protection. If a row 30 ft long provides too many vegetables to be conveniently used, then half the row may be sown in mid-April, for example, and the other half in early May. There is no rule to say that a row must be sown completely in one go. The same technique can be used for sowing a part or even a third of a row of lettuce seeds to provide a succession. By the way, the so-called beetroot seeds are, in effect, corky capsules which contain at least two shiny black seeds. This means that half the seeds you sow are thinned out and thrown away in any case.

Pelletted seeds In recent years various attempts have been made to popularise pelletted seeds. These are smaller seeds that have been coated to make them bigger and more easy to handle. In the case of beetroot, pelletted seeds mean that the shiny black seeds have been extracted from their capsule and there will be only one seed in the pellet instead of the two or more found in the corky capsule.

On the whole the British gardener has not taken kindly to pelletted seeds, mainly because of an apparent reduction in germination. This may be due in some degree to the pellet formulation but certainly in all cases which I have investigated, it has been found that dryness of the soil has been the cause. It must be remembered that the pellet must absorb moisture before this can be transmitted to the seed and unless the soil is very damp, germination may be retarded or will not take place.

Making a wide drill This can be easily done by putting down a line and taking out a shallow scraping or, with a shovelling motion, take the top inch of soil and put this to one side of the drill. Ideally the seeds should be covered with specially prepared soil. This involves mixing up a proportion of the excavated soil with equal parts of peat and sand putting this through a ¼-in sieve. Then dust this over the

Sowing seeds in dry weather

Where there is the slightest suspicion that the soil is not sufficiently moist or, because of the current weather, likely to dry out, drills should be soaked before sowing. The most satisfactory way to do this is to use a can without the rose on but with a small plug of wood or cork fitted into the spout. The plug, which should be about 1½ in long, should fit securely. Make a V-shaped cut in one side with a knife or hacksaw so that a trickle of water can escape when the can is tilted.

Take out the drill in the dryish soil slightly deeper than normal and with the trickle of water, wash down the sides so that the bottom of the drill is liquid mud. Sow the seeds on the mud and cover with the dry soil tamping down lightly with the flat of the rake head. The object of this is to moisten the soil where it is needed, not to superficially wet a large area with the rose on the can. Otherwise this will be rapidly evaporated by wind and sun and soil moisture will actually be sucked up from lower down. After sowing seeds in this fashion there is no need, however dry the conditions, to water overhead.

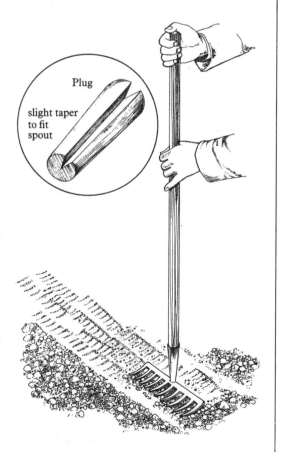

Plug

slight taper to fit spout

surface by hand, ensuring that the seeds are at the correct depth, which is approximately ½ in.

Whether V-shaped drills are taken out with a special tool, a piece of stick or a corner of the hoe, they are invariably made too deep and, unless the operator is very skilled, irregular in depth. A hand covering ensures a more precise depth. I have always been impressed with the results that blind gardeners obtain and have come to the conclusion that much of this is due to their meticulous precision in measuring not only depth, but spacing. It is very little trouble to make a depth gauge for sowing fine seeds, which is about the thickness of an ordinary match box.

Successional sowing and planting In the days before the importation of vegetables and fruit by air all the year round and the introduction of the freezer, professional gardeners were expected to maintain a supply of fruit and vegetables throughout the year from their employer's garden. Even in the largest establishments the only aids were the hot bed and the ice house. The latter being a cave dug into a hillside or a specially constructed building in the woods which was filled with ice laboriously cut by handsaw from the lake and stacked in the ice house in winter. This would last, with luck, to the end of August. Hot beds which were fermenting heaps of manure and leaves covered with frames were used to accelerate growth.

When growing vegetables very often it is a case of feast or famine but these surpluses and poor crops can be evened out by the use of a freezer. To make the best use of the freezer, varieties most suitable for freezing should be carefully selected from the catalogue. To avoid a glut, or if the summer holiday coincides with the maturing of the most desirable crops such as peas or beans, due regard must be given to sowing or planting times. With regard to vegetables most of them mature from 12 to 14 weeks after sowing. Therefore calculation of sowing times should be made backwards from the time that you need the crop. Such calculations, however, cannot be precise because of variable weather conditions and it is advisable to make three sowings at ten-day intervals. Supposing, for example, you want something ready on August 20th. You calculate back 14 weeks which brings you to mid-May so your sowings will be the first week in May, mid-May and then another 8 to 10 days later.

This brings us to the question of varieties of vegetables designated as early, second-early or mid-season and late. This refers to the time of maturity. For example, an early variety of pea may take 90 days to come to maturity whilst a late variety may take 100 to 110 days. This means that you can sow an early variety late because it will mature more quickly than a late variety. So in the case of peas it is possible to use one early variety sown at 12- to 14-day intervals to provide cropping right through to October. By using some form of protection such as cloches at each end of the growing season, another fortnight can be gained.

In the milder parts of the country, subjects like spring greens, lettuces and broad beans can be sown in October along with the overwintering hardy crops such as spinach, seakale beet and lamb's lettuce. These together with the hardy brassicas, such as savoys, winter cabbage, and stored white cabbage mean that greens can be had all the year round.

Intercropping Intercropping means slotting in early-maturing crops between those which take longer. For example, starting at one end of the plot with the hardiest crop of broad beans the next sowing would be of early round-seeded peas leaving a 3-ft space which later on, when the soil has warmed up, could accommodate two rows of beetroot or carrots. Then comes another sowing of beans or peas with a space between for lettuces and any other dwarf crop. This enables more of the ground to be covered by foliage so there is less moisture lost from the soil and the watering can be left to nature.

Vegetables to grow

Although there are nearly 80 kinds of vegetables which can be grown in the British Isles, some more readily in the south than the north, not more than a third of these are grown regularly. There are fashions too; for example, just prior to a recent severe winter perennial broccoli was being widely advertised and sown with the promise that such a broccoli would produce curds for many years. However, after seeing it reduced to mush by the long frosts its popularity is likely to fade.

Probably as soon as some enterprising seedsman discovers a source of the cauli-sprout (it produces sprouts on the stem and little cauliflowers on the top), this member of the cabbage family will make a comeback. A similar sort of thing happened with the colewort or collard which made a temporary come-back during the last war and is now surfacing again under the name minicole which, by the way, is the basis of commercial coleslaw.

Another vegetable which unfortunately will have only a limited use in our gardens because of unpredictable weather is the Chinese cabbage, also called pe-tsae or Chinese leaves. Unfortunately it tends to run to seed as soon as it is ready. It has to be sown directly into the ground and needs continuous moisture, so is probably cheaper to fly from America, as happens with celery, than it is to grow it here.

The vegetables we can and do grow very successfully, can be roughly divided into three groups. Brassicas, of which we eat the leaves or the stalks and flower buds as in sprouts and cauliflowers; root crops, under which I shall include potatoes, the vegetables which produce their edible roots and tubers under ground; and legumes or pod crops which embrace the pea and bean family.

I shall not be giving long lists of any varieties of vegetable for two reasons. The first is that new varieties and F_1 and F_2 hybrids are being developed-at such a rate that some of them would be out of date before the book was even printed. The other is that varieties vary from seed house to seed house and it would be less than fair to select a certain variety or varieties currently listed in a particular catalogue. There are so many varieties available today that the names of seed houses are probably of more importance than varieties which have a limited life. My advice is, however, if you are satisfied with the varieties you are obtaining from a firm then stick to these for your main sowings. However, do be a little bit adventurous and try out in a limited way new varieties which take your fancy.

As I have said before, if your soil will grow a good crop of weeds then it will grow anything else, and this is particularly true of the vegetable garden, because quite a number of the vegetables normally grown belong to the same families as the weeds. In deciding what is to be grown, the likes and dislikes of the family should be considered, even if it upsets those neat cropping plans, often laboriously drawn up. However, there is something to this business of crop rotation, it is not just a fad of a few cranks with nothing better to do but is a proved method of getting the best out of the land and controlling the pests and diseases which specialise in one particular crop. Without sticking to a rigid garden plan, divide the vegetables roughly into the three groups already mentioned, root crops, leaf crops and pod crops. These can be rotated or changed about for the very practical reason that some crops, with their roots at different depths, take more food elements out of the soil than others, but pod crops provide a practical bonus by virtue of the nitrogen fixing nodules on their roots.

These pods crops actually enrich the soil with nitrogen; this helps to make bigger leaves so if legumes are followed by members of the brassica family these will benefit and grow bigger leaves. From this it is fairly obvious that you follow crops that require trenches with pod crops. For example, when trenches are made for leeks and celery you can either change over the trenches from celery to leeks or vice versa, or follow in the same trenches with peas and beans. The reason for using trenches is to provide a concentration of manure and to give plants a deep moist root run.

Perennial Vegetables

There are many such subjects and on the salad and onion side we are very well catered for. My list reads as follows: Welsh onions, Egyptian onions, chives, sorrel, dandelion, watercress, parsley, seakale, mer-

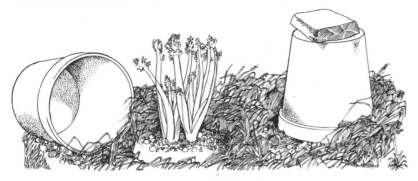

Seakale is a delicious
vegetable not often seen
nowadays. It can easily be
forced out-of-doors.

cury, nine-star broccoli, spinach beet, Jerusalem artichoke, globe artichoke, cardoons, asparagus, rhubarb, horseradish, runner beans and, of course, herbs.

This is a fairly long list and would be capable of supplying a wide variety of vegetables which require the minimum of attention. The yield of most of these is such that pickings could be taken so that vegetables and salads of some variety were available every day. To maintain a supply of young succulent growths, the main requirement initially is a deeply-dug well-manured land given regular mulchings of compost or of rotted manure and an occasional dusting of Growmore fertiliser during showery weather. In the winter some form of protection may be necessary; not that the plants will be killed but any young growth exposed will be slow to develop in the spring and could even be on the tough side.

Whether anyone would want to have a garden composed entirely of perennial subjects is a matter of personal choice, but quite a number could be successfully included. Most of these are readily obtainable either from seed or from plants, but there are one or two items for which you will have to search round. Having lived through the shortage of onions, for example, in two world wars, I retained my old wartime friend the Welsh onion. Welsh onions are like perennial spring onions, similar to but larger than chives, and can be used all the year round for salads and for cooking. All you have to remember is every time you take some away from the parent clump, split a few up and replant them. On a more ambitious scale they can be divided up and grown in rows. The Egyptian onion produces its small bulbs on the tops of the stem, they are like small shallots and very useful for stews and salads. To perpetuate the stock all you need is to press a few of these small bulbs into the ground at any time of the year. They will soon sprout and grow whilst the base or the old bulb continues to send up new growths. These two members of the onion family can be dotted about in almost any odd corner of the garden as they are not too unsightly.

Although I have mentioned dandelions and sorrel, I have not

Egyptian onions

107

mentioned nettles, because no one is proud of having a bed of nettles in the garden, as in most country districts they are there for the taking and a very good vegetable they are too. The cultivated dandelion is worth taking seriously as this can be blanched, it is every bit as good as endive or chicory and a lot less trouble. The two artichokes present no problems as the globe looks very well in the herbaceous border and the Jerusalem artichoke is an excellent alternative to the potato having approximately the same nutritional qualities. Indeed, in the old herbals, it is quoted as being far superior to the potato for diabetics.

As far as asparagus is concerned, no one needs to be afraid of the difficulties of producing this as a vegetable crop because it can be grown in rows across the garden as simply as potatoes. No need for elaborate beds; you can either earth it up to blanch and have white asparagus or you can leave it to its own devices and have a green type.

Mercury, also known as Good King Henry, is an easily-grown leafy vegetable that has been a favourite of mine because of its superb flavour. Spinach beet can be sown in spring and early summer and if thinned out to about 6 in will produce nice plants for the winter. In mild weather it can be used right through the winter, although it may need a little protection with cloches to keep it young and tender. The following season it must be prevented from going to seed by cutting out the flowering stems in just the same way as you would for rhubarb.

Every year there are shortages of one thing or another, due to weather conditions and crop failures so it does pay to have a back-up of hardy perennial subjects which can be relied upon to fill the gaps. Why not make an inventory of what you have in your garden and reserve a special portion for perennial or perpetual subjects? Or, if you have only a small garden, introduce subjects such as the Welsh onion which in addition to using as a salad crop can be used, tops and all, in soups and other cooked dishes. It doesn't take a lot of trouble to keep them all in good order and what is probably best of all, very few of these perennial subjects succumb to the normal pests and diseases of their respective tribes.

Brassicas

The word brassica is a group name, the preserve of the botanists in the days when a gardener lumped the members of this family together under the term 'greens'. Greens perhaps describes the group more accurately as it covers that group of vegetables where the portion consumed is above ground as distinct from roots, where the part below soil level is eaten.

Brassicas all developed from a common wild type, remnants of which are still found round the coasts of the British Isles and many

European countries. Over thousands of years, without the aid of man, it has divided itself neatly into such diverse plants as cauliflowers, sprouts, hearted cabbage and many other variations. The hybridist has just improved on nature's first diversity of form. What seems to have happened, however, is that with the improvement in size, flavour and texture, all the groups appear to have lost hardiness – as shown by the devastation of green crops during severe winters.

Working perhaps from the observed resistance of the wild cabbage of the coastline to severe weather and that the salt spray gave the leaves resistance to frost, gardeners treated their brassicas with salt and recommended the use of a cube of salt per plant in autumn. (The measure was made from a potato with a cubic inch cut out).

What appears to cause the breakdown of the leaves of modern brassicas is alternate freezing and thawing. I have found that by giving individual plants a teaspoonful of salt, the modern equivalent of a cubic inch, a resistance to freezing is developed; just like topping up the radiator with anti-freeze. Not only does it work but it gives an improved flavour, particularly to sprouts, savoys and winter cabbage.

The brassicas do not need to be coddled in any way. They require space so that air can circulate through the leaves; in fact they will grow in a field more happily than in the garden. They are not fussy about soil, provided that it is well drained, moisture retentive, alkaline (limy) rather than acid and enriched with farmyard manure or compost. The ubiquitous peat is not recommended. A slight exception to this is the cauliflower which can be regarded as the queen of the brassicas and, as befits a lady, should be treated more delicately. Cabbages and Brussels sprouts can be dibbled in to even undug ground but the cauliflower is better transplanted from the seed bed, lifted with a trowel and planted with a good ball of soil.

All brassicas may be sown in prepared drills in early spring; the times depending on district. In the more favoured districts they may

Baby cabbages

Spring cabbages can be made to produce a second crop after the heart has been cut. Remove all the outer leaves and slit across the top of the bare stump with a knife making a plus sign. Feed with a dessertspoonful of sulphate of ammonia or nitrate of soda and water this in if the soil is dry. In a few weeks time at least four nice little cabbages can be expected to carry through into late autumn.

be planted the year before in August or September to stand in their rows during the winter months. Sprouts require a longer season of growth than any other member of this family, so they can be started early in gentle heat by sowing seeds thinly in boxes, frames or under cloches.

The worst form of plant, but the ones which are most likely to be bought, are those which are sown thickly in rows in a nursery bed and just yanked out, tied up in bunches and offered for sale. Far better to raise one's own plants as the worst enemy of the brassica tribe, club root, can easily be imported. They are easily raised and the number of seeds in a packet is still generous. So millions more plants than necessary must be raised and wasted every year. By the way, brassica seed will keep approximately four years and, curiously, plants from two-year-old seed seem to come better than first-year seed.

It is far better to sow very thinly in drills 4 in wide than in a V-shaped drill where all the seeds fall to the bottom and come up too thickly, becoming leggy and drawn with a poor root system. When thinning never pull them up but ease them with a hand fork. Although the roots are tough and resilient there is no point in growing good roots just to break them off by rough handling. When planting

Preserving winter greens

Cauliflowers are plentiful in the summer time but as the season advances and frost threatens, the late curds need some protection to prevent them being discoloured by heavy dews, frost and rain. The late cauliflowers or broccoli are to a large extent self protecting with their incurving leaves but often something more is necessary. This can be achieved by bending some of the leaves over the curd but this is not always adequate.

To keep the curds white and clean and well protected against frost, I use an old gardener's trick of inverting the leaves of a plant which has already been harvested for the curd. To do this, cut out the curd removing as few of the outer leaves as possible, then cut off the top complete to the hard stalk. Invert this over the top of the curd of its closest neighbour, just like an umbrella, and it will be found that the leaves fit neatly in between the upright leaves of the growing plant. This inverted cone completely protects the curd underneath from rain, fallen

leaves, soot, frost and also bleaches the curd white. Incidentally, this is a trick well worth remembering if you wish to keep the curds of summer cauliflowers required for exhibition in perfect condition.

any of the brassicas, with the exception of cauliflowers, use a dibber with a blunt end as distinct from a pointed one.

All brassicas, no matter what the soil conditions, are, in my opinion, best planted in a drill about 4 in deep made with the corner of a draw hoe. The reason is that brassicas emit roots from their stems so that if the roots are damaged, either by cabbage root maggot, root gall or even club root, the plants have a chance of survival. Cultivation through the succeeding weeks will gradually fill in the drill, covering up the stems. Towards the end of the season over-wintering crops such as Brussels sprouts, broccoli and savoys can be earthed up another 4 in to sustain and support them during winter gales without the need for staking.

Blown sprouts One of the most annoying things to happen to Brussels sprouts is for them to open as rosettes instead of tight buttons and this, in many cases, is due to spongy soil and wind rock. Always heed the recommendation to firm in at planting and periodically draw up soil round the stem using the heel to firm it.

Remove blown sprouts and any yellowing leaves to improve air circulation. When harvesting gather progressively up the stalk leaving the tops until the very last when they will provide succulent greens in late April.

My weapon against cabbage root fly damage is aluminium foil. Wind a narrow strip around each brassica seedling before planting out

Cabbage rootfly One of their biggest enemies is the cabbage root maggot which is the larvae of a fly which lays it eggs near the stems of the plant. When these eggs hatch the little grubs make their way towards the plant, possibly by smell, and start to feed often devouring the whole of the root. The result is that the plants, and in particular cauliflowers, never grow but turn blue and topple over.

Over the years, however, I have managed to circumvent this villainy by armour plating the stems. My method has been to use strips of metal foil cut from the inside of tea chests but in recent years I have sneaked aluminium foil from the kitchen. This is cut into ½-in wide strips about 6 in long and wound in a spiral around the plant as low down into the root system as possible gradually working upwards overlapping the previous turn as far as the base of the leaves. It is then planted in the normal way so that at least an inch of protective foil is showing above ground. In this way I have never lost a single plant; it beats all the dusts and powder and is well worth the effort.

When planting with a dibber, particularly in dry weather, it pays to draw the plants carefully from the seed bed, easing them up with a fork. Then lay all the young plants in the same direction in a seed tray so that the roots are not unduly disturbed when handled. Have handy a square of cloth or hessian soaked in water to cover the tray. Make a hole with a blunt-ended dibber, or the roots may dangle. Fill in the hole with water as you go along. When the end of the row has been reached go back again to the beginning and push in the sides of each hole with the dibber taking care to keep the foil just above the surface. This may sound a lot of work but often makes the difference between a good crop or no crop at all. The numbers are not great, because no one should plant more than they can reasonably use.

Caterpillars Other pests of the brassicas are the caterpillars of the large and small cabbage white butterfly and it isn't long after the first appearance of these marauders before the leaves are turned into lace curtains. A lot can be done by manually destroying eggs and a co-operative family is most useful. When you see the butterflies flying about look under the leaves in the evening for clusters of little yellow or orange oval eggs and carefully rub these out with finger or thumb. This is far better than spraying the caterpillars.

Spraying with Jeyes fluid at the time that butterflies are active will deter them and I have watched with glee butterflies flying across a neighbour's patch, rise into the air avoiding mine to come down to attack those on the other side. Alternatively, the whole cabbage bed can be covered with plastic fruit netting. Cabbage butterflies will not go through netting.

If weeds between the rows are kept down by spraying with Jeyes fluid or similar specifics at the rate of one part of fluid to 35 parts water, the weeds will be killed and residue in the soil will confuse and destroy predators such as the flea beetle. It will also deter cabbage root fly and other objectionable insects as well as acting as a mild fungicide. Avoid splashing the foliage of your plants or it will kill them too. My secret weapon is a plastic funnel with the narrow end pushed onto the nozzle of a pressure sprayer which enables me to get right up to the stems without damaging or spotting the foliage. Not being a chemist or a scientist but a practical gardener, I have noticed that all strong smelling plants such as celery, chrysanthemums, carrots and onions attract a particular insect. If I can disguise that smell I find that there is less danger of attack.

Club root Finger and toe or club root is a fungus disease which is confined to the cabbage family and thrives in acid soil. Until now there has been no effective control of this disease. But now, with the introduction of thiophanate-methyl used as a pre-planting dip, prevention is possible.

Runner Beans

Runner beans have been with us some three hundred years, but recently their behaviour has left a good deal to be desired with regard to fruit setting. It is probable they still have not become fully accustomed to our weather. Runner beans rely a great deal on insects for pollinating their flowers and, if the summer is wet and windy, insects are not likely to linger on exposed flower trusses. It used to be thought that syringing with water assisted flowers to set but the benefits of this are doubtful. I find hosing the plants with a fairly powerful divided jet to be more effective.

The arrangement for training, I feel, has also some bearing not only on the setting but on the shape and straightness of the pods. Commercial growers must of necessity grow in straight rows to facilitate cultivation and picking but the home gardener is not usually bound by these considerations and can modify methods of cultivation and training to suit his own conditions. Because the runner bean is one of my favourite vegetables, I have experimented and tried out several methods of cultivation and training, both outdoors and under glass.

Training Where a fairly large quantity is required I prefer to plant two rows some 3 ft apart and incline the strings or canes to a central wire making a tent-shaped structure. The individual strings are placed 9 in apart and attached to a low wire as one might grow tomatoes. The alternative to this is to use a specially designed plastic net with a wide mesh. The advantage of the inclined support method, especially in exposed gardens, is that the trusses form on the outside and are exposed to light so when the beans form they hang down inwards. Hanging at an angle keeps them straight, prevents them from chafing and, as they are not exposed to weather, the skins are much more tender and generally more presentable. A variation on this method for the small garden is the tripod with the corners some 18 to 20 in apart. Rather similar is the quadrupod which consists of four canes inclined and tied together at the top.

Another variation is an adaptation of the method I use for sweet peas for the back of the herbaceous border, in fact bi-coloured varieties of runner beans are often used for this purpose too. The device or pillar consists of a central pole, either of wood or metal, about 7 ft high, to which is attached at the top and the bottom a square or circular hoop of wood or metal about 3 ft across depending on the materials available. The lower hoop is secured some 6 in from the ground and the top suspended by two wires across the hoop and stapled to the top of the post. Strings are then stretched 12 in apart between the two hoops or frames and the sweet peas or scarlet runners trained up the strings. They look most attractive when grown in this way and are, in my opinion, far better than beans grown in single rows across exposed gardens.

Growing conditions It has been very gratifying for me to see that the recommendations I have been making for the last 25 years have been proved on experimental stations to give better results than those distances and spacings which have been slavishly followed for many years.

Crops vary in their individual needs. In some cases, where the flowers are required to be fertilised by insects, it is not so much the plants that need protection but the insects themselves, as they cannot be expected to work easily and comfortably in a howling gale or strong draught created by buildings. I feel fairly certain that the improvement in the pod length of runner beans has in some way affected the setting qualities. For instance, if a short-podded variety produced eight beans to the cluster the taller varieties may only produce two or three but the weight gathered is roughly the same. This suggests that the vine can only carry a certain amount.

Weather too seems to affect varieties differently. In some years one variety will do extremely well but in wet windy conditions may fail badly. For consistent cropping I find that the shorter-podded varieties seem to set better and such old varieties as Princeps can always be grown as a standby. The varieties Crusader and Kelvedon Marvel are consistently good too. With Crusader grown for exhibition, Kelvedon Marvel a reliable cropper and the old Painted Lady as a decorative variety, the grower can be reasonably assured of a crop, no matter what the weather.

Manure of some sort is, I think, a must for producing good runner beans. When planning the vegetable garden I try to arrange the rotation so these trenches or any other heavily-manured ground can be used the following year for runner beans. All that is then required is to add bonemeal or superphosphate to the site.

Incidentally, if the bean rows are spaced about 3½ ft apart a superb row of parsley can be grown underneath, benefiting from the shade and possibly from the nitrogen-storing nodules. Seven feet is a good height at which to stop the beans. This stopping helps to encourage laterals to develop and anything higher than this is awkward to gather, although I have noticed lately that very few beans are produced above 5 ft. The average summer is seldom dry enough to worry beans in well-manured soil but they do appreciate phosphates and an occasional watering with liquid fertiliser. Loose soil or too much nitrogen induces too much foliage to the detriment of the formation of flower trusses.

Runner beans are true perennials. However, although I persevered for many years in saving the fleshy rootstocks the resultant crops were not worthwhile. From a single seed one gets a single vine but from overwintered rootstocks, five, six or even more shoots form and these have to be reduced to not more than two to get any worthwhile growths out of them. In warm sunny districts with a fair amount of irrigation these extra growths may produce worthwhile crops, but I have never been able to manage any to my satisfaction.

Blackfly is about the worst pest I have met and a constant watch must be kept during the early part of the year, especially if broad beans are grown in the vicinity. I try to make sure that the beans are free from pests before they start to bloom as later spraying may harm pollinating insects. To combat this pest I like to use either derris or pyrethrum as I always remember that I have got to eat the beans eventually.

Garden Peas

Garden peas are, without doubt, the most tasty and succulent of all the vegetables grown in our gardens, but in this day and age there must be millions of people whose only knowledge of the pea is the frozen one. I don't wish to disparage the frozen or even the tinned pea, for without them there would be millions of people who would never taste the delights of anything approaching a fresh variety.

Unfortunately, except in country districts where peas are grown, picked and placed on the market stall within a matter of hours, even those offered for sale in the greengrocer's shop bear little or no resemblance to a really succulent well-filled pod fresh from the garden. This is a great pity because a generation is growing up that despises the flat unfilled pods with rotting ends and the little wooden balls that make up what are optimistically offered as fresh garden peas. No wonder that most folks, especially those eating out, prefer the frozen kind which are at least uniform and of good flavour.

Every hour that a vegetable is out of the ground or off the vine it loses flavour and certainly the commercial pea grower appreciates this. I have watched with interest the pea-gathering machines working all night and the villagers kept awake by tractors rumbling through with lights on heading for the processing factory to get the peas frozen within an hour or so of harvesting. If peas are grown in the garden only for the pleasure of eating them fresh from the vine they would be a worthwhile crop.

Quick-maturing varieties have been developed for freezing and it is advisable to check the catalogue or packet to see if a particular variety is specifically recommended for freezing. Unless you have had experience of particular varieties it may be that one which cooks well when freshly gathered loses its subtle flavour after being frozen for a month or two. Talking of flavour, even fresh peas can lose this by being overcooked in too much water.

I should state here a particular interest in cooking vegetables which stems from my early days in private service. I got so tired of taking splendid vegetables to the kitchen and finding afterwards their flavour had been impaired by poor cooking. I find many people cook vegetables badly, often leaving them on the stove whilst they do chores elsewhere. As far as peas are concerned they need the minimum amount of water and young tender peas, freshly gathered, need no water at all. The best way that I know is to put a few lettuce leaves in the bottom of the dry pan, place the peas on top with a knob of butter and a half teaspoonful of sugar. Then, with the lid tightly fitted, bring gently to the boil and cook for the minimum time.

Peas are either wrinkled or round-seeded. The round-seeded are the hardiest and in some districts can be overwintered after an autumn sowing. Personally, I think the round-seeded varieties, in spite of their earliness, are so tasteless that it is worth waiting a few days longer and sowing the better-flavoured wrinkled types.

I prefer to make trenches for peas, unless the soil is deep. As well as benefiting the pea crop this is a way of breaking up a good depth of soil, so that ultimately the whole vegetable plot has been cultivated and organic matter worked in to the depth of two spade's blades. Furthermore, as one digs along to make a trench some of the lower soil (not the top soil) can be laid on the surface between the rows where it will improve enormously by exposure to sun, wind and rain.

Pea guards

Attacks by birds can severely damage your peas. To counteract this problem guards made from wire netting, plastic mesh or cotton may be used, as can cloches which, of course, also protect the crop from the weather.

A simple device which I have used for 50 years is to make a number of squares of wood nailed onto pointed stakes so that they can be pushed into the ground about 12 or 15 in and 1-in round nails hammered round the outside of the wood squares about an inch apart. Three of these squares will suffice for a 30 ft row, place one at each end and one in the middle. Strong black thread is then stretched and looped round the nail heads and may be left on long after the need for bird protection has passed allowing dwarf peas in particular to grow though. They need no other support for even if the tops do fall, the pods will not trail on the ground.

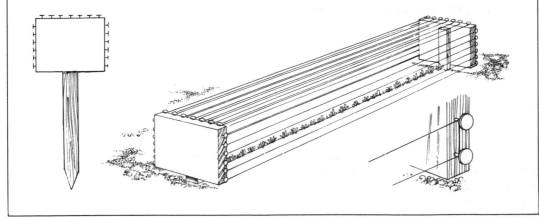

This inevitably leaves the surface of the trench some 2 in lower than the level of the rest of the plot. This is beneficial to young seedlings which will be sheltered from cold, cutting winds.

Fungal infection can be a problem. To guard against this, puff a fungicidal powder into the packet and shake the seeds around well to coat them before sowing. Mice can often be troublesome and very destructive once they get the taste for peas. There are several proprietary powders which can be added to the fungicidal dust and shaken up in the seed packet. Another simple precaution is to water newly-sown peas and beans with a solution of Jeyes fluid. Most animals and insects find this distasteful and it disguises the natural smell of their food supply. Dry soot dusted lightly over the surface of the newly-sown rows will deter mice. This is a particularly effective treatment under cloches where it remains dry.

Rows of single seeds may be sown where exhibition plants are required but for ordinary purposes a trench wide enough to take four single rows about 1½ to 2 in apart each way will produce a high-yielding row. Half a pint of seed will be enough to sow a 15 to 20 ft row at this spacing.

By the way, when sowing rows of peas or beans always sow a dozen or so extra near one end so that if there are any failures or gaps in the rows these extra seedlings can be carefully transplanted to fill in the gaps. Furthermore, if, due to inclement weather, bad soil conditions or any other reason you are unable to sow peas and beans as early as you would wish, damp a 5-in pot heaped full of peat, mix the seeds into this and put them somewhere under cover out of the way of mice. Then sow the mixture after the seeds have germinated to the point where the root has started to emerge from the seed. The distance between the rows should be as near as possible to the stated height of the variety grown. Do not worry if this is 4 or 5 ft in the case of tall varieties because the space between can be utilised for other crops which will enjoy the shade and protection of the taller peas.

Sugar pea

Sugar pea or *Pisum japonicum* is not nearly as well known as it should be as it will provide a supply of delicious vegetables over a very long period. Unlike the garden pea it keeps on producing its edible pods and as the whole pods are eaten there is no question of a glut occurring followed by a gap in supplies. The culture is simple for it will grow in practically any soil and is not subject to so many diseases and pests as the ordinary garden pea.

The seeds can be sown in March or April in drills 6 in wide and about 2 in deep. The plants spread laterally in the early stages but need little in the way of staking, only requiring a few twigs or some string supports along each side. The flowers are a beautiful deep-red colour and look most attractive.

The sugar pea is cooked in its entirety in much the same way as a French bean. It can either be sliced or, if gathered very young, cooked whole. If the pods are allowed to grow too big they become rather stringy.

Swedes and Turnips

As a 'swede basher' (a native of Norfolk) I have always been interested in the cultivation and, of course, the eating of swedes. As a vegetable they are fast regaining the popularity which they enjoyed some 20 or 30 years ago and make a nice change in the wintertime, either as a separate vegetable or mixed with mashed carrots and parsnips. From a nutritional point of view the most valuable parts are the blanched leaves and young shoots.

In Norfolk, where they are grown to perfection, it used to be the practice to pull up three rows, trim off the tops and tails and throw them together where they were ploughed in to remain during the winter and from where they were carted; as swedes, unlike mangolds, do not lend themselves very well to clamping. When they were ploughed out in the spring, it was the custom that children should be allowed to take baskets and gather the blanched growths. Some were boiled as a vegetable and others allowed to cool and pickled in vinegar. Although I have tried to trace how this custom arose, I have been unable to find the origin; it seems to have arisen out of necessity as a treatment for scurvy after a winter without fruit or green vegetables. When growing large quantities I always pile a few hundredweight of swedes under straw in an outhouse, so as to get one or two boilings of blanched tops.

I mentioned that they are grown to perfection in Norfolk, a county of broad acres and wide open spaces which are necessary for the production of good swedes. Field varieties of swedes grown in a sheltered or enclosed garden never reach the same size or quality of those grown in an open field and this necessitated the introduction of a special garden swede suitable for garden conditions. This is, of course, partly due to the fact that the field swede produces an enormous swollen root weighing 30 lb or more which is uneconomic in the kitchen and unsuitable for the greengrocer to handle. Though when it comes to actual quality, I would rather have field swede than a small garden swede any day.

Swedes belong to the same family as the cabbage and are subject to the same diseases, including the dreaded finger and toe or club root, although the varieties Wilhelmesburger and Bangholm are resistant.

Swedes, like wallflowers, need to be sown in early May and need a good rich soil, preferably one manured for a crop the previous season, plus the addition of superphosphate at the rate of 2 oz per sq yd. I found, by accident, that the addition of sulphate of potash, although reducing the actual size of the root, gives it a firm texture and reduces the risk of some of the other diseases to which swedes are liable.

Swedes, white turnips and the yellow-fleshed garden varieties, are traditionally drilled in and thinned out. However, I have proved to my own satisfaction that they give far better results if a small patch can be reserved for them, the seed broadcast and the seedlings then thinned out to about 8 in apart. Why this should be so I have no idea, but it certainly produces results. When singling, care should be taken not to damage the small seedlings as this early damage may set up not only scars but open wounds into which diseases penetrate. These can cause a soft rot which reduces the inside of the swede to a pulpy mass.

In the field, swedes are singled with great dexterity and skill with a 10-in drag hoe going through the rows cutting out the unwanted ones. The remaining small clumps are later singled to one at approximately 10-in stations.

Rotten material left on the garden can harbour disease which in turn infects the soil. This can then be carried on the boots or on barrow wheels all over the plot infecting other members of the brassica family including wallflowers. Cruciferous weeds are also attacked and these provide host plants not only for diseases but pests as well.

These remarks would appear to suggest that swedes are difficult to grow and are attacked by many diseases and pests. This is not really so but as the brassica family is large, and suffers from so many pests and diseases, it is best to pay attention to hygiene and to remove promptly infected roots.

Varieties In country and farming districts many varieties are available which are not readily available to the town dweller who should perhaps settle for a garden swede such as Purple Top Improved, which is a refined type of field swede. In the larger gardens, a Purple Top variety such as Johnson's Favourite is a very fine swede both in shape, hardiness, quality and crop. On club-root-infected land plant Bangholm for purple tops or Wilhelmesburger for almost pure green ones. Both are excellent varieties and resistant to the disease. From the point of view of flavour there is little to choose between the green and the purple but I prefer the latter for early use and the green for long keeping. In the smaller gardens it would probably be better to grow the turnip Golden Ball for summer and autumn use and a few purple tops for winter storage. Turnips, on the other hand, can be sown successively as they mature in six to eight weeks. A little item of interest; turnip seed has an average life of from five to seven years and only half an ounce is required to sow approximately 30 sq yd.

Potatoes

Garden lore is permeated with myths and one of the most misleading is that growing potatoes will break up the soil. Potatoes do nothing of the sort; it is the person who plants and grows them that does this job. Although potatoes will grow in almost any soil, except that which is continuously waterlogged, and produce a crop of sorts, they require a rich well-broken up soil more than any other vegetable. True, after growing potatoes the soil is pretty well broken up. First of all by the digging, then the earthing up and subsequently by lifting the crop; no other crop receives these three manipulating operations. The condition of the soil following a crop of potatoes is better because, in addition to this manipulation, the sprawling and dense foliage tends to smother out annual weed seedlings. All the same, unless the hoe is used freely or the weeds between the rows are sprayed with weedkiller they could easily take over and smother out the potatoes.

Probably the most important preparation for potatoes is the breaking up of the soil as finely as possible. Lumpy soil not only impedes the development of the tubers but actually distorts them – as an examination of imported potatoes which have been grown on dryish soil will reveal. Do not use ashes or other gritty materials to improve heavy land for potatoes as these scratch the skins of the young tubers and can actually cause a rough scabbiness which should not be confused with a disease called scab. Rotted or composted organic material is always good for potato land but it should be kept below the planted tubers.

A word of warning about the indiscrimate use of chemical fertilisers on potatoes, this can not only damage planted tubers, but can also have the most undesirable effect on the cooking, eating and keeping qualities of the harvested tubers. Lime should never be applied to soil before planting potatoes. Even small quantities of lime coming into contact with the young tubers will damage the delicate skins. With regard to the fertiliser, it is better to use only that which is formulated specially for potatoes and even this should not come into contact with the sprouted sets.

Seed potatoes The word 'seed' as applied to potatoes does not mean the true seed but refers to the selected tubers which are planted and could be more correctly described as parent potatoes. The true seed is contained in the so-called potato apples which are the result of the flowers being fertilised. Incidentally, not all varieties produce potato apples, with many varieties the flowers simply fall off without setting seed. The potato apples turn purple when ripe and it is from these seeds that new varieties are raised. These potato apples are not edible but neither are they as poisonous as some people believe. However children should be prevented from eating them as they contain solanine which could cause tummy upsets.

Potato varieties are divided into three groups: early, mid-season or second-early, and lates. This applies to the length of time which it takes them to come to maturity. In districts which are suitable and because they give a heavier yield, late varieties can be grown as 'earlies', but because they are immature they are often tasteless, as so often happens with imported potatoes. For example, a popular variety such as King Edward is imported immature and because the tubers have not developed sufficiently they lack the true Edward flavour. The true early potatoes develop their flavour before they are fully mature, as in the case of the renowned Jersey Royals.

Buying seed potatoes Because of the high cost of carriage it is unwise to buy by mail order except for special varieties, particularly as nearly every large store has its own horticultural department where tubers can be visually assessed. When choosing potatoes for seed buy those with shallow eyes (the eyes are the indentations usually found at one end of the tuber). This is important because deep-set eyes make potatoes difficult to peel and clean for cooking, especially when using a machine. The eyes are particularly important, it is from these that the shoots emerge and from the bases of the shoots the roots develop.

The tubers, too, should be sound, free from damage, sunken patches and discoloration. Don't attempt to buy 'ware' (eating) potatoes for seed, as these may have been sprayed with a growth inhibitor. This is very often done to prevent the tubers sprouting in store and to enable the farmer or stock holder to hold on to his stock until the last so that he can get the best price.

Seed potatoes are certified by the Ministry of Agriculture and should be offered for sale with an indication of their certification. This means that they are clean and free from certain prescribed diseases and have passed through a certain sized riddle or screen. It is advisable to buy fresh certified seed every year and not to replant tubers saved from your previous year's crop.

Seed potatoes are grown in Scotland and Ireland and to a lesser degree in the Isle of Man and the Isle of Arran. The reason for this is that in these areas the climate is conducive to quick growth and experiences almost continuous air movement which does not allow aphids, which are carriers of disease, to spread. If you are tempted to save your own seed to maintain the strain or for any other reason, then always select the seed potato when you lift the root and never from the store or clamp. This is because certain diseases reduce the size of the tubers to that traditional egg size. So you may think you have selected a fine sample but actually only picked out tubers carrying a disease.

Potatoes should never be exposed to frost as this breaks the starches down into sugar. When eaten they will taste sweet and quickly turn

Do not earth up potatoes to a sharp point but leave a depression around the stems to allow water to seep down to the roots

black when cooked. Frozen seed is quite useless and will rot in the ground without producing shoots.

It is normal practice, and has been now for many years, to chit seed potatoes. This involves standing them in shallow trays with the rose end upwards; the rose end carries the largest number of eyes. They should then be exposed to the light and a little warmth and the ideal position would be a shelf in a slightly-heated greenhouse. The tubers will green and thus be more resistant to disease. This chitting, which is roughly equivalent to pre-germinating seeds, encourages the shoots to develop. These can then be thinned out by removing the weakly shoots and reducing the rest to about three at one end.

Despite the fact that commercially tubers are passed through a riddle, they can come through endways on so occasionally you will have a large long tuber which may lend itself to cutting. In times of scarcity due to wartime or weather conditions, any piece the size of a small hen's egg carrying one or more strong shoots can be planted. A potato can be cut with a clean knife and the pieces exposed to sun and air with the cut surface facing upwards. This cut surface soon becomes covered with a corky layer and there is really no need to dust these surfaces with either lime or sulphur as often advised. If, however, they are suspect then they may be dipped or sprayed over with a commercial fungicide such as you would use for spraying roses for mildew.

Potato Planting Chart

	Early Varieties	Second Earlies	Main Crop
Distance between plants	9 in	12–15 in	16–20 in
Distance between rows	18 in	24 in	30 in
Quantity of seed per 30 ft row	4 lb	4 lb	4 lb
Planting dates*	early April	late April	April/May
Average yield per 30 ft row	30–50 lb	30–50 lb	30–50 lb

*this will vary from one end of the country to the other

The aim should be to produce stubby purplish-coloured shoots about 1½ to 2 in long. Sometimes, due to poor light conditions and excessive heat, the shoots may be much longer than this. If this should happen there is no need to rub them off but when planting lay the tuber on its side. This of course rules out planting with a dibber.

Methods of planting These are many and varied. If the soil has not been previously dug then the tubers can be planted as the digging proceeds but this is only really feasible on a friable medium to light soil. On heavy soils every spadeful turned over will have to be well broken up with a fork and this means the whole clod of soil and not just the top surface.

Any organic matter added at this stage should be at least half decayed and put at the bottom of the trench and any fertiliser used sprinkled on top of this and then covered with about 3 or 4 in of soil. The object when planting is to see that the sprouts, either upright or horizontal, are 3 in below the finished soil level.

Culture Potatoes are very susceptible to the slightest touch of frost and a late frost can ruin the whole crop. So when the tops appear, cultivate between the rows with a hoe or cultivator to destroy seedling weeds. This hoeing will also loosen the surface so that the soil can be drawn completely over the potato foliage to protect it. This growth will not appear evenly in the rows, some tubers being more precocious than others, and for a time the area may look as if moles have been busy making hills. But it is important that a watchful eye should be kept on this early foliage and it should be covered as it appears, until all fear of frost is past. Incidentally, a draw or drag hoe is the best tool for this job.

When the plants are about 6 in high give a dressing of potato fertiliser or a compound fertiliser containing potash at about 2 oz per yd of drill. Hoe this in with a Dutch hoe and two or three days later drag this soil with a draw hoe from the space between the rows up to the plants on each side. The object of earthing up or ridging is partly to support the hollow stems which are easily damaged by wind and partly to cover the bases of the stems on which the tubers are formed. This prevents the tubers from greening. Other methods are to cover the space between the rows right up to the plants with straw or, alternatively, plant under black polythene. With main crop varieties a second earthing to increase the height of the ridge may be necessary. The ridge should not be drawn to a point but left with a 'V' so that rain can percolate down and not run off a steep-sided ridge.

Harvesting There is no infallible way of seeing when the new potatoes are ready for digging. The early varieties, which mature more quickly, will be ready first. The fact that the plants may or may not be flowering is no indication either as this varies from one variety to another. The simplest and most elementary method of finding out when the tubers are ready is to move away carefully some of the soil at the ridge with your hand and if you find two tubers which you consider big enough to eat then you can begin to lift.

Only practice will determine how close you should place the fork to avoid stabbing the tubers, but probably the best way is to put it in between the plants and then throw the soil and tubers forward.

Make sure all the tubers are lifted up as any left behind, however small, not only encourage wireworms but can carry over disease and

WRONG

The fork has been thrust in too close and at too sharp an angle so the danger of spearing a tuber is great

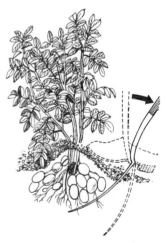

RIGHT

The original angle of entry (dotted outline) is well away from the tubers. The fork is then eased forward to lift the crop

provide food for keel slugs. They will also pop up and grow in all sorts of odd places the following season. Normally first earlies are ready for use in June, second-earlies in August and the main crop during September to October.

Lift when the weather is dry and leave the tubers on the surface for an hour or two before collection for storage. The object of this is to allow the tender skins to harden and so not scuff when handled. Never lift more potatoes than can be collected in any one day.

Method of storing Potatoes may be stored in boxes or sacks, in a dark well-ventilated shed which is free from frost. Do not use plastic sacks unless they are provided with holes to allow air movement otherwise the tubers will sweat. Large quantities may be stored in a clamp.

Site your clamp on an elevated sheltered spot which will not be flooded. Mark a circle on the soil and cover this with a 2-in layer of clean straw and stack the tubers in a conical heap, keeping varieties separate. Cover this pile with a layer of straw 6 to 9 in thick. Then, starting about 12 in out from the base of the circle, dig a trench turning the top loose soil over the straw-covered potatoes. When the mound is covered, finish off by patting down the soil firmly with the back of the spade. At the top of the clamp leave a few wisps of straw poking out to form a sort of chimney so any gasses generated can escape.

Growing under black polythene

Much has been made of this method of growing potatoes, particularly by the manufacturers of black polythene. It is feasible only if a comparatively small quantity is to be grown as it probably involves more work than the methods previously described.

When growing potatoes under black polythene make a cross-shaped slit over each of the sprouting tubers to allow them to grow up into the light. The polythene sheeting should be gently tucked in with the edge of the spade to a depth of about 4 in

In essence the soil is manured, cultivated and fertilised as for any other crop and the tubers are merely pressed into the prepared soil at intervals with the sprouts uppermost. The strip of polythene, usually about 2 ft wide, is then unrolled the whole length of the row and the edges pressed in to a depth of about 4 in with a spade. Alternatively, a shallow drill with a straight side can be made, the edge of the polythene is then tucked into this and the drill filled in. This is to prevent the polythene blowing away. After the sheet is in position, make two slits over the planted tubers with a knife. This is to allow the stems and foliage to grow through into the light.

One advantage of this method is that all weeds which germinate under the polythene die from lack of light. The big disadvantage is that the polythene affords absolutely no protection against frost. This can only be achieved by covering the young growths with straw or peat – a time-consuming job.

Pests and diseases

The main physical damage caused to potatoes under ground is by slugs, particularly the black keel slug. I find the best way to tackle this is to anticipate their attack. One way is to scatter a few slug pellets along the trench as the tubers are being planted or in the hole if a dibber is used. By the way, if a dibber is used then it should be blunt ended and not pointed. Dibber planting is only feasible on light soils as the dibber compresses the base of the hole. There are various commercial preparations including carbaryl which can be used in the soil but probably the most effective is to mix 1 lb powdered copper sulphate with 7 lbs of hydrated lime and work this thoroughly into the soil at least three weeks before planting. Copper by itself is a plant poison but is neutralised by the action of the lime; even so it should not be used on soil where crops are growing. One of the most effective methods of escaping damage in slug-infested soil is to dig up all varieties of potato, whether early, mid-season or late, before the end of September. The reason being that if left, young slugs can gorge themselves on these before descending to lower depths to escape the rigours of winter.

Millipedes can be a pest on some soils. Where these have been turned up while digging treat the ground with a proprietary soil insecticidal powder. This also applies to wireworms which are more prevalent where pasture has been dug up to make a garden. Above ground, aphids or greenflies may be troublesome and at first sight these should be treated by spraying the foliage with a systemic insecticide as greenfly are vectors of disease. Nearer the soil cut-worms, the larvae of a moth, may tunnel into the hollow stems of the plant both upwards and downwards causing the stems to collapse and wither. As they are hidden and protected inside the answer is to cut off carefully the haulms and burn or bury them deeply.

On the whole, diseases of potatoes are much more serious than pests. The first line of defence is never to plant a discoloured tuber which shows evidence of storage rot or one with depressed areas indicating some other disease. Here again I stress what has been said about the purchase of certified seed to ensure a clean start. My own philosophy, as an old boy scout, regarding disease in the garden is the tested motto 'Be Prepared'. It is always better to be safe than sorry and to give the crop a precautionary spray. July is the month for fungal diseases due to its high humidity, so spray with a liquid copper fungicide or dust with Bordeaux powder.

There are two scab infections which attack potato tubers, common or brown scab and corky or powdery scab. There is little one can do about corky scab but the common scab merely disfigures tubers rendering them unfit for exhibition. They have to be peeled a bit more deeply before cooking and usually do not keep as well. The cause is a micro-organism called actinomyces. Heavy liming, naturally alkaline soil, dry conditions and lack of organic matter in the soil favour development of this disfiguring infection. In practice the burying of greenstuff at planting time (such as old sprout leaves which are usually ready for clearing at this time), the addition of some peat, and dusting the trench with flowers of sulphur at the rate of ½ oz to the yard of row can help. Planting time also coincides with cutting grass so lawn mowings should be used liberally but not if the lawn has been treated with a hormone weedkiller.

For the rest of the problems such as eelworm or leaf curl which show their signs and symptoms after the crop has started growing, it is too late to do anything about them and the best advice is to clear the crop as early as possible. The young tubers, if large enough, are edible but should never be saved for seed. Potatoes should not be grown in that infected area for as long as is practicable.

New potatoes at Christmas

I have heard of all sorts of methods of producing new potatoes at Christmas but in most cases they are simply potatoes dug at the normal time which have been sealed up in biscuit tins or other containers and then buried in the soil. This is my method. After I have planted out all the seed potatoes I need, I string unsprouted sets on a fairly stiff wire. One end is bent to prevent the potatoes sliding off and they are simply skewered on a 2 ft length with the rose ends to the side. As each medium to large tuber will produce from 5 to 8 oz of new potatoes, you merely calculate how many old tubers you require to give you the quantity of new potatoes that are needed. A hook is bent on the other end and the string of potatoes hung on a nail on the outside of the potting shed wall.

The strings are left hanging until there is danger of frost in the autumn, which is roughly about the end of September. They are exposed to all weathers and they will make strong sturdy purple shoots. The only attention they require is to keep them free from greenfly which can be done by spraying with an insecticide. Normally when I spray roses with a mixture of insecticide and fungicide I merely spray the potatoes too as a matter of routine. Any tubers which go rotten or show signs of decay should be removed straightaway.

All that is required when you take the tubers off the wires is to lay them in boxes on a bed of dry peat with the tubers about 2 in apart. For many years I have had in my possession long wooden banana boxes but any receptacle about 5 or 6 in deep will do. Cover completely to a depth of about 2 in with more dry peat and store in the garage or shed, and simply leave them until you want them. They need no watering. What actually happens is that the small tubers are produced on the old mother tubers and the largest new potatoes will attain the size of a golf ball with several smaller ones. You can, of course, remove the large ones and put the others back to develop which they will continue to do until they have drained the old tuber quite dry of food.

Thread seed potatoes onto a length of stiff wire and hang outside to sprout until about the end of September

Most people will have seen this actually happen at the bottom of sacks or boxes which have been left and it is merely a controlled method of developing what potatoes do naturally. The sprouts will not develop very much, seldom more than 1½ in. They will be very thick and fleshy and the new potatoes will form just where the sprouts join the old tuber, extracting moisture and plant food from these swollen shoots as well. Over the last 40 years, I have found this a much more satisfactory method than cluttering the greenhouse up with pots of potatoes. They really do taste like new potatoes and only need to be cleaned with a soft brush.

With regard to variety, I find very little difference whether you use early, mid-season or late but a heavy cropping variety will, of course, give better results than, say, Golden Wonder which is not a very heavy cropper. Generally, white potatoes are more productive than coloured ones, although Arran Victory does very well.

Carrots and Parsnips

All crops which grow fully or partially underground appreciate soils which are free from lumps and do not compress the expanding underground portion which we eat and which, for the plant, is a store of food to produce seeds the following year. Where this soil does not occur naturally then it must be well worked and if necessary gritty material added and as much organic matter incorporated as possible. By the same token, however, this organic material must be well decayed for, if it is not, the existence of lumps will cause the roots to fork.

Few people are aware of the multitude of fine fibrous roots which are attached to the carrot which we blithely pull or dig up. In doing so we strip off fine delicate roots which can extend 9 in or more on each side of this central core. In the case of the carrot and the parsnip the point of attachment of these roots can be seen in the wrinkles.

For carrots which can be pulled and eaten in an immature state, the broad drill method as previously described is probably the best. Parsnips are probably best in a single drill, again in very deep well-worked soil. The best advice is to sow thinly and not to thin out. Parsnips can be sown in early March if large roots are required but a month or six weeks later is usual for stump-rooted varieties which are probably better for the kitchen.

The harvesting of carrots should be done when the tops die down and they can be clamped in the same way as recommended for potatoes, whilst parsnips are best left in the ground until required for use as the frost sweetens them. For convenience a number can be dug up and buried close to the kitchen door so that when the soil is frozen solid they can be unearthed.

Pests and diseases Both are subject to the same pests, notably the carrot fly which can attack at all stages and ages and, in a favourable season, can produce as many as five broods. Carrots range from little round ones through short and stubby kinds to those long pointed roots. On soils which are not so deep the round and the stubby short-horn varieties are the best. They also have the merit of being early and can be sown in succession. Where carrot fly is very troublesome they tend to escape attack if sown after the first week in July.

An interesting thing about the carrot fly is that for countless years they have been used to attacking the root at ground level. If the seeds are sown in an elevated position, either in a specially constructed box-like arrangement or even as individuals for exhibition in tubes or drainpipes, the roots will escape attention. Various soil fumigants are available to counteract this pest but now the swing is back to crude naphtha. In fact almost any strong smelling substances such as Jeyes fluid, whizzed naphthalene and Stockholm tar will deter the female from laying her eggs alongside the seedlings which are the intended meal for the young grubs.

Spraying with TVO or fuel oil will not only deter the carrot fly but keep down the weeds. The tops of the carrots will turn almost black but it does not harm them in the same way that it harms other vegetation and they will soon grow out of it.

Carrot fly will attack the parsnip, and although the grubs do not penetrate so deeply they will score the surface of the root and allow the entry of rust fungus which is so disfiguring and damaging. There are one or two varieties, such as Avonresister, which are less susceptible to rust but one of the best methods of warding off an attack is to see that the shoulders of the parsnips, which tend to protrude from the soil, are covered either with sand or fine peat which can be impregnated with substances such as carbaryl or Jeyes fluid. The latter acts both as a mild fungicide and pest repellent.

Both parsnips and carrots are very desirable exhibits at the local shows and all sorts of devices are used for growing the biggest and the longest. The method of so-called spieling, that is sticking a crow-bar into the ground as far as you can, waggling it to and fro in the shape of a parsnip and then filling in with specially prepared soil, has little to commend it as the pressure exerted by the crow-bar tends to harden the sides of the hole. Far better to use a drain pipe or a large plastic tube.

Shallots

There are at least half a dozen sources of the onion flavour and I have selected the shallot because it is the least trouble to grow and is very productive. It suffers from the fewest pests and diseases, stores well, can be used green to pep up salads and can also be pickled. It will grow almost anywhere on any soil and is perhaps the least wasteful of any of the onion family.

Shallots, or more correctly 'eschalots', are one of the earliest crops to be planted and, indeed, it has long been a custom to plant on the shortest day and harvest on the longest day. This is not always possible due to weather conditions, but even in difficult districts, or where they are required for exhibition, they may be started early in 3-in peat pots with no more protection than that offered by a cold frame. Although they are natives of Palestine, no heat is required as they are perfectly hardy and remain unharmed even if frozen solid.

When weather conditions are suitable and the tops have been exposed and are not too tender, they may be planted out with the pot sunk below ground level. John Innes No. 1 potting compost or something similar is perfectly satisfactory for planting and is best sifted through a ½-in riddle, no roughage in the bottom of the pot being required.

Shallots are, as a rule, more popular in country districts than in urban areas. They are always represented on the show bench and are often the biggest entry. In some northern districts special prizes are offered.

Shallots of late years have been divided into two classes: large and small. Some schedules stipulate a diameter of 1 in for the small ones with no limit for the larger Russian types. The popularity of the green or white versus the red varies from district to district. Some schedules legislate against seedlings, but the only objection to seedlings is that they have to be very carefully selected each season because of their tendency to run to flower. However, the real enthusiast will continue to grow from seed and select and re-select until he has produced a worthwhile strain.

Commercially there is not a great deal of choice, but if you shop around you may come across a variety Hative de Niort. This variety gives few offsets to a clove but they are perfectly shaped without the annoying flat side of our English varieties. The Jersey shallot is as large as a small onion with grey-green foliage and a thin red skin but is not such a good keeper. For producing the large varieties rich fertile soil is desirable and extra feeding can be given during the growing season, but for the small pickling onions a dryer, poorer and harder soil produces better and more bulbs of the pickling type with a much stronger flavour. Perhaps their popularity in the country districts stemmed from the fact that no outdoor worker went to work without a few shallots in his 'frail' basket to eat with his bread and cheese.

Planting Like onions, shallots require a firm soil and the bed should be trodden several times after breaking it down and raking it. This often leads to trouble later on if bulbs have been pushed into the soil. If they are pushed with too much force the top part of the bulb may be bruised and damaged. There is a risk, too, of damaging the basal plate on a stone. These two things can have the effect of the bulb producing a large number of very small offsets in the resultant cloves. In extreme cases the bulb may rot after first trying to sprout. Perhaps the most serious effect is that, as the roots form, they push against the hard pan caused by pressing in the bulb and rise out of the soil. There they are easily tipped over by birds, especially sparrows looking for new fresh green for their young. Worms, too, can tip over bulbs, so it pays to remove loose dead scales.

Irreparable harm can be done by pressing back sprouted bulbs as this will break off succulent roots. As the bulbs emit roots from a basal plate and are monocotyledons, these damaged roots cannot produce secondary growths and new roots must be formed from the basal plate itself. The damaged roots can rot and this can spread back up into the plate and inhibit the production of new roots. The answer to this is always to plant with a trowel or pointed stick. Shallots should be planted so that the shoulders are just covered. This is impossible to do on too firm a soil with the result that they are often planted too shallowly to start with.

The distance between rows and bulbs will depend on whether they are being grown for exhibition or for culinary use. Make no mistake about it, they are excellent for use in the kitchen, being stronger in flavour and much more handy for the housewife. Nine inches between bulbs is not too much for exhibition with 12 to 15 in between the rows. However, 6 in between bulbs and 12 in between rows is sufficient for the smaller varieties.

Growing Shallots are singularly free from pests and diseases but in their early stages the tops may be attacked by greenfly. In some districts the keel slug and also millipedes may attack the base of the bulbs. Because they are planted so early there is a great risk that the tops may be affected by cold, and, particularly, drying east winds. This shows itself in the whitening of the top inch or so of the leaves.

All onion types are short of leaf area and any damage to the foliage is a serious matter as this reduces the food conversion surface. In country districts, branches of hazel or other twiggy growths used to be spread over the shallot bed and a windbreak of holly or spruce used on the windward side especially in the eastern counties where the wind is a serious problem. Shallots can suffer from other onion diseases but when well grown with not too much nitrogen in the soil they are seldom affected.

As the shallot grows and develops a keen exhibitor will mark and select those which produce fewer, but better-shaped bulbs in the cloves while those that make a great number are discarded. This characteristic is inherent in the bulb and by selection a near perfect strain can be developed. This is a far more satisfactory method than selecting seed after the crop has been harvested.

Harvesting This is a simple job. Shallots mature, in a good ripening year, in late July or early August and they may be allowed to remain on the soil until the roots virtually die off. This is better than artificially breaking the roots by easing them with a fork. On heavy soils it may be necessary to remove a little soil from the base of the bulb to ensure complete ripening. This should be done with the finger rather than with any hard tool.

Lay the cloves unbroken on a sack on a hard dry surface or on fine mesh wire netting until they are dry, putting them under cover at night. Do not allow them to become wet again. I prefer to lay them under a shelter of some kind with the sides open, as during the summer there is a risk of heavy thunder showers. Moisture, if trapped under the top layers of ripened skin, can produce a very moist steamy atmosphere in which a black fungus flourishes. Finish off the ripening process by lightly rubbing off dead roots and scales but do not overdo this. Finally store in nets in an airy place.

Shallots as scallions In addition to the main bed of shallots I always put in a couple of rows of bulbs planted about 4 in apart. These are reserved for early use as spring onions or scallions, every other bulb being pulled. These make excellent fillings mixed with egg for sandwiches and are crisp and succulent additions to salads.

This is a crop that can be grown virtually anywhere; in troughs or containers on balconies, in small gardens, even amongst the roses. It is one crop that can be grown under virtually any soil conditions in the tiniest of gardens and there is not the slightest excuse for not having a supply for salads. With a little more room you can also grow bulbs for pickling and for cooking.

Exhibition Leeks

Our gardening friends in the north-eastern counties of Durham and Northumberland have made the growing of exhibition leeks very much their own. Strains and seeds are very jealously guarded and are even handed down from father to son. Some of the so-called 'pot' leeks (these are virtually unblanched) may be anything up to 5 in diameter. But this does not mean that leeks cannot be grown elsewhere. What they need is a long, cool growing season. But there is more to growing these monsters than just putting in the seed and feeding the growing plants prodigiously through the summer.

The flower head of a leek contains a number of tiny plantlets known as pods, as well as seeds

Raising the plants Leeks can be propagated in three ways: from seed, from pods, which are little growths which appear in the seed head, and from offsets which are small leek-like growths which appear at the base of the main stem.

All varieties of leeks have to start initially from seed, but there is often great variation in a sample. The best plants are allowed to run up to form a seed head the following year. In the drum-stick-like flower head are tiny plantlets known as pods as well as seed. These pods form in July but they do not develop very quickly and are capable of living on practically nothing, in fact I have kept old seed heads until the following spring when the pods have still been in first class condition. They are very tenacious and live on the little moisture in the seed head and the atmosphere as they do not actually put out roots until they are planted. It will be found that the seed will shake out quite easily but, just to be on the safe side, put a paper bag, not a plastic one, over the head and secure it with an elastic band so that any seeds which have already ripened will not be lost. Use a thin white bag so that the pods do not suffer from lack of light. When all the seed has been taken, the heads can be stood in a cool but not too dry a place (by a window in the shed will do admirably) where they will keep quite green and plump until December when the pods can be carefully removed and pricked out into boxes of sandy soil and kept in the greenhouse.

This vegetative propagation is the only way of ensuring that the 'children' are exactly like the parent. However, it has the disadvantage that after a time deterioration sets in and vigour has to be reintroduced by raising new plants from seed taken from selected plants. This needs to be done roughly every fifth year. This may sound complicated, but it is no more difficult than taking the cuttings from violas and over-wintering them in a cold frame. This process of selection each season ensures that a superior strain is built up resulting in the production of these huge specimens.

Just as a point of interest, there is no fundamental difference between what is known as a pot leek and a blanched leek. Both start off the same but the latter is blanched and elongated either by earthing up or blanching with cardboard or paper collars to produce a stem which may be 2 ft long or more. On the other hand, pot leeks simply sit on the ground and are not blanched except for the lower 5 in or so.

Soil preparation and feeding There are several other niceties which have been evolved over the years, but the main thing about leeks is that they need a rich soil, a fair amount of feeding and, as they are surface rooters, the soil surface should not be unduly disturbed by hoeing. Unless you have a very deep fertile soil, growing leeks in a deep trench does more harm than good, as it reduces the amount of good soil under the roots. This method of growing leeks and vegetables such as celery, peas and beans in trenches was evolved in the large private gardens where the good soil was some 2 or 3 ft deep. The trench method facilitated the flooding of the trenches with water or liquid manure and the subsequent blanching. As few of us have soils which have been worked continuously for hundreds of years and trenched and manured during that period, my advice is to grow these crops on the flat with as much good soil and manure under them as is possible.

Dig in as much manure and compost as can be spared. Ideally half a barrowload per square yard, plus 2 oz superphosphate, 1 oz bonemeal and about 1 oz sulphate of potash. Work this in thoroughly to a depth of at least 12 to 15 in and tread firm the soil a few days before planting. Any subsequent feeding should be mainly nitrogenous, preferably organic such as dried blood or liquid manure. During dry periods water thoroughly and apply soot water. All sorts of weird and wonderful feeds are often given to leeks, including beer, stout, sugar and water and other less pleasant concoctions. Actually these substances do not feed the leeks directly but stimulate fungi and bacteria to break down more of the available raw materials in the soil.

Growing and blanching To ensure a good long period of growth, seeds and pods should be started off in gentle warmth in January and the subsequent small plants potted up individually into 3½-in or 4-in pots and grown on in a minimum temperature of 7.5° to 10°C (45° to

Two drainage pipes filled
with peat blanch the stem of
a fully grown leek

50°F) until about April when they can be planted out either under cloches or, as so many leek growers do, under glass jars. This ensures continuity of growth without any check.

For pot leeks, a few inches of soil pulled up round the plants from the end of June to the end of July will be sufficient, but drainage pipes should be used for obtaining a long blanched stem. About the end of June, place one 6-in diameter pipe over the plant and leave this for a week or two until the leaves become elongated. Then start by putting about 3 in of peat in the pipe and gradually increase this. When the first drainage pipe is about half full (that will be to a depth of roughly 6 in) place another pipe 3 in in diameter over the leek so that it rests on the peat in the larger pipe. Gradually raise this by adding more peat. In this way you will obtain 18 to 20 in of beautifully blanched leek some 2 in in diameter. Next time you see bundles of these amazing cylindrical leeks at the large shows, you will know exactly how it is done and the amount of work it entails.

Leeks for the kitchen You can, of course, sow from January to April in boxes or a nursery bed for ordinary culinary purposes. For home use I recommend the varieties The Lyon, Musselburgh and Giant Winter. Plant out from late April onwards in 6-in deep holes made with a dibber spaced 6 in apart with 15 in between the rows. Drop one young plant into each hole. There is no need to put any soil in the holes as it will gradually fall in, giving you 6 in of blanched stem. In dry weather fill the holes with water at planting time. Leeks have few, if any, pests but suffer from the same diseases as onions.

Salads and Salading

The basis of almost any salad is the lettuce, which can be grown anywhere in the British Isles. In a rather off-putting way a salad could be compared to a compost heap in that anything organic can go into it and once, when I made a huge salad in the afternoon for evening use, it actually heated up. Apart from the recognised ingredients of a salad, nearly anything goes: blanched dandelions, beetroot, cucumbers, cress, tomatoes, small cherry tomatoes, cold peas, beans and potatoes. If you are partial to potato salads some of the continental varieties are useful as they remain firm when diced or sliced cold. Try any of the following varieties cooked in the normal way: Aura, Eigenheimer, Étoile de Nord, Fir Apple, Jersey Royal, Kipfler, Purple Congo, Red Craig's Royal, Red Cardinal. As most are early varieties they can also be grown in pots in a warm greenhouse or a cold frame.

Lettuce, with the assistance of cloches, cold frames, plastic tunnels or any primitive shelter, can be grown for use for at least nine months of the year. If you can be bothered, it can be grown indoors too in

The pipes are removed to
expose a superb long white
stem of exhibition quality

pots, trays or boxes. There has, I think, been more development and new varieties added to lettuces than to any other crop. Many old favourites with household names have had to give way to strange-sounding continental varieties such as Magiola, Novaran or Hilde. No longer is there just the sharp division between the soft cabbage lettuce and the tall crisp cos but many variations in between, including the crinkly and the buttercrunch type.

It is claimed that there are more vitamins in the green leaf than in the blanched crisp heart, although my personal taste is for the solid heart of a variety like Webb's Wonderful or the crisp nutty flavour of the reddish-brown variety Continuity. However, in the small garden the buttercrunch or non-hearting types are probably better value. These will last for months and can be robbed almost daily.

Continuity is one of the best varieties for use early in the season as its young leaves are very dark and not easily seen by sparrows. This is a big advantage, particularly in town gardens where a batch of this variety will be left alone whilst most others may be completely decimated by birds, especially in early spring. The flavour, incidentally, is excellent.

Raising plants There are several ways of doing this. They may be raised in gentle heat, in boxes or pots and pricked out, raised in frames in containers or sown direct into the frame and planted out directly into the soil when it warms up. The soil should have a good tilth, contain plenty of organic matter and be firm but not hard; lettuce needs moisture and extra watering during periods of drought. The essence of lettuce production is little and often, bearing in mind that transplanting lettuces adds 10 to 14 days to the time they take to mature. This is important as a small quantity may be sown in a drill and, when large enough to handle, thinned out and selected plants left without further disturbance. Those remaining will mature a week or 10 days earlier than the transplated ones. There is no need to drill lettuce seeds right across a plot. Just allocate the space for a row of lettuce plants and sow a drill about a yard long. When large enough thin out and use the thinnings to almost complete a row leaving about another 2 ft for sowing a little more seed. This technique can be adopted in most districts from about mid-March to mid-July. No seedling should be transplanted after the end of July. Covering with a cloche at the beginning of the season can advance the sowing date by a fortnight or three weeks and extend the cutting period at the other end of the season by five or six weeks.

Probably the worst pest is the root aphid which attacks the roots under ground and its presence is not suspected until the plant begins to look pale and sick. It is more prevalent during a dry spell. Watering with an insecticide such as malathion will give effective control in most cases.

Varieties Fortunately the lettuce has been cleaned up and now most varieties are free from lettuce mosaic virus. Varieties like Avon Crisp are resistant to mildew and the variety Irma has a high resistance to bad weather conditions and is slow to bolt. The varieties Reskia and Sanno Mosaic Tested are also disease resistant. For the tiny garden, for the front of the herbaceous or flower border, window boxes and balcony gardens, the variety Tom Thumb is the best. The seedlings can be planted a few inches apart and will make beautiful little hearts.

Strangely enough cos or tall lettuce are popular on the table but not so popular in the garden. There has been less change in these varieties than amongst all the other types of lettuce and Density, Little Gem, Lobjoit's Green and Vaux's Self Folding still dominate. As the latter grows tall and curves its leaves inwards there is always a risk that greenfly will establish itself inside these protective leaves and make them virtually inedible. In windy areas cos lettuces may have to be staked and, unless a self-folding variety is grown, may even have to be tied to prevent them opening out and sprawling.

Growing Outdoor Tomatoes

The tomato is probably the heaviest yielding crop per yard of ground that we have in this country, beating even crops like potatoes and onions. Tomatoes grow easily and well, require the minimum of attention and are sufficiently hardy to withstand the rigors of an average English summer, as anyone who has seen masses of seedlings growing on sewage waste tips will know. There is one trouble with these summer hardy plants and that is that the season isn't long enough for them to develop fruits unless they start their life indoors.

This means that they must be raised early in the season and planted out as reasonably well-established plants, but not before the soil warms up, which will probably be early June in most places. In consequence they have a comparatively short fruiting life. This can be extended by planting them close to a sunny wall which holds and reflects its heat during the night or by arranging some form of glass or plastic covering in the early stages to protect them from cold winds. With regard to varieties, practically all those which will grow under glass will grow outdoors. However, there are certain varieties which have been specially bred for outdoor growing which do not do at all well in greenhouses.

Some of the bushy varieties lend themselves very well to cloche culture and require no staking. They include such varieties as Sutton's French Cross, Pixie and Tiny Tim. I appreciate it is not much use mentioning the varieties to start from seed unless there is some form of artificial heat available for this but plants can be bought. The most important thing for tomatoes when grown outdoors is that they should have been prepared for it by hardening off. Taking plants straight out of the greenhouse, even if unheated, and planting them directly outdoors is a sure way of delaying growth. If you buy your plants in pots all well and good, but if dug up from a seed box then it is worthwhile potting them up so that they can be kept mobile. In the early part of the year in many districts days can be warm but nights extremely cold. So it pays for the first few days at least to stand them out in pots in a sheltered place in the sun and then at night put them under cover, even if it means taking them indoors. Standing them outdoors even in hot sun will cause the leaves to harden so that they do not get a check. If you check the growth of a tomato plant it can put it back 10 days or a fortnight and time is precious.

The soil at the base of a wall or fence, not a living hedge, should be prepared and soaked well in advance. (I do not advise planting at the base of a hedge because of root competition and drought.) Personally I prefer a raised bed against a wall. This can easily be achieved by using two layers of bricks, a wooden edge or any other device to help contain the raised soil. The existing soil should be thoroughly forked up and any rotted manure or compost available should be incorporated. The top of the box-like containment area should then be filled with soil of the quality of John Innes No. 2 or an equivalent soilless compost. An alternative is to use growing bags, now widely marketed by various firms.

In more favourable districts tomatoes are often grown as a field crop. They can be planted across the garden in just the same way as potatoes. I find it best to put in one or two strong posts so that about 3 ft is left out of the ground and stretch a wire across the top. The tomato plants are planted about 18 in away from the centre line and

Growing tomatoes in a tent arrangement allows the foliage plenty of light while the fruit stays clean and protected hanging down inside

trained up canes or strings inclined to the single wire. The advantage of this is that the leaves grow outward to the light but the fruits, by virtue of their own weight, will hang in the centre and are thereby protected by the foliage. It does not matter if you do not see the fruit; this is all to the good. There will be less attraction for blackbirds and thrushes and the protected fruit will have skins almost comparable to those grown under glass. Tomato fruits grown either in the greenhouse or outdoors will ripen quite happily without benefit of direct sunshine.

One of the usual complaints about outdoor tomatoes is that they are ugly and gross in size and are of more use for cooking than for the table. This is often dependent not only on variety but on soil preparation and feeding too. My own method when growing five acres a year was to plough and rotavate the soil, working in about 3 oz of a complete fertiliser to the square yard. After planting in rows with about 20 in between plants, the soil was carefully drawn from the centre and the plants earthed up leaving a depression where water could be applied if necessary. This also left an outer ridge along which the hose pipe could be laid. Before planting the soil was thoroughly firmed by rolling or treading, making it almost as compact as an onion bed. This compacting controlled the size of the fruits and there were few if any 'seconds'. Incidentally, I noticed that in a lot of the smallholdings on Tenerife which produces the Canary tomatoes, the same sort of technique is employed.

The plants should be 'stopped' at four trusses with one or two leaves beyond the final truss left so that they can send back food. Never leave a truss stuck out on its own either under glass or outdoors as manufactured food travels down a plant not up it. On ordinary garden soil which has carried a reasonable crop the previous year, little or no extra feeding is necessary. Applying all sorts of fertiliser only makes for big fruit which is difficult to ripen and I, for one, hate tomato chutney.

The Fruit Garden

Judging by the sales of fruit trees, more and more people are attempting to grow at least some of their own. True, many gardens are not big enough to sustain large trees, but the smaller bush-trained trees and even the cordons produce considerable quantities of fruit; often enough to supply the needs of a small family for a good many months of the year.

Varieties are much more limited today than say 50 or even 100 years ago, when it was a matter of concern and pride to grow varieties of apples which would mature during every month from August until April of the following year. Apples and pears not only have times of ripening but also times of maturity after storing and once upon a time when there were many connoisseurs of fruit, they would be rejected from the dining room if they were the slightest bit mealy, which means that they were literally 'over the hill' and as unappetizing as a fuzzy turnip. Nowadays hardly anyone knows whether they are eating a crisp apple or coloured fuzz ball and even with a beautiful apple like a Cox, half the time it is eaten in a state that a discerning palate would reject. It is a case, I suppose, of where ignorance is bliss.

If the pattern of the last few years is followed a considerable number of fruit trees will be planted and although the range of varieties is greatly restricted, it is well worthwhile checking up on the particular qualities and maturing times of those varieties selected or offered.

Storing fruit

In the case of apples, if you have no possible way of storing them then it pays to grow a variety that you can eat off the tree such as James Grieve, Worcester Pearmain or Beauty of Bath, which literally have no shelf life. Blenheim Orange, on the other hand, is a dual-purpose apple (cooker or eater) and will keep well into the New Year and improve for the keeping. For the early cookers, Victoria or Keswick Codling are amongst the earliest and there is, of course, nothing to beat a good Bramley followed a close second by Lane's Prince Albert. There are, many others, but suppliers tend to, what is termed, 'rationalise' their list and cut down on varieties offered for sale.

Grapes can be stored through the winter if they are kept in a cool room with their stems in water

Obviously, before you can store fruit it must be gathered and the decision when to gather is not an easy one to make as not every apple on the tree matures at the same time. When you have five hundred acres to pick a compromise must be made but in the home garden with fewer and more accessible fruits they can often be taken at the peak of ripeness. When ripe, apples and pears should part readily from the branch without tearing off a chunk and should be handled carefully without squeezing. They should be placed gently in a basket lined with two or three folds of soft material, like a piece of blanket. Don't use anything as rough as a sack as the skins of the fruit, especially when gathered warm, are very tender and the slightest bruise will reduce keeping time. Similarly when removed from the basket they should not be tipped out on to a hard surface.

The fruits generally stored today are apples and pears. Gone are the days when grapes were kept with their stems in bottles of water until the following spring, medlars were bletted and chestnuts, walnuts and filberts stored in every cottage. The requirements for successful storing are that the place should be cool, dark and with ventilation, but without moving air. The latter tends to extract moisture. The materials on which the fruit is laid should be clean, sterile and free from taint; so disinfectant or strong soaps should not be used to scrub boards and wood wool is out because that, too, may be strong smelling due to possible resin content. Similarly musty sacks or baskets should not be stored in the same place as fruit but, on the other hand, it is as well to remember that other things can also take up the smell from ripening fruit. The places in which fruit can be stored range from a clamp or a hole in the ground, cellars, old air-raid shelters, cool cupboards, a properly constructed fruit house and, going back to my childhood days, under the bed on the scrubbed floors where they gave off tantalising scents and nearly drove my brother and me mad because we knew the penalty for unauthorised filching.

Tree forms

The choice of tree for the small garden, as far as apples and pears are concerned, is generally limited to either the dwarf open-centred bush or one of the more restricted tree forms which are generally summer pruned. The restricted forms most generally planted are the cordon, the dwarf pyramid, the espalier and the fan. The more recent spindle bush is not generally well-known to the home grower. However, it is now being widely used commercially as it is perhaps the most productive form of growing, although not suitable for every variety of apple or pear.

Without doubt the dwarf open-centre bush with its varying length of leg is the simplest form to maintain and is probably the most productive. It is available on varying rootstocks but M9 is probably the best. Unfortunately this information is not always available at garden centres and you should always enquire what stock the tree is grafted on as its dwarf nature depends upon this. Cordons and dwarf pyramids are two other useful forms which can be planted closely together. Cordons should be spaced 2 or 3 ft apart in the row while dwarf pyramids need to be planted 3½ to 4 ft apart in the row with 6 or 7 ft between rows. Both require a lot of attention in the way of summer pruning, for if this is neglected the trees soon get out of hand. The espaliers and fans can be grown against walls or used to define boundaries. They can be planted behind a flower bed or even to edge paths where they can look most attractive; but again they require a considerable amount of attention otherwise the fruiting spurs become very long and are not nearly so productive as the bush form. The spindle bush is basically very much like a pyramid with a vertical central stem on which are carried the cropping laterals. The central spindle must be supported by a stake and it may be necessary to insert more canes to tie down the young laterals in the formative years.

Varieties

Having decided on the form of the tree, the variety is the next consideration and where only a few trees can be accommodated then due consideration should be given to their compatibility for cross pollination. The following table gives a brief list of varieties which are readily available and from them and by using the suggested pollinator most requirements can be satisfied. For example, taking Bramley's Seedling with the pollinator James Grieve, you have an excellent cooking variety and a fine dessert apple in James Grieve, although it is not a good keeper. Again, take Lord Derby as your cooker and Laxton's Superb as its superb dessert pollinator, and so on. It does require a little bit of thought if you are going to take your apples and pears seriously but it is well worthwhile. It should be noted that even with self-fertile varieties, better results can be obtained if a pollinator is provided.

Pollination Charts

Fruit		Fertility	Flowering Period*	Examples of Suitable Pollinators
Apples				
Allington Pippin	D	PSF	9–16	Ellison's Orange
Arthur Turner	C	PSF	9–16	James Grieve
Blenheim Orange	DC	PSF	13–21	Newton Wonder
Bramley's Seedling	C	SF	11–19	James Grieve

141

Fruit		Fertility	Flowering Period*	Examples of Suitable Pollinators
Charles Ross	D	SS	11–19	Seabrook's Monarch
Cox's Orange Pippin	D	SS	9–16	James Grieve
Crawley Beauty	C	SS	29–36	Royal Jubilee
Early Victoria	C	PSF	15–21	Lane's Prince Albert
Edward VII	C	SS	19–27	Orleans Reinette
Ellison's Orange	D	PSF	9–16	James Grieve
Grenadier	C	PSF	9–16	James Grieve
James Grieve	D	PSF	9–16	Cox's Orange Pippin
Lane's Prince Albert	C	PSF	15–21	Lady Sudeley
Laxton's Epicure	D	SF	1–12	Laxton's Exquisite
Laxton's Superb	D	PSF	13–21	Rev. W. Wilks
Lord Derby	C	SF	13–21	Laxton's Superb
Lord Lambourne	D	SF	7–15	Worcester Pearmain
Peasgood's Nonsuch	C	SS	9–16	Allington Pippin
Rev. W. Wilks	C	SF	13–21	Early Victoria
Ribston Pippin	D	PSF	5–13	Beauty of Bath
Stirling Castle	C	PSF	5–13	Beauty of Bath
Warner's King	C	SF	5–13	Stirling Castle
Worcester Pearmain	D	PSF	9–16	Cox's Orange Pippin
Pears				
Beurré Hardy	D	SS	14–24	Laxton's Superb
Conference	D	SF	6–16	Emile d'Heyst
Doyenné du Comice	D	SS	18–28	Glou Morceau
Louise Bonne of Jersey	D	PSF	4–14	Conference
Pitmaston Duchess	DC	PSF	16–26	Dr Jules Guyot
Williams' Bon Chrétien	DC	SF	14–24	Beurré Superfin
Winter Nelis	D	SS	12–22	Josephine de Malines
Plums and Damsons				
Belgian Purple	DC	PSF	Late	Cambridge Gage
Coe's Golden Drop	D	SS	Early	President
Czar	C	SF	Late	—
Farleigh Damson	C	PSF	mid-season	Cambridge Gage
Giant Prune	C	SF	mid-season	—
King of the Damsons	C	SF	Late	—
Kirke's Blue	D	SS	mid-season	Cambridge Gage
Merryweather Damson	C	SF	mid-season	—
Oullin's Golden Gage	D	SF	Late	—
Pond's Seedling	C	SS	Late	Czar
Victoria	DC	SF	mid-season	—

*based on the average flowering period of 36 days, although this may vary from season to season.

Planting

In an age of containerisation it is possible to buy and plant fruit trees at any time of the year but, in my opinion, it is still advisable to plant whilst they are in a state of dormancy or, at the very latest, just as the buds are beginning to burst. The main reason for this is that they are usually transported from the garden centre in the boot of the car and are very liable to damage at an advanced state of bud development. Bare-rooted trees are less frequently sent out nowadays unless large quantities are being supplied. In their case they should be unpacked as soon as they arrive and, if conditions for planting are not suitable due to frost, snow or for any other reason, they should be heeled in. This is possible even if snow has to be removed or a slight crusting of frozen soil removed, provided you can get down to unfrozen soil and is far better than leaving them in a shed or garage. Take out a trench to accommodate the roots, put back the soil and tread firmly. It will do no harm if any snow is put back over the top. In the case of bush fruits where it is obvious that the tops have been dried then the whole lot, stems and all, can be laid horizontally in the trench and completely buried for anything up to a month before planting. During this time moisture will be absorbed by the canes which will plump up the buds.

After selecting positions for the trees, the hole should be dug larger than the full spread of the roots and of such a depth that when the roots rest at the bottom, the final soil level (when filled in) is at the same height on the stem as it was in the nursery. This depth can be found from the soil mark which will be clearly visible on the stem. In the case of containerised trees, soak them thoroughly and allow them to stand for a few hours so that the water can percolate through the whole of the roots.

Remove the container by slitting on both sides and if the root ball is very compacted the roots on the outer side of the ball can be released by gently picking at them with a pointed stick, taking care not to damage them more than is necessary. The roots of open field trees may be damaged as they are now often lifted with a plough instead of the spade, and any jagged ends should be trimmed neatly with secateurs making a sloping cut so that the underside of the cut faces downwards. When digging the hole make two heaps putting the top soil on one side and the lower spit to the other. Break up the bottom of the hole thoroughly with a fork and mix in compost or well-rotted manure, working in just a handful of bonemeal but no other form of artificial fertiliser.

Bang in a stake and then carefully position the tree in the hole. Fill in using the top soil and work this well around the roots by gently jigging the tree up and down. This will not be possible with the containerised root system so the top soil should be put in the space between the root ball and the side of the hole. When half the soil has been used, break down the edge of the hole with a fork and gently firm by treading with one foot only. Fill in the remainder of the soil and top up with the bottom soil even if this be almost pure clay.

With a container-grown tree there is bound to be a surplus of soil, so dispose of this about the garden and do not mound it up around the stem of the tree. Don't be worried if the surface is then covered with clayey soil as this will break down quite quickly under the influence of rain, sun and wind, or, in winter, by the action of frost. With heavy clay soils do not leave the surface trampled down but lightly prick over the footmarks and mulch with compost or well-rotted manure; the emphasis being on well rotted.

Planting is carried out between October and March, October being preferable. Spring planting entails the risk of drying out so unless the soil is moist to wet, pour in a bucketful of water when the hole is half filled in. As far as the age of the trees is concerned, preferably they should be three to four years old for most types but in the case of cordons two- to three-year-old trees are the most suitable.

Planting in grass or open ground The fact that in old grassy orchards apples and pears produce heavy crops of well-coloured fruit tends to give the impression that this is the best and easiest way to grow them. The fact of the matter is that in nearly all cases these trees were intitally grown in well-tilled, well-cultivated, weed-free soils and over a period of time have been deliberately grassed down to save labour. There is no doubt about it that the fruit from grassed-down orchards is of high colour and in the past exhibitors used to take advantage of this by gathering apples and pears a few days before a fruit or flower show and letting them lie in the grass or covering them with mown grass for a few days. However, grass does militate against the apples growing in it in the following ways:

1. Lowering the water supply
2. Decreasing some elements in the food supply
3. Reducing the amount of humus
4. Lowering the temperature of the soil
5. Diminishing the supply of air
6. Adversely affecting beneficial microflora
7. Forming a toxic compound that affects the trees

I mention this because there are occasions when it seems a nice idea to have an apple tree on the lawn or to make a piece of rough grass productive without any trouble. In these instances it is necessary to retain a cultivated area at least 4 ft in diameter, either square or circular, round the tree. Keep this area clear for at least twelve or fifteen years until the tree becomes thoroughly established.

Feeding Whether apples are grown in grass or in cultivated soil – cultivated incidentally only with a view to providing a well tilled but not deeply cultivated soil around the trees – they should be fed at least twice a year. Once in early spring and again as the fruit is swelling after the flowers are fertilised. The early spring feed should be high in nitrogen using a fertiliser such as urea, nitrate of soda or even sulphate of ammonia. In contrast, the early-summer feed should be of a complete compound containing nitrogen, phosphates and potash, such as commercially available Growmore fertiliser. This basic general fertiliser contains 7% nitrogen, 7% phosphates and 7% potash.

Pruning

Since the period when I was pruning fruit trees and bushes daily from October until March I have taken a great interest in the job. In fact at that time one had to stop oneself going clean mad by the sheer repetition. This means considering every single bush and every single growth as a separate problem because no two bushes or two branches are alike, and this must be recognised if the job is to be done intelligently and successfully. True, one can get by for a short time by just slashing off any old bit but sooner or later, and often sooner than later, the bush or tree will deteriorate in shape and ultimately in yield. So it is really well worth while thinking about it, observing and even noting down the effects of a particular method.

So far I have said nothing about the tools to use. These consist essentially of a pair of secateurs, short or long handled depending upon the job, a saw and a sharp knife, preferably a hooked pruning knife. It would be invidious to mention any particuar design of secateurs as the better quality designs are equally good. There is the type where the blade cuts onto a soft metal anvil simulating the knife blade on the ball of the thumb and is, incidentally, a lot less painful. Then there is the type with scissor blades where the cutting blades cross and have a guillotine effect. Although cheap secateurs are often an attraction, they have a limited use. They may be good enough for small jobs but very soon the blades become strained and one might as well use a pair of pliers to crush the shoots to be removed. Many of the growths which are pruned away are hollow or contain only soft pith which offers little or no resistance to strained, ill fitting, poorly designed or badly sharpened secateurs. These bruise and damage the branch with the result that the mangled wood dies and allows spores of disease to breed in it which may eventually even kill the plant. This happens more often with roses than most people could believe

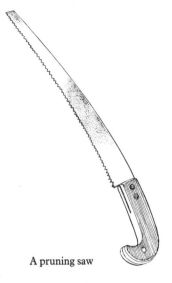

A pruning saw

possible. Apropos of this, if salesmen demonstrate to you showing how their secateurs can cut through hazel twigs thicker than your thumb, ask to see them cutting something which is hollow. Any sort of secateurs will cut through solid wood but not all will stand up to the test of the hollow tube.

The saw is needed to cut through any growth more than ¾ in in diameter and, preferably, a specially designed pruning saw should be used. In any case, a saw to cut green wood should have sufficient 'set' to provide clearance and all cuts should be made on the underside first, cutting in as far as is possible before the weight of the branch nips the saw blade. The object of this is to prevent tearing when the branch falls. A clean pared surface heals and calluses over much more quickly than a ragged edge where the bark has been chewed about by the teeth of the saw, and this is where the sharp knife comes into the picture. The surface of the wood should be pared and particular attention should be paid to the bark, beneath which is the cambium layer. This consists of an active living and growing group of cells which will continue to grow and in time completely enclose the severed portion of the branch.

As active growth only takes place in the cambium layer, the central portion of the severed branch must be regarded as dead wood. In fact the branch will begin to decay very soon unless protected, and cause a hollow to form which may penetrate eventually right down the centre of the tree. Personally, I have found nothing better than either grey lead priming paint or aluminium-based priming paint to cover these wounds. Gloss paints often form a skin which eventually peels off and does little towards the permanent protection of the exposed wood. Painting over the cut surfaces is not just to make them look tidy, but prevents the entry of water and fungus spores which set up the rot.

The pruning or the lopping off of large limbs, be they from fruit trees, ornamental or even forest trees, is best done during a period of dormancy. In the case of conifers this should be just before active growth commences in early spring. In spite of this, large wounds may start to weep profusely and the sap will even drip out like water from a leaky tap. Nine times out of ten this corrects itself and does no harm, even with subjects such as vines. Speaking from my own experience, the only harm done that I have ever seen, even after copious bleeding, is that the sugary sap of some trees congeals on the cut surface and fungus spores breed in this sweet jelly-like substance. Under these conditions when bleeding has actually stopped, the solidified sap can be washed off with detergent and the wound painted with disinfectant solution such as one part Jeyes fluid to twenty parts water.

Cuts of any kind are best made at an angle for two reasons. One is that it is easier to cut obliquely across the grain than at right angles to it. The other is that if the cut is inclined so that the face is pointing downwards, then the rain will run off. Never cut so that the sloping face is uppermost, because if the angle is acute then water can collect. Young wood, particularly, has a tiny core of pith which decays and leaves a channel for spore-laden water to percolate.

When pruning stone fruits such as plums and cherries, be they fruiting or ornamental, special care has to be taken. Even with the greatest care and skill in the world the removal of large branches may result in disaster. Along with magnolias and other shrubs which dislike pruning, plums and cherries should never be allowed to reach a stage where large branches have to be removed. Although very often when one inherits trees like this it can be a problem and one hesitates to do anything about it until it reaches the stage when massive surgical operations have to be undertaken.

Retraining a neglected tree

Where trees have been trained artificially, such as espaliers or cordons, and have been neglected, it is advisable to ignore the original pattern and adapt them to suit the state in which they are now. For example, the tiered espalier lends itself very well to forming a pyramid. Shorten the bottom tiers to 4 ft on each side of the trunk and reduce the upper tiers by 6 in successively, taking a centre growth up to form the trunk. The shortening of the tiered branches will induce growth from all round the trunk, so instead of being a flat hedge-shaped espalier it becomes a rounded shape.

Cordons which have escaped control can be made into bushes or half standards by trimming off the lower growths close to the trunk. For bushes clear 1½ to 2 ft of trunk and half standards up to 4½ ft. The top should be cut out leaving two or four closely-spaced side growths which will form the framework of the new shape. All these operations can be done as soon as the leaves fall.

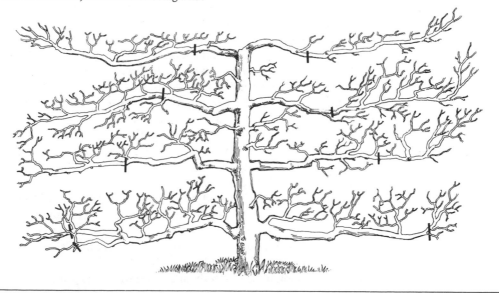

I doubt very much whether the single operation of pruning fruit trees adds a pound of fruit in terms of quantity, which inevitably raises the question, 'Why bother?' The answer, of course, is that it materially improves quality and improves the general health and well being of the plant, as well as lengthening its life. Pruning to me is an art and has no end in itself but the successful training with all its benefits which result from good pruning.

Improved fruiting Most people can argue that they have large old trees in their gardens which fruit regularly, and never receive the slightest attention, either from knife or saw. This is perfectly true, but these trees have reached the stage of stability where the actual fruiting acts in the same way as early pruning. The pruning is a method of early training and formation. When the tree reaches a certain maturity it settles down and becomes self regulating.

There are, however, a few basic principles of pruning which if mastered would enable one to produce bigger and better fruit as well as increasing the fruitful life of the subjects. First of all, forget all you have ever read about ring barking, root pruning, driving in nails and all the weird and wonderful things that are supposed to make unfruitful trees bear fruit. In many cases the results would be far better if the trees were left alone. For a start, hacking a tree about doesn't make it fruit any better. Cutting off large branches very often does no more than produce scores and scores of little whippy growths which are no good to anyone and do more harm than good to the tree.

A very young tree is like a young child or animal which needs training. The way a tree is pruned depends a great deal on the type of training decided in the nursery, be it standard, bush, fan, espalier or any one of the many different forms. The normal, and perhaps most useful, type of apple tree for example, is the bush. When well grown this is roughly like a wine glass in outline and without central growth. A pyramid, on the other hand, is a tree with a central growth with branches coming out all the way round, roughly like a child's idea of a Christmas tree. So, obviously, if the centre was taken out of a pyramid-trained tree then it would become a bush because the secondary growths would come up to replace the central stem. For all practical purposes, whether one is training a young tree or renovating a very old one, it is important to see that the branches are well spaced and that air and light can reach the centre of the tree.

When a tree is very old and has been allowed to grow its own sweet way, then invariably branches will cross and, in crossing, often rub against one another. Whether it is an apple, pear or plum of any age, this must be eliminated or prevented. So as soon as the leaves have fallen off your trees have a look at the branches, get under them if they're big, look up through them and see where they are crossing and rubbing. This rubbing causes wounds into which disease penetrates;

cankers and all sorts of troubles start from here. Most old trees can do with at least a third of the wood cutting out to let in air and light. All cuts should be made cleanly and any cut over ½ in thick should have the edges pared with a sharp knife after using a saw.

Staking Although at first sight planting has little to do with pruning, it is nevertheless very important to see that for the first year or two of its life the tree is adequately staked. On the fruit farm where I was employed in Norfolk, I helped to cut, cart, sharpen, and drive in, literally hundreds of thousands of stakes and in all cases two stakes per tree were used with a cross bar to which the tree was tied. This is certainly an ideal method in an orchard, as it allows the driving in of stakes without risk of damage to the head of the tree by the mallet and the stakes may be placed farther away from the roots which at that time will be small. Of later years, I have experimented with the use of short stakes and find that these work very satisfactorily, not only for fruit trees but for ornamentals too. The stakes are about 3½ ft long,

Double staking of a fruit tree was much more common when I was a boy. The tree is tied firmly, but not too tightly, to a cross bar nailed to two upright posts

pointed at one end and driven into the ground at least 18 in so that they are perfectly solid and rigid. A pad of either cloth, rubber or felt is placed between the stake and the trunk as a protection against chafing. The bottom part of the trunk is then secured so that there is no movement of the roots.

I got this idea from an old Scottish grower who had assured himself that if the trunk of a tree was allowed to flex itself and bend it developed more elasticity than if tied rigidly to a stake. It certainly prevented the head being snapped off at or just above the tie. There is a danger, of course, that where winds blow consistently from the same direction the tree will develop a lean unless a taller stake is used. The important thing is not the top but the roots, for if these waggle about the tree takes a long time to settle down. Constant breaking of the roots will cause suckering, particularly with stone fruits such as ornamental cherries, plums and almonds.

Tap roots

Occasionally, something is triggered off and the tree starts to make an exceptional amount of growth but ceases to fruit. In some cases the roots may have reached a layer of soil, clay or a water supply which makes the tree unbalanced and this is often attributed to the formation of a tap root. Tap roots can, of course, form on practically all trees and shrubs, but they are less common than one is often led to believe.

How does one find a tap root? The only way is to look for it and, in the case of a small tree, a trowel may be used carefully to dig in towards and under the centre where a root may be found growing straight down, very much like a carrot. In the case of larger trees a spade must be used, but care should be taken not to cut more fibrous roots than is absolutely necessary. If such a root is found then a small pruning saw can be used to cut out about 2 or 3 in of the root. This entails making two cuts; one close to the point of attachment and another one a little lower down to form a gap, as sometimes a single cut through may not be effective. Cases have been known where this has been done and the two portions have grown together again.

It is sometimes advised given that all new trees should be sat on a brick, slate or flat stone to prevent the formation of tap roots.

Personally, I have never found this necessary and if a tree does make one then it will ignore the brick and simply grow down to one side of it. Actually, the irritation caused by the movement of the tree against the brick in its early stages may cause more harm than good.

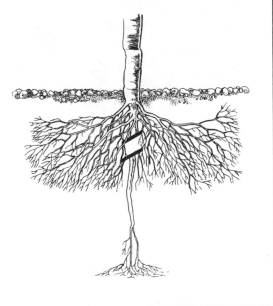

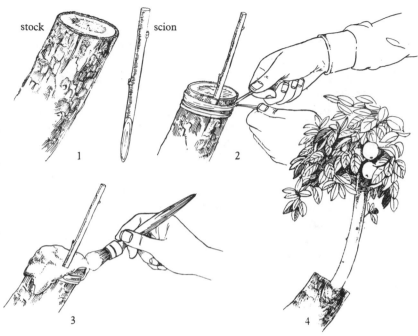

stock   scion

1

2

3   4

Crown grafting

1. Prepare the stock and scion in winter when the tree is dormant. The bark of the stock is slit and peeled back and the scion has a long sloping cut where it is to be inserted
2. The scion is inserted under the bark and bound into place with raffia
3. The whole is covered with grafting wax to exclude air
4. The successful result of a crown graft

Rejuvenating old fruit trees

To wade into an old fruit tree or bush with saw and secateurs is not the answer to this problem as, nine times out of ten, the hard cutting will only produce a mass of young brash growth. This is especially true of apples and gooseberries. If the fruit of an old and neglected apple tree is worthless, inferior or it is one of those semi-precious trees grown from a pip which has never fruited it pays to cut the trunk hard back and crown graft with a good variety. If the old tree forks at a height of under 5 ft from the ground, the cuts may be made through the thick branches about 9 in from the crotch. Crown grafting, which may be done in March or April, need not deter even the veriest novice as it is the easiest and most certain of all the forms of grafting.

If the variety is good, but the tree has got completely out of hand, it may be cut down as above which will encourage dormant buds to sprout. Then it is only a matter of rubbing out the unwanted shoots and keeping the best placed ones to form a new framework. Many old trees, however, do not require such drastic treatment and only need the cutting out of branches which cross the centre. A particular problem which arises here is the very thick branch which has crossed from one side of the tree to furnish almost half the opposite side. In this case, trim off any smaller branches arising from it which are choking the centre. This cleaning out of centres cannot be over emphasised. This job is essential even if nothing else in the way of pruning is done. Thick branches carrying no leafy twigs can fold over each other in the centre as much as they like provided they do not rub or chafe, it is the host of small ones cluttering up the middle that matters.

Plum trees are best cut back before or soon after leaf fall, and if very thick branches have to be removed, I prefer, where possible, to do this over a period of two years. This not only reduces shock which may cause death, but reduces the resurgence of growth which often takes place producing masses of wand-like branches with widely-spaced buds, more suitable for walking sticks than fruiting wood.

Neglected gooseberry bushes should be tackled boldly and the whole centre removed, but if the bush is not growing on a leg it is far better to strike cuttings to make new bushes and scrap the old ones. Bushes which have been formed by division or growing up from a 'stool' or a cluster of growths from the ground are nothing but a nuisance, as they spend half their time making useless wood. Nothing can be done to get such a bush back into shape, as the leg is formed by removing approximately two thirds of the bottom buds before inserting the cutting into the ground.

Stone Fruits

Peaches and nectarines require no pollinators, but cherries and plums are in a different category. So far soil conditions have not been mentioned but generally speaking apples and pears will do well anywhere hawthorns and wild roses thrive, but as you go further north there are areas where the springs are cold and wet and here pollination can be patchy. In the case of cherries and plums, if the soil is not naturally alkaline (limy) then lime must be added. A good natural indicator to the presence of lime in the soil is the wild sloe.

There is no real dwarfing rootstock for the plum, peach, nectarine, apricot or sweet cherry, although experiments on the latter are promising. Cherry trees can get quite large, particularly in the warmer parts of the country where they can grow to 30 or 40 ft high with a very wide spread. Not only is the size of the cherry tree inconvenient but there is very little that you can do to protect the ripening fruits from the ravages of birds. Therefore, if you are thinking of cherries then a wall-trained tree is your best bet.

Most plum trees vary in size from medium to large and as they grow fairly slowly, and even slower as you go further north, one or more could be accommodated in gardens of moderate size. Here again in the north the choicer plums should be grown against a wall. Incidentally when choosing the wall, length is more important than height as the older the trees grow the more productive they are on the new extension wood.

Plums and cherries bloom early in the year. This means that the further north you go the more dangerous a mild winter becomes because the blossoms may open early only to be followed by cold winds which inhibit pollinating insects and then frosty winds damage the embryo fruit if you are lucky enough to get them set. The damson and kindred varieties of plums are hardier but may not always set. It must always be remembered that the actual time during which the flowers are open is very short, maybe only ten days, and as half of this period can be cold and wet the time during which the flowers can be pollinated and fertilised is very short. In cold districts late-flowering varieties of plums, such as Belle de Louvain and Belgian Purple, should be used. My own two favourite plums are the old English Greengage and the Victoria. Fortunately Victoria is self fertile, producing marvellous fruits even in the north on a sheltered wall and the greengage can be fertilised by Victoria. The Giant Prune is also another marvellous plum for training on a wall. Incidentally, most top fruit can be grown very satisfactorily in large plastic tubs especially if you can accommodate them in a plastic tunnel or unheated greenhouse. My own peaches spend most of the time outdoors, being brought under a glass-covered verandah when the flower buds start to show pink, kept there until the fruit has been gathered and then stood outdoors again to ripen off the new growths.

Perhaps one of the biggest cultural problems with the plum family is that they will produce suckers and these should be removed carefully, not just chopped off with a hoe. Growing anything, including trees, against a wall means that provision should be made for watering.

Years ago the cherry used to be a much more popular fruit than it is today and having worked in a cherry orchard I can understand why. All the same they have been with us for somewhere around 3501 years and if only people would realise that a ripe cherry plucked off a tree bears no relation to the often miserable things one buys in shops there would be many more grown. So if you have a sunny wall facing from east through south-west grow sweet cherries and on a north wall, which never gets any sun, you can plant the Morello or sour cherry.

Incidentally, single-stem cordons take up very little room and are easily protected. They produce ropes of cherries on fruiting spurs on the older wood and also on buds formed at the base or along the greater part of the shoots of the previous year's growth. The Morello cherry is slightly different and fruits more like the peach, that is along the length of the new wood. However, not every variety grows well as a fan or cordon, but here are a few: Frogmore Early, Early Rivers, Governor Wood, May Duke, Late Duke, Bigarreau, Waterloo and in the case of sour cherries, just Morello. One or two of the cherry varieties are partially self fertile but fortunately all can be fertilised by the Morello provided they all bloom at the same time.

I did mention that a long low wall was suitable for plums, in the case of cherries a high wall is necessary, especially for some of the more vigorous varieties. Many are very suitable subjects for the gable end of a house, always remembering to use the north end for the Morello and the warmer end for the sweet cherries.

The apricot

Of all the fruits, in my opinion, a freshly-gathered ripe apricot is the finest fruit of all. Inclement weather, cold winds and frost in early spring are the only deterrents to growing first class fruits and, given suitable conditions, the apricot can fruit from one end of the country to the other. In the south and up to the midlands they can actually be grown as standards in the open garden. However, as a general guide the shelter of a wall insures a reliable and good crop. As a rule, experience has shown that apricots succeed best on west walls in southern England, south walls in the midlands and an angled south and west shelter for northern gardens. The objection to an eastern exposure is that the early morning sun reaching the flowering trees will cause failure if the blossom is even slightly frosted. They are excellent subjects for a cold greenhouse, porch or conservatory and can be very successfully grown in plastic tubs about 14 in in diameter.

Incidentally, apricots come reliably true from seed and can be grown and trained from the stones. They are generally in three forms, dwarf fan trained, tall fan trained and cordons and it is these trained forms that you are likely to buy. If you are growing your own from seed then you can use standards for sheltered gardens. Because they have fallen so much out of favour, goodness knows why, the choice of varieties is very limited and most fruit nurseries only offer a few varieties. Moor Park is the most common and has been with us for some 200 years. It can be grown practically anywhere in the country. This has large roundish orange yellow fruits which turn brownish red on the sunny side. The flavour is superb, very juicy and rich and the tree comes into bearing early in September.

The soil for apricots as well as for peaches and nectarines, to which all the following cultural conditions apply just as well, should be a well-drained medium loam; avoid extremes although heavy soils can be ameliorated by adding grit and old mortar rubble. Sandy soils can be made more retentive by adding clay.

Under good conditions fan-trained trees can cover a large area and 18 to 20 ft should be allowed, although if you have a long wall the spaces can be filled in temporarily with cordons planted 2 ft apart. Even when grown from seed they can quickly furnish a wall. The best time to plant is from the middle of September to the end of November, whilst the soil is still warm enough because, like most members of this family, they make an early start. Apricots, together with other members of the family like almonds, bloom early in the year, often in March, so even in the most favourable of districts provision should be made for the protection of the blossom. This is not as difficult as it sounds as a double thickness of ordinary fruit netting hung in front will suffice. Next time you are visiting an old walled garden you may see brackets projecting about 18 in from the top of the wall and wonder what purpose they serve. These were used to suspend nets in front of trained fruit trees to protect the blossom from frost and later the fruit from birds.

Provision must be made for training the branches and, as with any other wall-trained tree or shrub, this is best done by affixing battens permanently to the wall and leading wires through vine eyes screwed into the battens at about 9-in intervals. This allows air to pass up behind the trees and is essential on a south-facing wall as in summer these walls can get hot enough to cause damage. It also reduces the risk of red spider mite which loves hot dry conditions and, to a lesser degree, peach leaf curl spores which rest and overwinter on the wall.

In the old days the new growths used to be affixed to the wall with cast iron nails and strips of cloth and on cold winter days I have knocked many painful chunks off my fingers doing this. Just as a matter of interest we used to find that strips from the coachman's cast off overcoat was the best and most durable stuff for this job.

Tying in laterals

Keep an eye open for greenfly when the young leaves start to form and regularly examine ties to see that they are not cutting into the wood. Young wood grows very quickly and the diameter increases proportionately and what was a loose tie may, in a few months, strangle or cut into the young wood. The danger here is that gummosis can be induced which, as its name implies, is the formation of droplets of gum on the branch and for which there does not appear to be any cure. So carefully avoid any damage or chafing. When making the ties on to the wires, take the tying material, preferably soft string, one turn round the wire and fasten at the front. The twist round the wire will prevent the branch sliding away.

Sometimes the wires are stretched, for example 9 in apart and the shoot appears to be hanging loose or out of control. If this is the case tie string to the wires above and below, making sure it runs in the same sloping angle as the branch, then tie the shoot to this extra support.

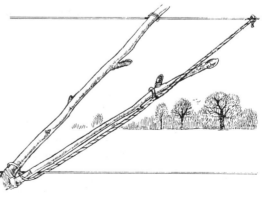

Apricots and peaches bear their fruit on the shoots of the preceding year's growth, also on spurs formed on older growths. However, to make sure of fruit being borne, these growths must be well ripened or only wood buds will form. As with any other bud formations the fruit buds are the roundish and plump ones whilst the growth buds are usually farther apart, smaller and pointed. This is where summer pruning comes in because not only are the best placed shoots selected during this operation but they should be tied in to benefit from improved air circulation and exposure to the sun. Actually summer pruning is more important than winter pruning because by the winter it is too late to do anything but cut out the unwanted wood.

The first step in summer pruning is known as disbudding and simply means the removal of superfluous shoots. Certainly breast-wood and little shoots 2 or 3 in long must be removed. (Breastwood growths are those which come out at right angles to the main fan of the tree.) If done early enough these can be removed with the finger and thumb. The operation includes the selection of the strongest shoots to form future branches and you should lay these in between the older growths. Any that you don't want to lay in, even if they are strong, should be shortened back to about 4 in, and this is why the job should be done when they are soft enough to pinch. I never like leaving wood that has to be cut with secateurs. Incidentally, the shoots that you do lay in should not be shortened back. Sometimes a very strong shoot almost like a cane is formed but don't imagine this is a good thing; cut it right out close to the main branch. Space wood you wish to lay in at about 10 to 12 in intervals. The initial training after planting is of the utmost importance to secure the frame-work of the tree.

Fan-trained trees are usually sent out with about four to six growths when they have had the initial training. When planted and firmed in, take the outer growths and gradually pull them down at right angles to the trunk, that is pointing to nine o'clock and three o'clock. The next pair – one on either side – should be pulled down to within a foot of the first pair. This will leave the centre completely open to be filled up over the next three or four years. The reason for doing this is that after the branches harden and thicken it is impossible to pull them down and you will only get a fraction of the spread of the fan that is so desirable.

Setting the fruit is critical. The trees should never be allowed to get dry at the roots, the flowers should always be protected from frost and cold winds and, if the weather is dull, cold and not many insects are moving, you may have to resort to artificial pollination. This can be done by forceful syringing with clear water or touching the blossoms with the traditional rabbit's tail on the end of a stick.

As soon as the fruits are as big as walnuts they need to be thinned out to 3 in apart and if some set in clusters then these should be broken up by first removing the biggest fruit and then gradually thinning down to one. Clusters should be thinned out when the fruits are about the size of hazelnuts. Never do this in one operation, it is a progressive job because you may find that some of the small fruitlets will turn yellow and drop off at a touch. This is usually an indication that the roots are dry. Incidentally, the apricot stands up to drought conditions better than any other stone fruit.

Later on as the tree gets older, or if you are trying to tidy up an old neglected tree, you may have to make big cuts. If so paint over any wound with that old, now almost forgotten, remedy Stockholm tar. This old standby has many uses from tarring discs to keep off cabbage root maggot and tarring tow or string to lay alongside carrots. It is a wonderful standby and I have seen my father and old gardeners even dab it on cuts on fingers.

Silver leaf disease is a danger to apricots, peaches and nectarines especially if there are old trees or neglected orchards in or near the garden. It usually attacks plums, particularly Victoria, all stone fruits and sometimes apples. It is easily recognised by the silvery sheen on the foliage and later the fungus growing on the trunk. July is the deadline for rooting out and burning the diseased trees. Peach leaf curl attacks apricots as well as peaches, nectarines and almonds and it is advisable to give a precautionary spray with lime sulphur in February.

Blackcurrants

When you pass a thirty-acre field planted with blackcurrants I don't suppose you ever give a thought to who carries the prunings from the middle of the field to the edges. I do because that was a job I had for two winters as a boy. It is a lonely, heart-breaking and never-ending job. The pruners would advance across the field in a row of anything up to a dozen, laughing and talking and no one ever gave a thought to the lad picking up the prunings. In situations like this you either go wooden and numb and do the job mechanically or take a keen interest in why the job is being done. Fortunately I was interested and was eventually admitted to the ranks of the pruners. Later on I was to help the great man 'Spider' Davison himself, a great hybridist, and planted out the first cuttings of Davison's Eight.

Since then several more excellent varieties have come from the Westwick stable including the variety Westwick Choice, which has a high vitamin content. For some reason or another blackcurrants have come to be looked upon as an everlasting fruit bush and I have come across moss-covered bushes in gardens whose owners have proudly assured me that they must be at least 36 to 40 years old. All plants including trees have a definite age limit and with blackcurrants the average worthwhile fruiting age is 12 years. As a general rule they should be grubbed up after this and replaced. There is, however, nothing wrong with taking cuttings from healthy stock and turning them into new bushes.

New varieties are obtained from seed but for all practical purposes the usual way of increasing blackcurrants is either by cuttings, softwood cuttings in July or hardwood in late summer, or by division. The latter method is a useful one as fruiting bushes can be obtained more quickly provided the stock is healthy. The method is to trim up a big bush and then stand in the middle of it, pressing out the side growths and half breaking them below soil level. Soil is then thrown into the middle and trodden down firmly, further pushing out the partially broken portions. In about twelve months these will root into the mound of soil in and around the bush and the whole can be split up with a spade or mattock. The advantage claimed for this method is that a better stool bush is produced.

Blackcurrants fruit on both the old and the new wood but better, bigger and more fruits are produced on the young growth formed the previous year and naturally the stronger and bigger the growths the more berries they will carry. New growths form at any point on all wood, but the higher up they form the shorter they are and in very old unpruned bushes they may be no more than 4 to 6 in long whereas a better length would be 3 to 4 ft. The whole aim is the production of new stems from the base, and this formation is called a stool. Gooseberries, red and white currants differ from blackcurrants although they are members of the same family as they are trained and grown on a single stem called a leg.

The training starts at propagation. In the case of plants required to be grown on a leg the lower buds of the cutting are removed but where a stool formation is desired all the buds are allowed to remain on and the cutting is inserted with buds below soil level. Of the two types of cuttings the hardwood cuttings are easiest to root and are less trouble, but the one advantage of taking softwood cuttings about 3 or 4 in long in July is that if there is danger of big bud mite these cuttings can be rendered virtually immune by soaking for a few minutes in malathion. The big bud mite is a microscopic insect which moves very slowly, in fact the young growth grows faster than the mites move. However, they can be blown onto new growth, carried pig-a-back by insects or on the feet of birds so it is wiser to wash the cuttings thoroughly in a good insecticide. This means that the stock at least starts clean.

Blackcurrants should be pruned as soon as the crop has been gathered but I hold no brief for the method of cutting off fruit rods and carrying them away somewhere else to strip off the fruit.

New and old wood more than three years of age can be distinguished by colour; the older wood being black or almost black and the younger wood a light greenish brown. As a general rule sufficient cuttings may be had from the young growths at the tips or half way up old wood but they should be no thinner than an ordinary pencil.

Several cuttings of about 8 in long or even slightly less may sometimes be taken from one good young growth.

To distinguish the top and bottom of a cutting, which may be of almost equal diameter, cut straight across below a bud for the base and for the top cut at an angle of 45 degrees.

Blackcurrants will grow in almost any but waterlogged soils but to give of their best they require an annual mulch of farmyard manure with two or three applications during the growing season of a nitrogenous fertiliser such as sulphate of ammonia. In the ordinary garden, blackcurrants form an excellent wind break and should be placed so that they do not shade other crops for, under good conditions, they can run up to 6 ft in height. Planting should be at 5 ft intervals and for garden use I prefer to plant one-year-old bushes in preference to the older ones. If these are then cut down to within 4 in of the ground, excellent new growths spring from the base. For the home garden the large sweet variety Boskoop Giant is still really good. For the exhibitor, Laxton's Giant with berries almost as big as a cherry is superb. Westwick Choice has a high vitamin content, and for a good general purpose berry try Mendip Cross.

Aphids and big bud mite are the two worst pests of the blackcurrant and, for small plantings, regular and systematic picking off and the destruction of the buds is as good a way of controlling big bud condition as any that I know. Give the kids 5p a dozen for the big swollen buds and you will have little trouble from blackcurrant mite, but see that they are destroyed and not just thrown on the ground. Aphids can be controlled by spraying with malathion, paying particular attention to young shoots and the undersides of the leaves.

I think the most important thing with any fruit bush, and particularly with blackcurrants, is that if they develop an unthrifty, unhealthy look and produce poor or small fruit then do not waste time and money treating them but grub them up and replant. By the time the trouble has been identified and treated some of the other bushes may be infected as well. With the commercial grower the position is different. He is expected to know something about the bushes but the home gardener cannot possibly be expected to know everything that can happen to his fruits.

Gooseberries

There is an old saying, 'God caused the gooseberry to grow where the grape would not'. No doubt implying that the gooseberry was the alternative to the grape and, in my opinion at least, the flavour of many gooseberries is far superior to that of many varieties of grapes. The gooseberry is found wild in Europe and Great Britain.

It is one of the few fruits, perhaps the only one, to have shows and exhibitions entirely devoted to it. A few of these specialist societies still survive but 60 to 100 years ago they numbered many hundreds, particularly in the northern part of the country where the gooseberries were developed almost to perfection. Enormous weights have been recorded for individual berries and single fruits have been produced almost the size of a normal hen's egg. Generally, however, the flavour of the fruit decreases with size; the best flavoured ones being the smaller berries like Golden Lion and Golden Drop. Incidentally, these small-berried varieties make the best hedges as the wood and habit is generally stiffer and more erect and they fruit very well indeed.

The gooseberry fruits on old and new wood and indeed bushes will fruit for close on a hundred years even if they are never pruned. However, in this state they are simply a tangled mass of prickly vegetation and almost completely inaccessible so, for convenience of gathering and to preserve a shapely bush, they are generally pruned to a goblet shape – about eight main branches with the centre kept completely open. Furthermore those branches which form the frame-work of the bush are invariably pruned during dormancy back to a spur carrying three to five buds. The leading growths are also shortened back by about two thirds, partly because these immature growths would die off in any case following winter frosts and also to keep the bush balanced.

The gooseberry is not particular as to soil provided it is not completely waterlogged, but possibly no bush or fruit is so responsive to potash or lack of it. Except on commercial plantations and in expertly run gardens, practically all the gooseberries in this country are deficient in potash. This is shown by the death of the leaf margins and very early leaf fall. A dressing of sulphate of potash at the rate of 4 oz to the square yard should be given every year. This quantity is approximately two handfuls per bush but very few gooseberries get this amount in their lifetime. Alternatively you can use bonfire ash.

One great advantage of the gooseberry bush is that it can be trained into virtually any shape and can be grown under any conditions, I have even seen them grown by enthusiasts in window boxes and tubs in back yards in industrial towns. As they lend themselves to being fruited on a single stem with spurs, they can be any shape including single, double, triple or quadruple cordons, espaliers, fans, balloons, in fact any contorted shape that the grower can think up. The main advantage of this adaptability is that in a small garden they may be grown alongside a path or used as a screen measuring only 4 to 6 in in width. This means that even in the tiniest pocket handkerchief of a garden or even with no garden at all, gooseberries can be grown. When grown for exhibition it is advantageous to train the growths horizontally about 6 in from the ground, so that the ripening fruits benefit from the reflected heat and moisture; in fact, the real exhibitor will put saucers of water under selected berries.

Unfortunately, varieties are now restricted to a few commercial cultivars but if you are interested and search around you will still find exhibitors and collectors who have stocks of some of the old favourites. Few new varieties have been introduced of recent years and, as they are so easy to hybridise and propagate, someone with time on their hands might turn their attention to this aspect.

Original stock can be bought in as maidens, two- or three-year-olds and also as partially-trained plants in espalier, fan and low- or high-bush form. Gooseberries should be grown on a single stem or leg and they may be propagated from cuttings from which the lower six buds have been removed to produce this clean leg.

Commercial varieties come in four main colours and are exemplified by the following varieties:

Careless: white, mid-season.

Keepsake: green with large berries of excellent flavour and a regular and very heavy cropper.

Leveller: yellow, smooth oval berries, prolific and can be grown on to produce berries of about ten to the pound.

Whinham's Industry: red, oval and hairy, very sweet and hangs late. This variety will also tolerate a certain amount of shade.

Although nearly all gooseberries fruit about the same time, times of fruiting and hanging can be varied by siting them in different parts of the garden. For example, early ones can be produced on a sunny border and fruits can hang until late August on a sunless north border.

Red and White Currants

Because more exotic fruits are readily available in the shops and with the introduction of frozen fruits out of season, red and white currants are not nearly so widely grown and used as in former years. Where red currant jelly is appreciated as an adjunct to lamb or mutton, they will always be grown but the eating of red and white currants when cooked in their green state is not so widely appreciated as it should be. Curiously enough this delicacy was at one time so widely relished in this country that it was carried to the New World and from thence is now coming back home as something new. One of the detractions even in the best of the red and white currants is not so much the slight acidity of the fruit but the preponderance of seeds. This is often more apparent when they are cooked than when eaten as dessert. This objection disappears if the fruits are eaten green and before the seeds become woody. The other advantage is that this provides one of the earliest of the fresh fruits from the garden and those currants remaining benefit from the thinning.

The red and white currants have another advantage over all the small fruits except the gooseberry, in that they may be trained as fans, cordons and espaliers against a wall or on wires. The advantage of being able to train them on walls is that for the earliest fruits they should be given a sunny position and to extend the fruit until early September they may be grown in complete shade. Provided the fruit is netted, or the birds leave them alone, the fruit will hang without harm for five or six weeks after being completely ripe. More often than not fruit is spoiled by honeydew. This is a deposit from aphids which can be severe pests but regular spraying gives control and the fruit is kept bright and appetising.

Red and white currants will fruit on old wood, the base of spurs of old wood and on new wood, but the best and biggest strings come from the base of new or current growth which has been spurred back to about three or four buds. Red and white currants are grown on a leg as described for gooseberries and this is obtained by removing the lower half dozen buds from the cuttings.

In the bush form red and white currants are best pruned after leaf fall and trained to produce a goblet or wine-glass-shaped bush, with about eight to ten main growths springing from a central trunk. The side growths are shortened back and about a half to one third of the length cut from the tips, making a bush about 3½ ft high. When trained on a wall or on wires, the main branches can become more or less permanent as in the case of apples and pears and will in some cases reach a height of up to 10 ft. Every so often these growths should be cut out and replaced by younger wood.

Fortunately they will grow in any soil and both red and white currants are readily propagated from cuttings of ripened wood inserted in a V-shaped trench of sandy soil from late September onwards. They can be purchased as two- or three-year-old plants and early planting in late October or early November is essential if they are to carry a little fruit the first year. Unlike the blackcurrant there is no need to cut them back hard, but merely to shorten back the leaders if this has not been done at the nursery.

The berries on even the large-fruited varieties will deteriorate if not fed and to do them justice they should receive an annual topdressing of farmyard manure in the spring and at least one application of a compound fertiliser such as Growmore during the growing season. Where fairly large quantities of bush fruits are grown, the weeds may be kept under control by chemical spraying or by seeing that the ground is clean and spraying with a pre-emergent spray during the early part of the year. This will give control from all except deep-rooted perennial weeds and these can be individually treated by hormone weedkillers.

However, for the ordinary household only one or two bushes of red and white currants are required and these will provide green fruits for one of the finest fruit salads it is possible to make and also supply currants for dessert, for making cooling drinks and for jellies. A very palatable wine as well as red currant tea can be made from the fruits and with the renewed interest in home-made wines I can well recommend them.

There is not a great choice of varieties, Laxton's No. 1 is probably the best as this has the largest red berries with the smallest seeds, is a heavy cropper and will continue bearing for many years. Laxton's Perfection is another good variety with darker fruit and is suitable for exhibition as it hangs well into late August. Fay's Prolific is early, sweet, dark red and will provide the first of the sweets when green. Two good varieties of white currant are White Versailles and White Pearl. Both these have very thin skins, large berries and make a very pleasant dessert.

Raspberries

Raspberries are easy to grow and will thrive in any but waterlogged soil. They prefer plenty of manure and organic matter dug into the soil before planting. Afterwards, being shallow rooted, any dressings should be put on the top and any cultivation should be confined to the surface. After a long experience on fruit farms and in private gardens as well as commercial holdings, I have yet to find any better way of growing them than trained in a triangle. This can be applied to either a large or small planting.

The canes are planted 20 in apart in groups of three and a central stake driven in. Attached to this stake is a loop of thick galvanised wire which encircles the three groups of canes. One advantage of this is that if there is only room in a small garden for six plants then these can be accommodated as two groups of three and, if necessary, at the back of a border. The clumps themselves are some 3 ft apart and have the added advantage that if virus does develop it does not spread nearly so readily or rapidly as it does down a row. Furthermore, clumps can be dug up and replanted or replaced without interfering with the rest of the plants.

With fairly large plantings in private gardens, this grouping is further improved by covering the whole area with a layer of ashes from the coke- or coal-fired boiler. This produces conditions very much to the liking of raspberries, keeps the weeds down, and makes gathering a cleaner job. I commend this method to you unreservedly because it has proved itself over scores of years. Provided the canes are kept healthy and well fed by giving an application of a top dressing of manure or compost annually and one or two feeds of fertiliser during the growing season they will crop almost indefinitely as they are rejuvenated annually by young growths which spring from stolons.

It is important when planting initially that no reliance should be placed on the canes to fruit the following season. For example, if planted in November the canes should be cut down to about 9 in before they start to sprout the following season. The object being to induce the production of young canes. Some varieties not only produce a summer crop but an autumn crop as well, and in fact the old variety November Abundance will produce two quite good crops in one season. This autumn fruiting often worries people who wonder whether the canes should be cut down and the plants treated as summer-fruiting only. As the autumn crop is so light, this has no effect on next summer's fruiting provided the canes are well fed and the soil kept in good heart.

Once upon a time, maggots in raspberries were regarded as an act of God and inevitable and I well remember as a boy of thirteen that one of my first jobs every morning on the fruit farm was to skim off the maggots from the wooden tubs into which fruit gathered the day before had been placed. Fortunately, modern insecticides now take care of these pests. Raspberry canes and foliage are damaged more by aphids than most people appreciate and spraying with a good insecticide in spring should be routine. Possibly the two worst pests are the raspberry beetle which produces the maggots and the raspberry moth which damages the canes.

As raspberries do not flower all at once any spraying or dusting should be repeated at least twice and should commence as soon as the flowers begin to open. There is often a conflict here between dusting and spraying and the visitation of bees to which the sprays may be harmful. To avoid the wholesale destruction of bees and other pollinating insects it may be better to wait until a substantial number of flowers have dropped their petals for the dusts will still be effective on the embryo berries. My personal preference is for the use of derris dust in about mid-June, applied in late evening after the bees have gone to bed.

With regard to varieties my own feeling is that flavour has been sacrificed to size and vigour and for the small garden the seldom offered Pynes Royal is still the best garden variety. The fruit is large, dark, sweet and borne in great abundance but the canes are rather on the soft side and it is essential to support them. The variety Lloyd George, an improved New Zealand strain which has been raised from virus-free stocks, is a strong grower, produces a large berry of good flavour and crops on the young growths and laterals. It is an autumn fruiter as well as a summer cropper. Of the new Malling strains I prefer Malling Exploit because I find it stands up to winds and exposed conditions better than most. For very exposed districts Malling M with its short stiff canes is to be recommended although in my opinion the fruit is only moderately flavoured. For dessert I prefer golden raspberries which are not nearly so acid as the red ones. Such a one is Golden Everest, very prolific and strong growing which fruits during July and August. Other varieties include: Malling Jewel,

Malling Promise, Glen Clova, Malling Orion, Malling Admiral and Delight. The autumn-fruiting varieties are September, Zeva–perpetual fruiting raspberry and Fallgold.

Strawberries

*'The fruit is fragrant hence Fragaria, delicious
and universally esteemed'* – Louden.

A hundred years or so ago, strawberries were much more diversified than they are today. Over the years the species have lost their identity and become merged with the modern hybrids. This is sad in some ways because of the loss of taste and flavour. Our native wild strawberry *Fragaria vesca* and *F. chiloensis*, and its variety *F.c. grandiflora*, the pine strawberry, have all played their part in the building up of the modern strawberry. When I first started gardening, remnants of these could be found on the old country estates, and at one particular place we used to grow large quantities of wild strawberries culled from the woodland. These were grown on special walls and mounds to get the best flavour (see Strawberry Walls).

Amongst them could be found white, cream, mottled and red berries and some with greenish-pink fruits. The disadvantage of these old varieties was that the fruit was coarse, large and very irregular in shape; a good many pounds had to be gathered to get one good dishful for exhibition. Another failing was the large calyx and the fact that in some varieties the plug was not easily detached and the fruit had to be nibbled off. All this was fine for discriminating individuals but when produced commercially and distributed by the ton, or used for freezing and canning, a greater uniformity in size and shape of berry was essential.

The variety Royal Sovereign more nearly contains all the ideals than any other variety. However, it has certain disadvantages being more a variety for the southern half of the country than for northern districts because of its liability to disease where rainfall and humidity are high.

On the whole, however, the strawberry is a very adaptable plant and I have grown it at an elevation of 1,300 ft in a peat bog with excellent results. A deep root run is essential for strawberries and some of the older growers claim that the roots will penetrate to a depth of 2 ft. At the same time it does make surface roots which can be damaged by too deep cultivation. Where strawberries are grown for exhibition, or to produce extra fine berries for the table, there is nothing to beat the mound or ridged system where the soil is kept up by stones, bricks or thick wooden planks. The object is to produce a deep well-drained soil with a free circulation of air around the clusters of fruit, which should be held clear of contact with gritty soil. To this end such methods as growing in barrels are used. Incidentally I believe this was first used aboard sailing ships, and illustrations in old books appear where lettuces, endive, and other plants are shown growing in the same way to produce fruit and salads to combat scurvy.

In general, strawberries object to artificial fertilisers and prefer large quantities of manure, compost, leafmould, fish and bonemeal instead. On heavy soils, basic slag is ideal for digging into the soil when preparing a bed and I would never dream of preparing the soil for strawberries without putting in a good double handful to the square yard. On thin heavy soils I find that it pays to plant on ridges made up in the same way as for any other crop with the difference that the ridges are not subsequently knocked down. The method is to dig one spit forward and one on each side on top of this, adding manure to the middle and central trench.

There are many ways of growing strawberries and for at least forty years I have secured early runners or plantlets, potted these up and planted them out in groups of three about 4 in apart and cropped them the first year. Disbudded, these produce the finest and most shapely fruit and the group can be treated and the trusses supported as if it were one plant. If five or six berries are taken from each maiden then the clump becomes a worthwhile proposition.

On dry soils and in situations where it is not possible to have a strawberry bed as such, I like to use the raised bed method in the same way as alpines can be grown in chalky soils in a border of heaths and azaleas. An enclosure is made with three or five large stones about 18 in in height. The bottom is broken up and a good forkful of manure added. Then the space within the stones is filled with a good compost equivalent to John Innes No. 2 and three or five plants accommodated. The flowers look attractive and the berries hang down and colour on the warm stones to produce immaculate fruit. This is a technique which can be used in small gardens and as a variation an alpine or perpetual strawberry may be planted in the middle of this group, for there is no real reason why strawberries must be grown in rows.

Lifting them up in this way in a flower border provides interest and variation as the next enclosure may be of something entirely different. Under ideal conditions, strawberry plants will continue to bear from three to six years but after the third year the berries, although more prolific, become smaller. On one commercial planting where I worked, we used to allow them to go to six years and the fruits were almost entirely used for jam making. Today, three, or at the most four years, is considered the profitable limit. To be sure of good quality strawberries, it is a good proposition to have three beds or three rows which will be made up of maidens, two-year-old and three-year-old plants and, where space allows, as the three-year-olds are dug up they are replaced by a new batch, not on the same bit of land, but on the other side of the three rows or beds. Runners may either be taken from the two- or three-year-old plants, it makes no difference, but I stress again that they must be taken from healthy plants. Good cultivation will go a long way to keeping down disease, but there should be no sentiment about keeping a plant which begins to look sick and smaller than the others. I find there is no point in trying to treat individual plants for any sort of disease or stunting which may take place. The best thing is to fork them up, burn the plants and soak their stations with a good disinfectant.

The list of pests and diseases which attack the strawberry is a long one but in my opinion one of the worst is the aphid. This not only debilitates the plant but, in the case of the shallot aphid, causes severe damage by dwarfing the plants, curling the leaves and distorting the blossoms. Perhaps most serious is the fact that aphids are vectors of virus diseases. In the ordinary garden, not one person in a hundred

Propagating strawberries

Virtually everyone knows that strawberries are propagated and increased by runners but the question often arises as to whether the runners at the extreme end of the string-like stolons are as good as those nearer the plant. From the point of view of health and cropping ability the only difference is that the first one or two plantlets become established earlier and make bigger plants, because they are there first and can be potted up or planted out earlier than the smaller ones at the ends.

Where strawberries are a feature of a garden it is best to propagate from one or two good plants which are proven croppers and in extreme good health. This is far better than taking runners indiscriminately from anywhere in the bed just to get enough. Where space allows I would prefer to use one stockplant in the centre of an 8 ft square and peg down all the plantlets that radiate round it. For the ordinary garden it is sufficient to allow one or two plantlets to develop from the best plants, rigorously suppressing all others.

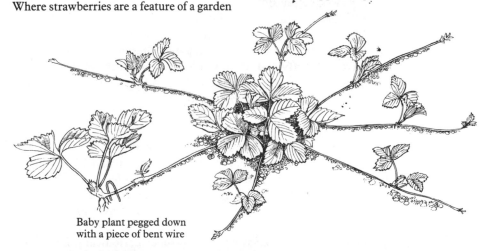

Baby plant pegged down
with a piece of bent wire

thinks of regularly spraying strawberry plants, but in my opinion that is most important and would more than halve subsequent troubles. It is also important when selecting runners to dip these in a good insecticide.

Leatherjackets and cutworms (surface caterpillars) can also play havoc with young and established strawberry plants alike, attacking them both above and below ground. If this is a problem HCH dust should be used.

Amongst the diseases botrytis or grey mould is possibly the most serious but this can be controlled by using captan or thiram. But it is essential to spray early and certainly not later than petal fall. Where special rings are pushed into the ground to support the trusses (these consist of a wire circle supported by a short cane) no strawing or matting is required. A free circulation of air round the fruit is provided and is, I think, preferable to strawing.

You may have guessed from my enthusiasm that strawberries are my favourite fruit, but it is also a fruit that can be grown practically anywhere under almost any conditions in town or country. If so desired, they can be grown in pots, boxes and even in window boxes. Furthermore they can be had over a longer period than perhaps any other fresh fruit. Advantage can be taken of a long fruiting season by planting early, mid-season and late varieties plus perpetuals and alpines.

Strawberries under cloches

This is a profitable and worthwhile method of growing strawberries and one which I have practised for a good many years. I find that it pays to give the site of the crop extra special preparation by digging in half-rotted manure and adding bonemeal and basic slag at the rate of 2 oz per running yard over the width covered by the cloche.

I find there is a tendency amongst present day home gardeners to leave soil puffy and unconsolidated; this is further aggravated by the use of small rotary cultivators. It is important to tread down the soil well after the row has been prepared.

In late summer, select the best and strongest runners and root these separately in small pots and, when well-rooted, plant them out with a trowel, making sure that the soil is packed in between the roots. I like to get the planting done by late September or early October at the latest. Water the plants if necessary to encourage root development before growth slows up. Keep them free from weeds and do nothing more except to remove debris or in some cases prevent them from making runners. Cover with cloches at the end of January or early February and beyond examining them periodically for aphids, they will require no attention.

Should the spring be dry, any watering should be done outside the cloches; on no account wet the surface of the soil underneath. This will discourage slugs from laying up under the leaves and attacking the crowns and will also almost completely eliminate attacks of mildew.

If aphids should appear the simplest way is to fumigate after covering the length of cloches with a sheet of thin polythene if glass cloches are used. Calculate the cubic capacity in the same way as one calculates the cubic capacity of a greenhouse, that is length by breadth by half the height.

Any type of cloche that has a height of 15 in or more at the ridge is suitable for strawberries. As a rule, the flower and fruit trusses will need little or no support but twiggy growths or forked sticks cut from privet or a similar shrub should be used to prevent the berries leaning against the side of the glass as this causes condensation and may trigger off an attack of botrytis.

As soon as all worthwhile fruit has been gathered the cloches may be removed and some transferred to the ordinary strawberry bed to advance some of the next batch. As the strawberries under cloches have not been really forced, the plants should be cleaned up, sprayed with an insecticide, given a good dressing of fish meal and then used for the second year as an ordinary bed of strawberries.

Where the cloches are wide enough, I have no hesitation in growing a few early carrots with the strawberries. Neither crop seems to mind this, the only danger being an aphid attack on the foliage of the carrots. I have grown strawberries under glass and glass-fibre cloches and the results have been equal, but under plastic or polythene film cloches the crop is slightly later and is vulnerable to frost which can cause black-eye damage. In fact, although no controlled experiments have been done, strawberries seem more susceptible to frost damage under polythene sheeting than when grown outside and protected by straw. All strawberries are susceptible to frost damage when in flower so at this vulnerable time protect them with either straw, not now so readily available, or with nets. If grown in a fruit cage you should always put the flexible net top on before they start to bloom.

The ideal strawberry cage is one with ½-in wire mesh sides with a removable top of plastic netting which should be removed after all the fruit has been gathered to allow birds to forage for insects. Never use a strawberry cage with a galvanised wire netting top as the drip, particularly in or near industrial areas, will contain traces of zinc which is poisonous to the plants underneath. Always avoid planting a strawberry bed at the base of a slope or in a low-lying area which may be a frost pocket, as the slightest touch of frost will damage the stamens causing them to have black-eye damage and the berry will never form properly.

The strawberry wall

If you want something different try a strawberry wall. This is a very efficient way of growing strawberries, particularly in a small garden. There are several variations but I think the most effective one is a hollow wall about 4 ft wide at the base with the sides sloping inwards at the rate of about 4 in in every lift, filled with soil and narrowing to about 18 in at the top.

The origin of the strawberry wall goes back beyond the introduction of the Virginian Red and the Pines from which all our modern strawberries descend. Before this it was only the wild strawberry which was available and gardeners used to go out into the woods to search for the best plants and, as with alpine strawberries, seeds used to be sown and plants raised from the best berries.

In my early days as a private gardener I had the opportunity of seeing a strawberry wall which seemed to be literally a mound of fruit. The best way is to run a wall east to west so that you can have early

Modified strawberry wall

I use a modified form of the wall using circles of plastic mesh. These are made by using 6-in wide strips of 1-in mesh plastic netting to make tiered beds. A strip about 7 ft long joined at the end will make a big enough circular bed which could be stood on paving, tarmac or anywhere you like and is completely independent of soil underneath it. This strip, which is joined at the ends, should be lined with black polythene and the space filled with soil. Another smaller circle is placed on top of this, lined and filled with soil in a similar manner and another one, if desired, placed on top of this. Strawberries can be planted all the way round the edge of each tier. The berries are clean and, what is more important, always free from mildew and botrytis as they get plenty of air circulating round them. They are also extremely easy to protect from birds and can be grown on roof gardens or on the patio or verandah.

fruits on the southern side and much later on the cooler northern side. Fruits from a strawberry wall on the southern side can be picked some ten to fourteen days earlier than those grown on the ground.

A variation is to make strawberry steps and this is a very useful way of utilising some of these horrible clay banks which are left by builders after they have levelled off a site for a house on a slope. The steps are just small terraces such as you can see in the hilly districts where you spend your Mediterranean or island holidays. The size will depend entirely on the materials you have available or can procure. In fact you could make a pyramid instead of a wall if you wish.

A typical wall in a large garden would perhaps be 20 ft long with the outer measurements 6 ft wide at the base tapering up to 2 ft at the top, and about 4½ ft high. Any size can be made as long as the proportions are the same. Hollow concrete blocks which are used for insulating or dividing walls are ideal as these can also be filled with soil. Start off as you would build any hollow wall by taking out a trench some 4 in deep and putting the first row of stones in, then infill with soil putting about 2 to 3 in extra on top of the stones. This levels them but also allows the plants to root. The soil used should be rich, containing plenty of organic material such as well-rotted manure and compost or the same mixture as you would use for tomatoes and chrysanthemums. This has to last anything up to ten years so incorporate bonemeal which will provide a steady supply of phosphates. As the work proceeds, vertical pipes of various lengths about 2 in in diameter can be inserted so that during dry weather watering will be sure to reach all levels. Plant the young strawberries as you go along, then put on the next layer of stones some 4 in in from the lower row, fill up with soil and continue in this fashion until you get as high as you wish to go. The alternative method of planting is simply to plant in the soil at the top of the wall and allow the runners to root as they hang down. This is the reverse of the so-called climbing strawberry. Watering and feeding is done at the top and growing the strawberries in holes in barrels is a variation of this.

It is best to plant rooted runners in September. There are some very good English varieties available and an abundance of continental varieties which lend themselves extremely well to this technique.

Index

*Page numbers in italics
indicate illustrations*

Aikman, Professor C.M.,
    42
Ampelopsis, 75
annuals: sowing, 91, 92,
    92
ants, 56, 57
aphids, 125, 159, 167
Apples: storing, 140
Apple trees:
    crown grafting, 151-2,
        151
    feeding, 145
    in grass, 144-5
    old: rejuvenating, 151-2
    pollination chart, 141-2
    tree forms, 140-1
    varieties, 141-2
Apricots, 152, 154-7
Artichoke, globe, 108
Artichoke, Jerusalem, 108
ashes, 36-8
    collecting, *37*
Asparagus, 108

bacteria: where found in
    soils, 19
Beans, Broad, 101-2
Beans, Runner, 112-15
Beard, Professor James, 51
bedding plants, 92-4
    planting out, 94
beds:
    planting, 94
    preparing, 92-4
    shaping, 93, *93*
Beech: as hedge, 77
Beetroot, 102
Berberis prattii, 77-8
    as hedge, 77-8
big bud mite, 159
Blackberries: as hedge, 81
Blackcurrants, 157-9
Blackthorn, 77
blood, dried, 32
bonemeal, 32

borders:
    designing, 89
    feeding, 91
    herbaceous, 89-92
    mixed, 89-92
    renovation, 89-90
    topdressing, 91
botrytis, 168
Brassicas, 105, 108-12
    pests, 111-12
Broccoli: protecting
        curds, 110, *110*
Brussels sprouts, 23
    planting, 109
    blown sprouts, 111
bulbs:
    naturalising, 97-8
    planting in grass, 98

Cabbage:
    planting, 109
    second crop, 109, *109*
cabbage root fly, 111-12,
        111
Camellia, 76
cane fruit: as hedge, 81
carrot fly, 128-9
Carrots, 102, 127-9
caterpillars, 112
Cauliflower:
    planting, 109
    protecting curds, 110,
        110
Ceanothus, 75
Chaenomeles japonica, 77
chafer grubs, 56
chemicals found in plants,
        26
Cherries, 152-4
    pruning, 147
Chinese cabbage, 105
Clematis, 73
climbers:
    on posts, 68-70, *68*
    training over wire or
        rail, 75-6, *75*
Clover: as green manure,
        32, 33

club root, 112
coleslaw, 105
Comfrey: as green
        manure, 33-4
compost heap, 27-30, *29*
conifers: needles, use of,
        40
container grown plants:
        planting, 65-6
corticium, 59-60
Cotoneaster, 77
    simonsii, 78
Crocus:
    naturalising, 98
    species, 97
crop rotation, 106
cutworms, 56, 125-6, 168
Cytisus battandieri, 71, 73,
        75

Damson:
    pollination chart, 142
    varieties, 142
Dandelion: as vegetable,
        108
digging, 11, 15-18, *17*
    double, 16
    manuring during,
        16-18
    strip digging, *33*
Dogwood, 86-7
dollar spot, 59
drainage sump, 44-5, *44*

earthworms, 20, 31, 58
eelworm, 126
Erythronium dens-canis, *96*

fairy rings, 60-2
Faulkner, R.P.: quotation
        from, 26-7
fertilisers, 34-6
    application to lawns, 64
    application whilst
        digging, 17-18
    danger of using lime
        with, 35
    dilution, 36

173

fertilisers, *continued*
  encouraging growth of
    moss, 53
  foliar, 36
  general, 35
  reading instructions,
    35-6
  salt as, 40-2
  slow-release, 34
  straight, 34
fish meal, 32
flea beetle, 112
foliar feeding, 36
footwear, 21-2
forks, 11
Forsythia, 76
  suspensa, 75
frost: salt as protection
  from, 109
fruit: storing, 139-40
fruit garden, 139-71
fruit trees:
  cane: as hedge, 81
  as hedge, 79-81
  neglected: retraining,
    147, *147*
  old: rejuvenating, 151-2
  planting, 143-5
  pruning, 145-9
  staking, 149-50, *149*
  tap roots: pruning, 150,
    150
  tree forms, 140-1
fungi: where found in
  soil, 19
fusarium, 59

garden centres, 65
Garrya elliptica, 71, 76
Good King Henry, 108
Gooseberries, 158, 159-61
  as hedge, 77, 79-80,
    80-1
  old: rejuvenating, 152
grafting: crown, 151, *151*
Grapes: storing, *140*
grass: as ground cover, 95
greenfly, *see* aphids
green manuring, 32-4
ground cover, 94-6
growing bags, 32
Growmore, 34

Hamamelis mollis, 96, 97,
  97
Hawthorn: as hedge, 77
hedges, 76-81
  fruit trees as, 79-81
  planting, 78-9, *79*
hoes, 14
Holly: as hedge, 77

honeydew, 162
honeyfungus, 85-7
Honeysuckle, *see*
  Lonicera
Hornbeam: as hedge, 77
Howard, Sir Albert, 27
humus, 19-20

intercropping, 105
Ivy, 72
  Buttercup, 72
  for cover, 72
  as ground cover, 95

Jasminium nudiflorum, 78,
  96

Kerria japonica, 75

lawns, 43-64
  acidifying soil, 64
  aerating, 54-5
  badly-laid: improving,
    45
  cannibalising, 48-50
  diseases, 58-64
  drainage, 43-5
  dressing with sand, 45
  edges, 49, *49*
  feeding, 45, 56, 64
  grass cuttings from, 51
    as compost, 40
  moss on, 53-6
  mowing, 50-1
    in new garden, 43
  pests, 56-8
  from seed, 46-7
  soil for, 43
    improving, 45-6
  topdressing, 62-3
  turfing, 47
  unorthodox methods of
    making, 48-50
  weed gullies, 49, *49*
  weeds, 63-4
  wheeling barrows on,
    24
layering, 86-8, *88*
leaf curl, 126
leaf miners, 38, 39
leafmould, 39-40
leatherjackets, 57, *57*,
  168
leaves:
  to avoid in leafmould,
    39
  texture, 39
Leeks, 132-4
  flower head, *132*
Legumes, 106
Lettuce, 102, 134-6

lime:
  danger of using with
    fertilisers and
    manures, 35
  testing for requirements,
    10
Loganberries: as hedge, 81
Lonicera (honeysuckle), 73
  fragrantissima, 69, 71
  japonica Aureoreticulata,
    68
  nitida, 77
Lupin, annual: as green
  manure, 32

Magnolia, 76
manure:
  animal, 25-6
    comparisons, 26
  danger of using lime
    with, 35
  green, 32-4
  organic, 26
manuring, 16-18
Mercury, 108
Michaelmas Daisy:
  dividing, 90
millipedes, 125
moles, 56, 58
moss, 52-6
  controlling, 53-6
  eliminating, 53
  fertilisers encouraging
    growth of, 53
  formation, 52
    after use of weedkillers,
    52-3
  harm done by, 52
  requirements for growth,
    53
  spreading of spores, 52
  on well-drained surface,
    53
mowers, 50-1
  maintenance, 50-1
  sharpening, 50-1
  types, 50, *51*
mulching, 20-1
Mustard: as green manure,
  33

Nectarines, 152, 154-7
nematodes, 58
Nettles: as vegetable, 108
nitrogen, 32, 34, 38
noise: barriers against, 66

oil storage tanks: screening,
  70-2
Onion:
  Egyptian, 107, *107*

Spring, 102
Welsh, 107, 108
organic matter: importance
      of, 26

Parsnips, 127-9
Peaches, 152, 154-7
pea guards, 116, *116*
Pears: storing, 140
Pear trees:
   as hedge, 77
   pollination chart, 142
   tree forms, 140-1
   varieties, 142
Peas, 104-5, 115-18
peat, 30-2
   advantages and
      disadvantage, 31
   as fertiliser, 31
   moss formation on, 52
   types, 31
Pe-tsae, 105
phosphates, 32, 34, 40
Pine needles: use, 40
pipes:
   covering, 68-70
   plastic mesh round, 69,
      69
Plums, 152-4
   Myrobalan, 77, 81
   old: rejuvenating, 152
   pollination chart, 142
   pruning, 147
   varieties, 142
Polyanthus, 97
Polygonum baldschuanicum,
      70, 75
posts:
   covering, 68-70
   plastic mesh round, 69,
      69
potash, 32, 34
Potatoes, 120-7
   culture, 123
   earthing up, *122*
   growing under black
      polythene, 124-5,
      124
   harvesting, 122-4, *123*
   new, at Christmas,
      126-7
   pests and diseases, 125-6
   planting, 122-3
   for school, 134
   seed, 120-2
   storing, 124
pot plants: fertiliser for, 35
pruning, 145-9
   tools for, 145-6
Pyracantha, 77
pythium blight, 60

rakes, 14
Rape: as green manure,
      32, 33
Raspberries, 163-5
Red currants, 158, 161-3
   as hedge, 80
red thread, *see* corticium
ridging, 18-20, *19*
root crops, 105-6
root flies, 38
Rose:
   for screening, 71-2
   shrub: for hedge, 77
   in walls, 100
   Zéphirine Drouhin, 69,
      72

salads, 134-6
salt:
   ancient uses, 40-1
   to give frost protection,
      109
   as manure, 40-2
   as weedkiller, 40
saw: for pruning, 146, *146*
scab, 126
screening, 66-8
   surveying height of, *66*
secateurs, 145-6
seeds: pelletted, 102-3
Shallots, 129-32
shrubs:
   against wall, 74-6
   aspect, 74
   diseases, 76
   preparing soil for, 76
silver leaf disease, 157
slash-and-burn techniques,
      26
slugs, 40, 125
snow mould, *see* fusarium
soil:
   acidifying, 64
   analysis, 9-10, *9*
   consolidation, 21-4
   cultivation, 20
   feel, 10
   fertility, 9, 26-7
   improving, 45-6
   judging from trees and
      weeds, 9
   organic matter in, 26
   organisms in, 8-9
   origins, 8
   puddling surface, 23
   surface cultivation, 21
   testing for requirements,
      10
   types, 8
   walking on, in wet
      weather, 24

soot, 38-9
soot water, 39
spades, 11-13
   sharpening, *12*, 13
Spinach beet, 108
staking, 149-50, *149*
stone fruits, 152-4
Strawberries, 165-71
   propagating, 167, *167*
   strawberry wall, 170-1
      modified, *170*, 171
   under cloches, 168-9
   wild: as ground cover,
      95
suckers, 83-5
Sugar pea, 117-18
sump, 44-5, *44*
superphosphate, 40
Swedes, 118-19
Sweet peas, 69

tanks: screening, 70-2
Tomatoes, 23
   outdoor, 136-8
tools, 11-15
   for pruning, 145-6
Tree heath, 76
trees:
   decay: treatment, 81-2,
      82
   holes in: treatment,
      81-2, *82*
   suckers, 83-5
Tropaeolum canariensis,
      69
turf, *see* lawns
Turnips, 118-19

vegetable garden: planning,
      101-5
vegetables:
   freezing, 104
   intercropping, 105
   pelletted seeds, 102-3
   perennial, 106-8
   sowing, 103-4
      in dry weather, 103,
      103
   successional sowings,
      104-5
Vetch: as green manure,
      32

walls:
   aspect for plants on, 74
   dry, 98-100
      construction, 99
      planting, 100, *100*
   hollow, 98-100
      construction, 99
      planting, 100, *100*

walls, *continued*
  preparing soil at base of,
    76
  shrubs against, 74-6
  supporting plants on,
    72-4, *73*
wasps, 57
water: feeling plants'
    requirements, 10

weedkillers: salt as, 40
weeds:
  as green manure, 32-4
  judging soil type from, 9
  on lawn, 63-4
  pernicious, 11
White currants, 158, 161-3
  as hedge, 80
White thorn, 77

Willow, 96-7
wind: barrier against, 67
winter garden, 96-7
wireworms, 56, 57, *57*, 125
worms, *see* earthworms

Yew: as hedge, 77